AT THE COURT
OF THE LAST TSAR

AT THE COURT
OF THE LAST TSAR

BEING THE MEMOIRS OF
A. A. MOSSOLOV

Head of the Court Chancellery, *1900-1916*

EDITED BY A. A. PILENCO
(*Formerly Professor in the University of Petrograd*)
AND
TRANSLATED BY E. W. DICKES

WITH AN INTRODUCTION BY JOHN VAN DER KISTE

A & F Reprints

First published by Methuen 1935
This edition published by A & F 2020
Introduction Copyright © 2020 John Van der Kiste

A & F Publications
South Brent, Devon, England TQ10 9AS

Typeset 11pt Charter

ISBN 9798621673758

Printed by KDP

CONTENTS

PART II

IV. THE COURT OF NICHOLAS II

INTRODUCTION

Alexander Alexandrovich Mossolov, was born 19 February 1854 in Ryazan, the son of Alexander Vasilievich Mosolov, a provincial secretary. He married Elizabeth Feodorovna Trepova, a maid of honour (1858-1920), daughter of F.F. Trepov, St Petersburg's mayor from 1908, and cavalry general, and they had three sons and two daughters, one of whom was killed in action during the Great War. Entering military service in 1873, he was appointed to the Life Guards Horse Regiment two years later, fought in the Russian-Turkish war of 1877-8 and commanded the convoy of Prince Alexander Battenberg. From 1900 to 1916 he was the head of the Chancellery of the Ministry of the Imperial Court. His responsibilities included court censorship, and carrying out under supervision the preliminary censorship of materials mentioning members of the imperial family. In December 1908 he was promoted to the rank of Lieutenant General.

At the end of 1916 he was appointed Minister Envoy to Romania, and after the revolution, he actively opposed the Bolsheviks in southern Russia. He is believed to have actively encouraged and participated in plots and plans to rescue the imperial family. After all hope was lost he left Russia for a time, lived in Constantinople, and later in England, Sweden, Finland, Germany and France before settling in Sofia, Bulgaria in 1932. In exile he was one of the organizers of the All-Russian Monarchist Congress in Reichengall (Bavaria) in May 1921 and a member of the leadership of the Union of United Monarchists. His first wife died in 1920, and he then married Countess Lydia Sergeyevna Cherkasova. For the rest of his life, they lived with the two children of her first marriage, Vladimir and Tatiana. He died in 1939 and was laid to rest in the Russian cemetery in Sofia.

His memoirs, first published in serial form in an Estonian journal in 1934, and then in Russia and England a year later, are an invaluable source of information about the Tsar and the imperial family during that time. As he got to know the Tsar better, he was struck by his positive qualities, as a faithful, loving husband and father; timid, courteous, thoughtful and affable towards all around him, even-tempered, and with a touching concern for the fate of the wounded in wartime. Nevertheless he had nothing of the personality of his father and little if anything in the way of leadership qualities, with 'an ingrained dislike of argument' and standing up to anybody.

As for the Tsarina, he was impressed by her efficiency as an organizer, particularly with regard to the installation of hospital trains, convalescent homes, and hospitals, and her ability to gather round her persons of ability and energy. The same could not be said for her concern with affairs of state, when she 'submitted herself to an occult and disastrous influence'. Her husband had been imbued with the principle that he 'was responsible only to his own conscience and to God', and in this he had her steadfast support. As a person she was very timid, devoid of social skills and with no time or inclination for 'society talk', a failing that earned her a reputation for hauteur.

His portrait of the Tsar's redoutable aunt Marie Pavlovna, Grand Duchess Vladimir, an overbearing and irascible but far more accomplished personality and born leader in society, and her 'rival court', which effortlessly eclipsed the official one, is interesting. He was a born peacemaker who had the gift of getting on with everybody, and just as noteworthy was his valiant if ultimately futile attempt to try and reconcile the Romanovs, particularly the Grand Duchess and the Tsarina as one after the dissensions caused by the murder of Rasputin, a mere three weeks before the revolution tore their world apart.

Mossolov also had the opportunity to observe other European royalties, notably the German Emperor William II, who 'had a special gift of upsetting everybody who came near him', and the far more affable, easy-going King Edward VII of England.

Of Rasputin, that 'degraded man', who did his best to try and ingratiate himself with Mossolov, he has nothing positive to say. He was not alone in discovering for himself that no servant at court, no matter how loyal, could ever cross the *moujik* and expect to retain the Tsarina's trust. It is implied that the Tsar's plan to appoint him as Minister Plenipotentiary at Bucharest may not have been simply a matter of coinciding with the entry of Russian troops into Roumania, but a way of removing him as he was not congenial to her. In this capacity he worked closely with King Ferdinand and Queen Marie (a cousin of the Tsarina). The latter originally found him 'a clever, rather sly-looking' character, but soon came to like and respect him.

He was there when they learned that the Tsar had abdicated. In 1918, he and various colleagues tried to secure German help and save

4

the Romanovs from their approaching fate, but in vain. Not long afterwards he retired to Paris, where he wrote his recollections of life at the imperial court, and died in 1939. They serve as a kindly testimonial to the sovereign whose reign and life ended in tragedy, but remained to the end a good man, albeit a weak one.

My thanks go to Greg King and Penny Wilson for much of the biographical information about Mossolov above.

John Van der Kiste

ILLUSTRATIONS

PART I

CHAPTER I

THE EMPEROR NICHOLAS II AND HIS FAMILY

I. THE TSAR

HIS FATHER AND MOTHER

Alexander III, son of Emperor Alexander II and of the Empress Marie Alexandrovna, Princess of Hesse-Darmstadt, was educated at home, as was the custom in his day, and did not attend any school. He had had one idea instilled into him above all others — that of the omnipotence of the Tsars of Russia, and of the consequent necessity of maintaining the prestige of the Imperial authority. On this latter point the tradition inherited from his august father and his grandfather Nicholas I was maintained in its full grandeur and integrity. The doctrine was continually impressed on the future Emperor that the Russian Tsars are the masters whom God has willed to bestow on Holy Russia in her boundless immensity. The Tsar was his country's guardian and a symbol of the national unity; he must stand forth as the last rampart of paternal benevolence and chivalrous justice.

Alexander's mother had taught him to hold in high honour the ideas of marriage and the family. She had, of course, been equally concerned that on its social side her son's education should produce a docile submission to all the rigours of etiquette and ceremonial.

In his personal sympathies he came much nearer to his grandfather, Nicholas I, than to the liberal spirit of his father, Alexander II. He considered that the evolution of the Russian people had to be slow and gradual — that too rapid a development of its political institutions would foster the subconscious tendencies towards anarchy that have always characterized the Slav race. He feared that precipitate reforms would be followed by disorders and would prejudice the true interests of the country.

It is well known what masterly expression Prince Troubetzkoy, a sculptor of exceptional talent, who had been charged with the erection in St. Petersburg of the equestrian statue of the great Tsar, gave to these conservative ideas of Alexander III. With an iron hand Nicholas II's father grips the tautened rein of his massive and almost clumsy palfrey. Every time I passed this marvellous statue in the Znamenskaya Square I used to say to myself, old cavalry general that I am:

'Slacken the rein! A horse is not to be mastered by forcing him to mark time!'

The second element in the character of Alexander III on which it is necessary to say a few words was his passion for everything that was characteristically Russian. Emperor William I and certain petty German princes had exercised far too much influence at the Court of Alexander II, and the reaction in the soul of Alexander III was correspondingly violent. He grew to detest everything that was German. He tried to be Russian down to the smallest details of his personal life, and that was why his bearing seemed less aristocratic than that of his brothers: he claimed, perhaps without reasoning it out, that a true Russian should not be too highly polished in his manners, that he should have a touch of something like brutality. He yielded to the exigencies of Court etiquette, but as soon as he came into a more restricted circle of friends he threw off every artificial form: he regarded ceremony as necessary only to German princelings with no other means of sustaining their 'dying' prestige and defending their claim to existence.

Alexander's consort, the Danish princess, mother of Nicholas II, had been brought up in one of the most patriarchal courts in Europe; and she instilled into her son an unquestioning reverence for the principle of the family; she also transmitted to him a great deal of the personal charm which had made her so popular in Russia. All the Princess Dagmar's children were smaller in stature than their uncles and aunts. The majesty of bearing that distinguished the earlier generation did not descend to the last of the Romanovs. That was why Count Freedericksz, the Minister of the Imperial Court, never tired of advising Nicholas II to ride on horseback when he had to appear in public. I remember the Emperor saying once, with a laugh:

'The Count loves caracoling in front of a crowd; I'm sure that is why he insists that I should not go in a carriage.'

In spite of his short stature the Tsar was an accomplished horseman; his bearing on horseback was very imposing.

HIS EDUCATION

Two of my friends, General Vassilkovsky, A.D.C., and Mr. Heath, the English teacher of the heir to the throne, have given me some details of the education of the children of Alexander III. According to them, the Emperor's children were not well disciplined. One might fairly say that their manners were much like those of the children of petty provincial nobles. Even when dining with their parents, they did not deny themselves the amusement of throwing pellets of bread at one another, if they knew that they would not be caught. They all had good health and spent a great deal of time at sports, with the exception of George Alexandrovitch, the second son, who had a weak chest and died in the flower of his youth.

Special attention was given to their language studies, and the tutors devoted a great deal of care to correcting their pronunciation of foreign words. For the rest, the children all had an excellent memory, especially for names and faces. His good memory enabled Nicholas Alexandrovitch to gain a wide knowledge of history. At the time when I first met him he was certainly a well-educated man. His parents had taken no particular trouble over the education of his brothers and sisters.

The future Emperor's tutor was named Danilovitch, and had been given the title of General A.D.G. My friend Vassilkovsky never called him by any other name than 'that old dotard of a — Jesuit'. Danilovitch started his career as head of a military school, and it was there that he was endowed with that sobriquet. He was in general charge of the education of Nicholas II, and trained him to adopt an impenetrable reserve, which was an essential trait of his own character. Alexander III was ruthless even with his children, and loathed everything that savoured of 'weakness'. The children and even the Empress herself were often obliged to conceal from him not only mistakes of their own but those of persons in their entourage. Thus a spirit of dissimulation and restraint was engendered in this family; and it did not disappear after the father's death. Many a time have I heard Nicholas Alexandrovitch speak in severe terms of people who had failed to keep their promise not to divulge a secret.

When he became Tsar, Nicholas II made it a fixed rule that he was in no way bound by his position as monarch to do anything that he did not want to do. In this his natural timidity played a part. He hated to have to investigate anything, to complain of anything, to 'stand up' to anybody. Following out his fixed rule, he never worried and never grew heated, even in situations in which an outburst of temper would have been only too natural. If he found anybody seriously in the wrong, he brought the matter to the notice of the offender's immediate superior; he commented on it in the gentlest of terms; and never in any case did he show the slightest sign of disapproval to the actual offender.

The teaching of the 'Jesuit' Danilovitch had borne its fruits.

I can bear witness that the Tsar was not only courteous, but thoughtful and affable towards all around him. His attitude was always the same, whether he was with a Minister or a menial; he treated all men with respect, whatever their age or position or social status.

He could part with the greatest ease even from those who had served him for a very long time. The first word of accusation breathed in his presence against anybody, with or without evidence, was enough for him to dismiss the victim, though the charge might have been a pure fabrication. He did so without the slightest regret, and without attempting to establish the facts; that, in his view, was the business of the victim's superiors or, if necessary, of the courts. Still less would it occur to him to defend anybody, or to examine the motives of the calumniator. He was distrustful, like all weak persons.

Was he a good man?

It is very difficult to penetrate the depths of another's soul, especially when that other is an Emperor of Russia. When he visited the military hospitals during the war he showed a touching concern for the fate of the wounded. In the cemeteries, before the thousands of crosses erected on 'fraternal' (collective) graves, he prayed with a fervour that could not have been feigned.

The Emperor's heart was full of love, but it was a 'collective love', if the phrase may be permitted; so that his feelings were very different from those which plain men sum up in the single word 'love'.

He had a sincere and intense love for the Empress and his children; I shall return to this later.

Did he love his more distant relations? I doubt it. Freedericksz was personally responsible for dealing with all requests, big and little, submitted by members of the Imperial family. The Tsar rarely refused one. Yet the Count told me many times over that the Tsar bestowed honours or money or property without the slightest sign of any satisfaction in the act. It was simply a part of his duties as sovereign. It was a nuisance, and sometimes contrary to the interests of the State; but it 'had to be done'. It was out of the question to offend an uncle or a nephew. Once the grant of the favour had been authorized, it would be some little time, the Tsar hoped, before the beneficiary came back with some fresh importunity.

He had more regard for his two sisters and his brother Michael. He felt a real tenderness towards his nephew Dimitri Pavlovitch, who had grown up under his eyes and whose youth appealed to him. As for the rest, he knew how to show just as much feeling as the proprieties demanded, just as much as was required in the due performance of his duties as Tsar, as much as would stave off any unpleasantness.

INSINCERE OR TIMID?

He has been charged with insincerity. Instances are quoted of Ministers who imagined that they enjoyed his entire confidence being called on, with staggering suddenness, to resign. That is not quite just to him.

These Ministerial dismissals were peculiar events; but whatever the explanation of the Tsar's actions, it must not be sought in any lack of straightforwardness. In the Tsar's eyes his Ministers were officials like any others in the service of the Empire. He 'loved' his Ministers in exactly the same way as he loved each one of the 150 millions of his subjects. If a Minister came to grief the Tsar regretted it, as every man of feeling would regret another man's misfortune. But Count Freedericksz was the only one who really enjoyed the Tsar's confidence.

If a Minister was in disagreement with the Tsar, if some accusation had been made against him, or if for any reason the Tsar no longer felt confidence in him, Nicholas was still perfectly able to give him a friendly reception, to thank him for his collaboration, and to shake hands warmly with him when he left — and then to send him a letter calling on him to resign.

This was certainly due to the influence of Danilovitch, the 'Jesuit'. The Ministers did not allow for the Tsar's ingrained dislike of an argument.

Almost always the same vicious circle recurred. When he had appointed a new Minister the Tsar would evince for some time the utmost satisfaction with him; he felt entirely happy with the new official. This honeymoon period might last quite a time. But then clouds would begin to appear on the horizon. They would come all the sooner if the Minister was a man of principle, a man with a definite programme. Statesmen like Witte, Stolypin, Samarin, Trepov, felt themselves on fairly solid ground when their programme had received the Tsar's approval; they imagined that their hands were then free in regard to all the details of its execution. The Tsar saw things in a different light. Frequently he would try to impose his personal views in matters of detail, such as the appointment of some subordinate official.

Confronted with this attitude on the part of their sovereign, the Ministers would act as their temperament prompted. Some, like Lamsdorff, Krivosheyin, or Sukhomlinov, temporized or compromised. Others were less compliant; they would try to get their way by some devious method, or would try persuasion. It was thoroughly dangerous for a Minister to turn to either of these expedients, but especially the former, which exasperated the Tsar.

It must never be forgotten that Nicholas II had very little of the combative spirit. He had a great capacity for grasping his interlocutor's thought halfway through its expression, of appreciating every delicate distinction in a report, of giving their true value to details which had deliberately been slurred over. But he made a point of preserving the appearance of acquiescence. He never contested the statements made by his interlocutor. He never adopted a definite and energetic attitude, an attitude which would have enabled him to break the resistance of a Minister, to bend him to his will and so to retain a useful servant in a post in which he had gained experience. The Tsar was incapable of unmasking his batteries, or of provoking his Minister to an energetic rejoinder that might have induced the sovereign to change his mind.

The Tsar's contribution to a talk was never sharp or direct, never argumentative, never hot-tempered, never made in other than even tones. The Minister would take his leave, delighted at having, to all appearance, carried his point. But he would be sadly mistaken. What he had taken for weakness was merely dissimulation. He had forgotten that the Tsar was absolutely without moral courage; that he loathed making a final decision in the presence of the person concerned. Next day the Minister would receive a letter from him — a letter of dismissal.

I repeat: the very idea of discussion was wholly alien to the nature of Nicholas II. We must not forget that he inherited from his father (whom he venerated, and whose example he followed assiduously even in small details of his everyday life) an unshakable faith in the providential nature of his high office. His mission emanated from God. For his actions he was responsible only to his own conscience and to God. In this view the Empress supported him with intense conviction.

Responsible only to his conscience, his intuition, his instinct — to that incomprehensible thing which in our days is called the subconscious, and of which the notion did not exist in the sixteenth century, when the Tsars of Moscow forged for themselves an absolute power. Responsible to elements that are not reason and at times are contrary to reason. Responsible to imponderables; to the mysticism that steadily increased its hold over him.

The Ministers relied exclusively on considerations that were based on reason. Their arguments were addressed to the understanding. They spoke in terms of figures and statistics, of precedents, of estimates and forecasts based on the principle of the weighing of probabilities; they referred to reports from officials, to the example of other countries, and all that. The Tsar could not have argued with them, and evidently had no desire to. He preferred to write a letter announcing his Minister's 'resignation'. The Minister had ceased to give satisfaction — nobody could say how or why.

For the rest, the Tsar, like so many Russians, believed that no one can run counter to his fate. What is to happen will happen! Everything will come right in the end, for Providence is watching over us.

HIS SENSE OF DUTY AS SOVEREIGN

In other words, the Tsar took his role of God's representative with the utmost seriousness. This was particularly evidenced in the sustained attention which he gave to the consideration of petitions for the reprieve of condemned men. It was this arbitrament over life and death that approximated him most closely to the All-Powerful.

As soon as a reprieve was signed, the Tsar would unfailingly urge me to pass it on with all speed, so that the message should not arrive too late. I remember receiving an appeal for reprieve late one night, during one of the Tsar's journeys.

I had my name sent in for an audience. The Tsar was in his own compartment, and seemed astonished at my, appearance at that late hour.

'I have ventured to disturb your Majesty,' I said, 'as it is a question of a man's life.'

'You did entirely, entirely right. But how can we get Freedericksz's signature?' (Under the law the telegram conveying the Tsar's reply could only be sent out when it had been signed by the Minister of the Court, and the Tsar knew that Freedericksz had gone to bed long before.)

'I will send the message over my signature, and the Count can countersign it in the morning.'

'Excellent. Lose no time.'

Next morning the Tsar returned to the subject. 'Are you sure,' he said, 'that the telegram was sent off at once?'

'Sire, it could not fail to be.'

'Can you guarantee that these telegrams containing my orders get priority?'

'Without exception.'

The Tsar seemed satisfied.

THE TSAR NEVER HAD A SECRETARY

As God's representative on earth, the Tsar conscientiously and systematically set himself standards to which the ordinary mortal could not aspire.

It is a significant detail, not, perhaps, generally known, that this Tsar of all the Russias never had a private secretary. He was so jealous of his prerogatives that he himself sealed the envelopes containing his decisions. He had to be very busy before he would entrust his valet with this relatively trivial task. And the valet had to show the sealed envelopes, so that his master could satisfy himself that the secrecy of his correspondence could not be violated.

The Tsar had no secretary. Official documents, letters not strictly of a private character, were written, of course, by third parties. Taneyev drew up the 'rescripts' to high dignitaries who were to be decorated. The Minister of the Court prepared the official letters addressed to the members of the Imperial family. The drafting of communications for foreign sovereigns would come within the province of the Minister of Foreign Affairs — and so on.

But there were other things that the private secretary to a sovereign could do — prepare reports, file papers, keep an eye on outstanding matters, receive correspondence, all sorts of things. There was enough of this work to occupy two or three confidential secretaries.

But that was the difficulty. It would have been necessary to take a third party into his confidence, and the Tsar hated to confide his ideas to anybody.

There was another danger — the secretary might magnify his position, impose his own personality, try to influence his master. To influence one who was not prepared to consult anything but his own conscience. The very thought of it was enough to make Nicholas II tremble!

The Minister of the Court encouraged His Majesty in this outlook, since it would not have been pleasant to him to see an interloper come between the Sovereign and his chief servant.

The Empress had a private secretary, Count Rostovtzev; the Tsar had none!

He wanted to be alone.

Alone with his Conscience.

I recall our return from Compiègne, where we had been present at a memorable review of the French Army. We had been among soldiers, and, needless to say, many hours had been devoted during the long railway journey to the study of a problem in which all were intensely interested — 'Is the French Army capable of holding in check the battalions of William II?'

The whole future of Russia's foreign policy depended on the answer at which we arrived. Some of our specialists held that the French troops were less disciplined and less stubborn in resistance than the Teuton phalanxes. Others declared that in the defence of his own soil the French peasant would fight like a lion; events proved that they were right. The disputants grew heated and excited. The Tsar spoke not a single word!

At Livadia, during the holidays that Nicholas II allowed himself from time to time, I had the honour of accompanying him on horseback on several occasions. I was a little inexperienced in those days, and supposed that it was my duty to 'amuse' my master and keep him in conversation. I began with the latest news from the papers, the big political events, the questions of the day. The Tsar replied with evident reluctance, and changed the subject to tennis, horses, the weather, mountains, and so on. Often, instead of giving any reply, he put the spurs to his horse and galloped on, making any discussion impossible.

It did not take me long to understand. The Tsar never talked of serious matters with members of his entourage, even if they belonged to the Imperial family. He disliked expressing an opinion. He was afraid that his opinion might be retailed to other people; in any case, he felt that he had enough important decisions to take already without needlessly adding to them. The Ministers were in attendance at the appointed times to receive his final decisions — that was quite enough.

It was all the easier for him to make this his rule since, whatever the occasion, he unfailingly remained outwardly imperturbable. I remember the arrival of the telegram reporting the total loss of the Russian Fleet at Tsushima. It came when I was with the Emperor on a railway journey. Freedericksz had remained a good half-hour in the Tsar's compartment; the Tsar had been utterly cast down. It was now impossible for us to win the war; the Fleet, the object of such solicitude on the part of the Emperor, was annihilated; thousands of officers whom he had met personally and had learnt to appreciate highly had been killed.

An attendant came to tell us that His Majesty was taking tea in the dining-car. We went in one by one. There was a dismal silence: no one dared to be the first to speak of the terrible news.

The Tsar broke the silence. He talked to us of the army manoeuvres then in progress, of various insignificant events. He went on talking for more than an hour. Not a word did he breathe about Tsushima.

He left us with the impression that he was entirely unconcerned at what had happened. Freedericksz undeceived us, telling us of the consternation that the Tsar had shown an hour and a half before.

'His Majesty wants to see the Minister of War, in his compartment.'

General Sakharov had a long audience. He, too, when he came back from the Imperial coach, told us that the Tsar had shown deep concern.

'His Majesty discussed the situation with me. He showed that he thoroughly realized the problems ahead of us, and he sketched a very sensible plan of action. His composure is admirable.'

Much later I discovered how seriously the disaster of Tsushima had impaired His Majesty's constitution, strong as it was.

'YOUR' PETER THE GREAT

In the whole of my seventeen years of service I only had occasion twice to talk politics with my Imperial master.

The first time was at the bi-centenary of the foundation of St. Petersburg by Peter the Great, that reforming Titan of our country. The newspapers were full of articles devoted to the victories and the reforms of the creator of modem Russia. One day I was talking enthusiastically of Russia's first Emperor. The Tsar did not seem to want to pursue the subject. I knew how non-committal His Majesty always was in conversation, but ventured to ask him whether he agreed with me.

After a short silence he replied:

'I recognize my ancestor's great merits, but I should be lacking in sincerity if I were to echo your enthusiasm. . . . He is the ancestor who appeals to me least of all. He had too much admiration for European "culture". . . . He stamped out Russian habits, the good customs of his sires, the usages bequeathed by the nation, on too many occasions. . . It was a period of transition. . . . Perhaps he could not have acted differently. . . . But to go on from that to say that I feel in any way drawn to him — '

As the conversation proceeded I gained the impression that the Tsar blamed Peter the Great for the 'showman' element in all that he did. I seemed to hear my august interlocutor pronounce the word 'adventurer'.

Apparently the Emperor long remembered the sympathetic interest that I had shown in Peter the Great.

One day, in the Crimea, when we were ascending to the plateau of Outchan-Sou, where a wonderful view is to be had of Yalta and its environs, the Emperor told me what a pleasure it was to him to come to the southern shores of the Crimea.

'I should have liked to be able to live here always,' he said.

'Sire, why not transfer the capital here?'

'I must admit,' the Sovereign replied, 'that the idea has often occurred to me.'

The other officers joined in the conversation. Some thought the mountains were too close to the sea, others that there was not room enough for all the public buildings.

'And,' said one, 'where shall the Duma be put?'

'On top of Ay Petri,' some one suggested.

'But Ay Petri is buried in snow in winter, and there would be no possible way of getting up there for. the sessions of Parliament.'

'So much the better,' said an aide-de-camp.

Half an hour later, on the way down, the Tsar was at my side on a narrow footpath. Turning to me, he said, with a little smile of resignation:

'No, it is impossible. Besides, once we had set the capital on the flanks of these mountains, I should certainly have ceased to love them. Castles in Spain!'

Then, after a few moments' silence, he burst out laughing.

'As for your Peter the Great! If he had conceived any such plan, he would have carried it out regardless of all the political and financial difficulties. He would never have asked himself whether Russia could benefit from his pet idea!'

That was the last time we touched on the subject of the 'Reformer Tsar'.

His antipathy for that great creator of modern Russia was in keeping, in any case, with the character and mentality of Nicholas II. It will be remembered how, at the very outset of his reign, the young Tsar received a deputation from one of the provinces of Russia, and gave them a rebuff that resounded from end to end of the country. These delegates were sincerely imbued with liberal ideas, and were all sincere constitutionalists. The Tsar made a short speech in reply to their representations. It was as brusque in tone as a command, and ended with this unhappily famous phrase:

'You must give up all these foolish dreams!'

This first public speech of the young Tsar's came as a thunderbolt to the intelligentsia, who had hoped for a moment that Nicholas II would return to the path of liberal reform on which his grandfather Alexander II had entered with such success, and from which his father, Alexander III, had at once turned back.

'IMPOSSIBLE TO BE TOO PRUDENT'

My only other political conversation with Nicholas II had reference to Bulgaria. It was in 1912. The war with Turkey was approaching its end; the Bulgarian army was exhausted after a series of superhuman efforts.

General Radko Dimitriev had sent me a letter asking me to inform the Tsar that the appearance of the Russian Fleet in the neighbourhood of Constantinople would be likely to modify the situation to the advantage of the Bulgarians. I determined to speak to the Tsar on the matter.

After some remarks on the general political situation he replied, in substance:

'I am sorry for Bulgaria. But I cannot sacrifice Russian soldiers to enable her to cover herself with laurels.'

Then, after a moment's thought, he added:

'It would be best for you to send no answer at all to Dimitriev. I do not want to drive him to despair. ... I am whole-heartedly on the side of the Bulgarians; I admire their brave little army. . . . . But the slightest intervention on my part might provoke a European war. It is impossible to be too prudent in these questions.'

He took up the reins of his charger, which went on at a quicker trot. We continued on our way in silence. Then the Tsar repeated:

'A pity! There is nothing I can do for your Bulgarians.'

And he changed the subject.

A MODERATE NATIONALIST

Like his father, Nicholas II was keenly interested in all that was characteristically Russian. I recall his words to Mme Plevitskaya, a singer well known and appreciated for her singing of peasant songs. After a concert at Livadia he said to her:

'I thought it would be impossible for anybody to be more Russian than I am. Your singing proved to me that it is not. I thank you with all my heart for that revelation.'

The Tsar had a perfect knowledge of Russian. Our language is exceptionally rich in terms denoting the degrees of family relationship; it has special names for every category of relationship by birth and through marriage, not excepting the most distant, and with particularly subtle shades of distinction. One day the Tsar had a list of the terms used by the peasants brought to him. It was clear to us at once that he was thoroughly acquainted with all of them, however quaint or obsolete. None of us was able to answer the 'posers' that he set us in this improvised examination — to the great joy of the children present.

'The Russian language,' said the Tsar, after abundantly demonstrating our ignorance, 'is of such wealth that it is possible to give Russian equivalents for every expression in any foreign language; no word of non-Slav origin should be allowed to disfigure our speech.'

I remarked to His Majesty that I had made it an invariable rule that reports submitted to the Sovereign should contain no expression of foreign origin.

'I think I have succeeded,' the Tsar replied, 'in getting the other Ministries also to adopt this excellent habit. I underline in red every passage in their reports in which I find expressions of foreign origin. The Foreign Ministry is the only one on which I have been unable to make any impression.'

I ventured to point out to His Majesty a foreign word which has no equivalent in the Russian language: What can one say for "on principle"?'

'Really,' said the Tsar, after a few moments' thought, 'I cannot find a Russian equivalent.'

'Sire, there is a word in the Serbian language which expresses the idea. They say satchelno, which means "behind the front"; this may be inlerpreted as "an idea behind the front" — "subconscious and preconceived".'

'Very interesting. I am going to ask the Academy to set up a special Commission to compile a dictionary of the Russian language, as is being done in France. We have no record providing an indisputable source of reference for Russian phonetics and orthography.'

There was only one field in which the Tsar admitted his nationalism to be qualified; and, in this instance, it is easy to understand it. He was very fond of music, and placed in the same rank two composers of whom only one was Russian — Wagner and Tchaikovsky. (The 'Ring' had been performed in the Imperial Theatres by the express command of the Sovereign, and repeated regularly every year.)

I may add that the nationalism of Nicholas II had not the extreme character of that of his 'monolith' father. Nicholas was far more cultivated than Alexander III, and he also lacked the energy for the outbursts that the latter had sometimes permitted himself.

Nicholas II used to wear a sort of *mujik's* blouse at home, and looked well in it. He had put one of his regiments, the Fusiliers of the Imperial Household, into similar garb. He had entertained an ambitious idea of abolishing all the modern uniforms of the Court dignitaries and replacing them by copies of costumes of sixteenth-century boyars. An artist had been set to work on the necessary models. But in the end the plan had been abandoned because of the expense it would have entailed. The boyars were clothed in extremely expensive furs, and wore too many diamonds and rubies and pearls.

The time had gone by (or perhaps had not yet come) for a combative nationalism to be able to take root at the Court of Nicholas II.

'WHEN THE TOMBSTONE . . .'

In one environment only did the Tsar condescend to associate on equal terms with others — among soldiers.

After the forced march referred to below, the commanding officer of a regiment asked the favour of permission to enrol His Majesty as one of the soldiers of his first squad. The day the request reached him, the Tsar sent for the military service certificate of a soldier of the lowest rank, and himself filled it up. He entered his name as 'Nicholas Romanov'. In the place for the date of liberation from military service he wrote:

'When the tombstone lies over me.'

How significant his action looks in retrospect, and how true to character!

The famous forced march provides a convincing proof of the extreme conscientiousness and sense of duty which inspired the Tsar as head of the army.

The Minister of War was at work on an important reform, the determination of the type of clothing and equipment to be worn and carried in future by every Russian infantryman. Those who have had army service, or have even had experience of hiking, well know the importance of the smallest object added or taken off when equipment has to be carried for ten hours a day. An ounce in excess of the unavoidable minimum, when carried by each one of millions of men, may be of capital importance.

When considering the modifications proposed by the Ministry, the Tsar certainly hit on the best of all possible ways of deciding with a full knowledge of the facts. He told only the Minister of the Court and the Commander of the Palace of his intention. They had the full equipment, new model, of a soldier in a regiment camping near Livadia brought to the palace. There was no faking, no making to exact measure for the Tsar; he was in the precise position of any recruit who is put into the shirt, pants, and uniform chosen for him, and given his rifle, pouch, and cartridges. The Tsar was careful also to take the regulation supply of bread and water. Thus equipped, he went off alone, covered twenty kilometres out and back on a route chosen at random, and returned to the palace. Forty kilometres — twenty-five miles — is the full length of a forced march; rarely are troops required to do more in a single day.

The Tsar returned at dusk, after eight or nine hours of marching, rest-time included. A thorough examination showed, beyond any possibility of challenge, that there was not a blister or abrasion of any sort on his body. The boots had not hurt his feet. Next day the reform received the Sovereign's approval.

William II wrote a letter congratulating the Tsar on his enterprise. It is interesting to note that the letter had a slightly bitter undertone. Our military attaché reported later that the German Emperor had asked to be supplied with all the cuttings from the Russian newspapers concerning the march. It seems that he showed a good deal of vexation — why had not that brilliant idea occurred to him?

As for the Tsar, he said afterwards, with obvious sincerity, that he greatly regretted having authorized the publication in the newspapers of the story of his forced march. He had made it entirely on account of military considerations, and the publicity given to it was distasteful to him.

'TO GO TO THE FRONT WITH THEM'

The Tsar regarded himself as a soldier — the first professional soldier in his Empire. In this respect he would make no compromise: his duty was to do what every soldier had to do.

Indirectly, and within certain limits, that was the cause of the downfall of the dynasty and of Russia.

The reader will have guessed my meaning. I am brought now to the subject of His Majesty's assumption of the supreme command during the Great War. It is one of the most enigmatical and most tragic pages of the history of the period with which we are concerned.

Nothing is more dangerous for a great country at war than to retire a Generalissimo who is surrounded by people whom he has learnt to know and to judge according to their merits, and to give the command to another Generalissimo. This step is only permissible in the last extremity; as a rule it can only be taken at the cost of an enormous sacrifice. For Russia, the taking over of the supreme command by the Tsar himself was bound to involve not only grave difficulties in the field of strategy but incalculable political consequences. We know now that a great war may cost a throne, even in a country much less ripe for revolution than was Russia.

The loss of his throne, with all the resulting convulsions, was the penalty that a Tsar who had placed himself at the head of his troops and had been beaten must inevitably suffer. I will pass in silence over the difficulties that followed in the administration of an immense country tormented by endless complications and deprived of the immediate presence of its Sovereign. The *Stavka* (G.H.Q.) was too far from Petrograd; the effective power passed into other hands than the Tsar's. It was a fatal risk to run.

The Tsar had two main reasons, military and political, for his decision. Military considerations certainly played as decisive a part as the political and dynastic considerations, with which I shall deal later.

To explain the considerations arising from the Tsar's feeling of military duty, I must recall my memories of the period of the war with Japan.

Everybody knows how disastrous that war was for Russia. The troops left in successive detachments, and the astronomical distances which separated us from the theatre of operations swallowed them up like an insatiable Moloch; every day there were fresh victims. Kuropatkin, the Generalissimo, said again and again, 'Patience, patience!' But the months went by without the smallest grain of good news to give us fresh courage. Already there was talk of dissensions between the principal military leaders — a very bad sign.

The Tsar was present at the departure of the troops whenever a large detachment was leaving. He made well-phrased speeches (the more entirely improvised they were, the more effective they proved), and distributed icons to each regiment as it left. I used to note how sad and careworn he looked as he came away in silence from these leave-takings.

One day he said in my presence:

'I ought not to be bidding them farewell. It would be better to go to the front with them.'

Few of those who were present had particularly noticed what he said. Later on I realized its full significance.

It was hardly more than a colonial war — a war in China, so remote that it took twenty days' journey by rail to reach the scene of hostilities — and the Tsar thought of going to the front! His duty, as he saw it, was to be in the midst of the fighting, at the point where danger was. He who would never accept promotion above the rank of Colonel of the Preobrajensky regiment — was fretting at his enforced inaction.

THE SUPREME COMMAND

The Great War.

The Winter Palace transformed once more into a huge factory for dressings and surgical apparatus.

The first successes.

My regiment of Horse Guards routing an enemy division. . . . My son's letters telling me of the splendid deeds of the Cossacks of the Guard, which he had joined. . . .

Then, the annihilation of Samsonov's army. . . . the general retreat . . . the inglorious surrender of some of our fortresses . . . the mass evacuations of the populations of territories abandoned to the enemy

. . . the stories of espionage. . . . Public opinion began to show signs of alarm.

People set about hunting for a scapegoat. There was a tendency, especially among the entourage of the Empress, to throw the blame for all the reverses on the Generalissimo, Grand Duke Nicholas Nicolayevitch. It was said that in spite of his forcefulness he was inclined to bow in passive resignation before 'Fate' — that defect of so many Russians who accept defeat in advance at the hands of what has been 'written in the decrees of Providence'. Instances were also being quoted of undue severity towards brave Generals: some had taken their lives in consequence of extravagant censure from the Grand Duke. . . .

The Tsar said nothing. Disturbed but undecided, he let no sign of his secret feelings appear. But for all his reticence he was anxiously watching what was going on around him. Then, one day, he sent for the Minister of the Court and announced his decision: it was his duty to take over the supreme command.

Freedericksz showed the utmost hostility to the idea. The Tsar discussed it with other persons in his entourage. He found some encouragement, especially in quarters attached to the Empress's Court. He considered that Nicholas Nicolayevitch and General Yanushkevitch had made serious mistakes. General Alexeyev was inclined to look on a battle-field as simply a chess-board; but he was an officer of exceptional intelligence, and if he were made Chief of Staff he might, the Tsar hoped, change the face of things.

The Tsar decided to go to his duty, the duty of active service.

THE SO-CALLED PLOT OF THE GRAND DUKES

From the political point of view the Tsar's decision is much more difficult to explain. What follows is no more than guesses and indications.

Nicholas Nicolayevitch, the Generalissimo, certainly had plenty of 'go'; he had a reputation for firmness and energy. The strong measures that he had taken against the civil populations of the regions that had to be evacuated were quoted in evidence of what he 'could do if he had his hands free'. The Left wing had claimed him for its own: it was constantly said that it was he who had wrung from the Tsar in 1905 the October manifesto, that first swallow of constitutional liberties; it was he who had championed Count Witte, the author of the legislation which had set up the Duma. The Allies were disturbed at the constant friction between the Government and the representatives of the nation, and it was only too natural that they should urge forward the only one of the Grand Dukes who could continue and bring to completion the work of emancipation begun in 1905.

It began to be whispered that the Empress was going to be sent to Livadia, or else to a convent. If the Tsar did not fall in with the plan, he would be deposed by a *coup d'état*. Nicholas Nicolayevitch would be made Victory Dictator, and when he had won the victory he would become Tsar.

At one time there was almost open talk in Petrograd of a coming Palace revolution. Had Grand Duke Nicholas Nicolayevitch himself been a party to the plot? I do not believe it. I am convinced, indeed, that the plot existed only in the imagination of drawing-room chatterers. The only courts then in Petrograd were those of the Grand Duchess Marie Pavlovna and the Grand Duke Nicholas Michailovitch; and neither alone nor in association could they possibly have taken any decisive action. All the other members of the Imperial family were at the front. After the Tsar took over the supreme command, the Grand Duke Nicholas Nicolayevitch stayed in the mountains of the Caucasus and Armenia. None of those who might have acted as his agents were in Petrograd. Just before his nephew's abdication in 1917 he wrote him the famous letter begging him 'on my knees' to abdicate; but that, I think, is the only false step that can be laid to his charge.

But the State police, the *Okhrana*, were certainly aware of the rumours that were so persistently in circulation in society circles. The Tsar could not have been in ignorance of them. Did any documents come into his hands? I do not know.

In any case the idea of falling back on the *Stavka* (G.H.Q.), where it would be virtually impossible for a *coup d'état* to be carried out, might have been considered for the political reasons that I have just indicated.

But I shall always hold that for Nicholas II as I knew him it was the military considerations that counted. The Empress may have been guided by motives of a more personal character; she is said to have been jealous of the ascendancy that Nicholas Nicolayevitch might gain with the mass of the people if the troops under his high command won a decisive victory.

DISTRUSTFUL

The aloofness which the Tsar made his rule of life was all the more pernicious since he distrusted even the persons in his own suite. The only exception was Count Freedericksz.

The Tsar came to the throne at the age of 26; his character was not then definitely formed, and he had not had the experience needed to enable him to acquire the art of judging people.

His only contact with the outside world up to then had been his stay in three different regiments, for about six months each. One may be sure that life in these regiments was made as pleasant and carefree as possible for the heir to the throne: 'Everything is in order in the regiment under my command' — that sacramental formula in the daily 'report' from every regiment, battalion or squad in the Russian army — will have been the outstanding leitmotiv of the initiation into military duties of Nicholas Alexandrovitch.

He soon realized that the formula was deceptive; and that destroyed his trust in people. He could detect a lie; but he could place no trust in truth. It was his distrustfulness that rendered the task of the Emperor's immediate suite so difficult.

He strove as best he could against 'unprofitable servants' among Ministers and members of his suite. And when he left for the front he took the opportunity to delegate his powers to the Empress: he credited her with a great deal of will power and strength of character.

I admit that his final abdication was the gesture of a tired man. He had lost courage through his own hesitations. And he had assumed that he would be left in peace, that he and his son would be able to 'cultivate their gardens' at Livadia. But his supreme motive was his desire not to have to shed blood in suppressing the revolution.

A FATHER WORTHY OF ALL PRAISE

The paternal love shown by Nicholas II was worthy of all praise. He adored his children and showed special pride in them. I shall never forget how the Tsar brought me for the first time into the presence of the Cesarevitch.

The child was a few months old. The Imperial family were cruising in the Finnish fiords, and the nursery of the Cesarevitch was in a sunny spot on the *Standard*'s upper deck. I came past the Tsar just as he was coming away from the nursery.

'I don't think,' he said, 'that you have yet seen my dear little Cesarevitch. Come along and I will show him to you.'

We went in. The baby was being given his daily bath. He was lustily kicking out in the water.

'It's time to take him out. Let's see if he'll be good in front of you. I hope he won't make too much noise!'

Alexis Nicolayevitch was picked up and dried, and did not show so very much resentment. The Tsar took the child out of his bath towels and put his little feet in the hollow of his hand, supporting him with the other arm. There he was, naked, chubby, rosy — a wonderful boy!

The Emperor covered him up again and gave him to me for a moment; after that we came away.

The Tsar went on talking to me of his son's strong constitution.

'Don't you think he's a beauty?'

He added, almost naïvely:

'His legs are in good proportion with his body. And, best of all, what lovely 'bracelets' he has on his wrists and ankles! He's well nourished.'

Next day the Tsar said to the Empress in my presence:

'Yesterday I had the Cesarevitch on parade before Mossolov.'

I had the impression that Her Majesty was not altogether pleased. Did she think her husband had been too hearty and unreserved for a sovereign?

LOVER OF HIS WIFE

Nicholas II was much more than a loving and devoted husband. He was literally the lover of his life's partner. He was a lover, and could not hide a slight feeling of jealousy of the persons who made up his wife's entourage, of her occupations and the things that belonged to her.

In every union there is one side that loves and another that lets itself be loved. Of the Imperial couple, it was the Emperor who loved with his whole heart; the Empress responded with an affection that showed her happiness in being loved by one whom she cherished and esteemed.

But she herself showed jealousy of everything that deprived her of the company of her husband. She had all the characteristic German conscientiousness, and she understood how manifold were the Tsar's duties. Not only did she never prevent him from working, but she actively encouraged him in his devotion to his duties as head of the State. She readily recognized that Nicholas II needed the long solitary walks that he took in order to be able to ponder over his decisions. But she set rather narrow limits to what she regarded as 'work'.

Any talks with people unconnected with 'the Services', any receptions not absolutely necessary for reasons of State, were, in her eyes, simply and purely a waste of time. She did all she could to reduce to a minimum the occasions when the Tsar undertook such 'duties'. She made no allowance for any exceptional circumstances or any enthusiasm, no matter for what: everything had to be planned out in conformity with the established routine.

Then there were the sacrosanct hours of reading aloud in the evening. I find it difficult to imagine any affair of State of sufficient importance to induce the Empress to forgo a single one of these fireside evenings, tête-à-tête.

The Tsar was a master of the difficult art of reading aloud. He could read in Russian, English (the language in which their Majesties were accustomed to talk and write), French, Danish, and even German (the language with which he was least familiar). The head of his private library, Mr. Stcheglov, was expected to provide the Tsar with about twenty of the best books of the month. At Tsarskoe Selo these works were placed in a room opening out of His Majesty's private apartments. One day when I came into this room the Tsar's valet saw me approach the table on which the collection was laid out. He asked me not to touch the books. 'His Majesty,' he said, 'himself arranges these books in a particular order, and he has forbidden me once for all to disarrange them.'

It was from this collection that the Tsar chose the book of the evening for reading to the Empress. Usually his choice would fall on a Russian novel giving a general picture of one of the social classes in his Empire.

'I can assure you,' he said to me one day, 'that I am afraid to go into that room. I have so little time, and there are so many interesting books! Often half of the books have to go back to Stcheglov without even having had the pages cut.'

He added, almost apologetically:

'Sometimes an historical book or a book of memoirs has waited here for a whole year, I so much wanted to read it. But it has had to go in the end.'

These readings aloud were at all times the favourite leisure occupation of the Imperial couple, who looked forward to the quiet homely intimacy of their evenings.

II. THE EMPRESS ALEXANDRA FEODOROVNA

'MY PERSONAL BUSINESS'

Alexandra Feodorovna never understood how the affairs of her family could interest the whole country. 'It is my personal business', she would say again and again during the Tsar's illness; 'I wish people would not meddle in my affairs.' She took up the same attitude each time the sick Cesarevitch had a relapse.

That attitude was to have important political consequences.

The Tsar was staying at Livadia when he fell rather seriously ill with typhoid fever. Before typhoid had been definitely diagnosed, Freedericksz asked the Empress, through one of her maids of honour, for an audience. The Empress came down into the garden, and when she learned that the Minister wanted to see the Tsar she categorically refused to let him. He had to explain at length that under the fundamental laws of the Empire the personal intercourse between the Sovereign and the Government could not be interrupted for a moment. If the Tsar was unable to receive his Ministers a regency would have to be set up at once.

The Empress indignantly rejected this last suggestion, but promised that she would let Freedericksz — but no one else — see the patient on the following morning. Freedericksz went away thoroughly embarrassed and in doubt what to do. He asked the Court surgeon, Dr. Hirsch, to convey to the Tsar at his next consultation the message that Freedericksz felt it important that he should be admitted every day without exception to the Sovereign's sick-room, even if only for a few moments. In that way the letter of the law could be considered to have been observed.

This was done. The Tsar's view of a regency was sought by an indirect reference to the question — Freedericksz asked whether he would not wish his brother Michael to be asked to come to see him. The Tsar sided with his wife:

'No, no! Mischa will get everything into a mess: he is so easily imposed on.'

In the end it was decided that Freedericksz should have a daily audience, and that all reports sent in by the other Ministers should be submitted to the Tsar through him.

It was not easy, indeed it proved impossible, to carry this out.

The Empress guarded the sick-room like a veritable Cerberus. She did not even admit people for whom the Tsar had sent. As for Freedericksz, most of his visits were reduced to a few minutes behind a screen, out of sight of the Tsar, and with no possibility of speaking a word to him. The consequence was an accumulation of urgent business.

It was at this stage that the Empress began to make a practice of giving 'orders' concerning affairs of state. Until then she had only had to do with her maids of honour and the female staff in attendance on the children. Suddenly, at a day's notice, we saw her take the affairs of the State into her hands.

At that time the Empress had three maids of honour. Princess E, Obolenskaya, Princess S. Orbeliani, and Mile A. Olenina — manifestly an insufficient number. She summoned back from Rome Princess Marie Victorovna Bariatinskaya, a former maid of honour with whom she had broken off all communications for some three years past. This lady, who had a great deal of energy and plenty of common sense, at once established herself as a sort of Chief of Staff to the Empress. She discussed with me and with Ministers the problems that the Empress wanted to settle, and 'prepared' solutions that would be satisfactory to her mistress. We saw at once that Her Majesty's 'orders' were going beyond the petty instructions to be given to 'Cutlet Colonels' (as the junior officers in subordinate posts at the Court, responsible only for matters coming within the very limited range of the affairs of the palace, were nicknamed), and were infringing the provinces of all the Ministers. The consequence was that Freedericksz found himself at times in a very delicate situation, especially as the maids of honour, in passing on the Empress's 'orders' to his subordinates, frequently asked them to 'keep these orders secret — don't tell the Minister of the Court'.

We began to realize the Empress's inadequacy to the task that she had determined to undertake.

THE GERMAN PRINCESS

She was a princess from a petty German principality, and she remained true to type throughout her life. An excellent mother, an economical housewife, 'house-proud', she had never developed the qualities that go to make a true Empress. She had not even succeeded in becoming Russian at heart or in sympathy. Right up to her tragic end she never brought herself to converse in Russian; she used that language, as is well known, only when talking to servants and to the Orthodox clergy. This was all the stranger since her own sister, the Grand Duchess Elizabeth Feodorovna, grew completely, radically 'Russified' in a very short time. Elizabeth filled all who knew her with deep love and admiration. The Empress never attempted to follow her sister's example.

I recall an incident that occurred during one of Their Majesties' visits to the Crimea. The Empress was expecting a baby. On leaving St. Petersburg she had told the Minister of the Court that she did not want to have any receptions on the journey or any watching crowds in the towns they passed through. Freedericksz informed the Minister of the Interior of this.

In spite of all the precautions of the police, as we came to one little station we saw a crowd of people in their Sunday best. At the sight of them the Empress at once had all the blinds of her car drawn.

The provincial governor was on the station platform, and urged that His Majesty should come for a moment to the window; he felt it would be a 'blunder' to make his police send away a crowd that had waited a good part of the night simply in order to catch a fleeting glimpse of their sovereign. The people there, he urged, were all filled with a feeling of veneration for their Emperor, and it was impossible to have them hustled by gendarmes.

Freedericksz went into Their Majesties' compartment and conveyed to them the governor's very reasonable representations. The Tsar made a move towards the window, but the Empress said to him at once that he had no right to encourage even indirectly 'those who were not carrying out his orders.' Freedericksz felt it necessary once more to press the matter. The Tsar gave way, and went to one of the windows. The enthusiasm of the crowd was indescribable. But the Empress would not move her curtain an inch. The children pressed their faces against the slits on either side between curtain and window frame. They too had received a strict injunction not to let themselves be seen.

Marie Feodorovna, the Dowager Empress, learned, I do not know through what channel, of Freedericksz's happy intervention. Her comment was:

'If *she* was not there Nicky would be twice as popular. She is a regular German. She thinks the Imperial family should be "above that sort of thing." What does she mean? Above winning the people's affection? There's no need to go in for what I should call vulgar ways of seeking popularity. Nicky himself has all that is required for popular adoration; all he needs to do is to show himself to those who want to see him. How many times I have tried to make it plain to her. She won't understand; perhaps she hasn't it in her to understand. And yet, how often she complains of the public indifference towards her.'

Freedericksz himself told me at length of this conversation, immediately after an audience which Marie Feodorovna had granted him.

THE CARRIAGE PROBLEM

That was not the only occasion on which the narrowness of the Empress's outlook — a narrowness instilled into her in the petty court of Hesse and on the Rhine — was productive of difficulties.

During the visit to Compiègne Alexandra Feodorovna made terrible difficulties over the famous question of carriages.

Etiquette required that the Tsar should ride with President Loubet in the first carriage. The Empress would follow in a second carriage with the Mistress of the Robes, Mme Naryshkin, by her side.

All went well until the Tsar had to go on horseback for the manoeuvres. The existing rules of procedure require that the President of the Republic shall not appear to the troops otherwise than in a carriage. It was thus impossible for him to follow the Tsar's example. He must appear in a carriage — but in what carriage?

'Why, of course,' M. Crozier, *Chef du Protocole*, explained to us, 'in the Empress's carriage, by her side.'

The Empress would not hear of it. The Tsar of all the Russias on horseback, to all appearance 'escorting' the President! It was impossible. The President must ride in a separate carriage from hers, although that would look as if he were in the Tsar's suite.

In the end we found a solution at Compiègne which avoided wounding French susceptibilities. We had to resort to a subterfuge. This message was sent to M. Crozier:

'The Tsar will start in President Loubet's carriage. On arrival at the manoeuvres, he will leave the carriage and mount his horse. Would it be possible at that stage to bring up the second carriage, the Empress's, and to arrange for Mme Naryshkin to get out of the carriage so that the President could take the place left vacant by the Mistress of the Robes?'

'President Loubet,' our Masters of Ceremonies hinted, 'will not think of subjecting an old lady, one of the highest dignitaries of the Court, to such an affront.'

The French, gallant as always, gave way to our arguments, and President Loubet remained in his carriage.

For the ceremonial review the discussions had to begin all over again. Up to the last moment the French insisted that the President must accompany the Empress in her carriage. But she held out, and left in a carriage in which Mme Naryshkin had taken her place beside her. President Loubet had to rest content with a second carriage, in which he was joined by M. Waldeck-Rousseau, the Prime Minister.

Next year, when President Loubet returned the visit of the Russian sovereigns, the same difficulties came up again. There could be no reason why the head of an allied and friendly State should not be found room in the Empress's carriage.

This time the Empress employed another stratagem. The Tsar would go on horseback; the President would be in the Empress's carriage. But the carriage would be transformed into a sort of family charabanc: there would be two seats at the back, for the Empress and the President, and two in front, facing the horses, in which the Dowager Empress and Grand Duchess Elizabeth Feodorovna would ride.

This vehicle was constructed.

But now protests came from Marie Feodorovna. The state coaches had no coachman, being conducted by postilions; consequently the front part, in which the Dowager Empress was to sit, looked like a coachman's seat — a box seat, indeed; for, to add to her disgust, it was raised up.

But the young Empress had the final say. The whole ceremony was carried through in the way she wanted.

THE *ALMANACH DE GOTHA* CENSORED

The Empress had her own peculiar notion of the omnipotence of the Tsars of Russia. I recall the incident of the *Almanach de Gotha*. Her Majesty imagined that in my capacity of head of the Court censorship I was in a position to impose her will on a work of reference published abroad.

One day, on the way back from Tsarskoe Selo, Freedericksz told me that the Empress had been extremely annoyed by a headline in the *Almanach*. She wanted this annual to be forbidden to use the following description in the chapter devoted to Russia:

'DYNASTIE HOLSTEIN-GOTTORP-ROMANOV.'

The *Almanach* must be made to delete the first two names, on pain of being excluded from Russian territory.

I had had plenty of trouble over this already. Regularly every year the editorial office of the *Almanach* sent me proofs of the pages dealing with Russia. Regularly every year I entered the names of the newly appointed dignitaries, and cut out the words 'Holstein-Gottorp'. And regularly every year the editorial staff, with equal care, made every change I had indicated except this last one: they retained the words 'Holstein-Gottorp'. In the end I wrote to them, and received the reply that in their view the name of the dynasty could not be modified, since it depended on the historic fact that the Emperor Paul was the son of the Duke of Holstein-Gottorp.

To ban this annual, so well known throughout the world, would, it seemed to me, be ridiculous, and I begged Freedericksz to submit a report from me to the Tsar, so that he could rescind the Empress's order. Freedericksz preferred to submit my report to the Empress herself. She sent for me at once.

'Are you really unable to get these two words cut out?'

'I have already written,' I replied, 'to the editor, and have been met with a refusal.'

'But suppose I authorized you to say that it is *my* wish that these two words should be suppressed?'

'We should run the risk of being given quotations from the historic documents which exist to prove that the dynasty should bear the name

Holstein-Gottorp-Romanov. They might also send a troublesome article to the Press.'

'Then there is nothing left,' she concluded, 'but to prohibit the entry of the book into Russia.'

'That, Madam, is even more impracticable. There would be a world-wide scandal. The story would go round everywhere that the most legitimist of all books, the aristocratic almanach *par excellence*, had been banned by the Russian censorship! The two words in dispute would at once be discovered, and irreparable harm would be done. As things are, the Russian public has not the least interest in this question of the dynastic title. If the decree banning the *Almanach* goes out, the one subject of conversation in every diplomat's drawing-room will be this particularly delicate problem.'

Finally I suggested that Grand Duchess Victoria Feodorovna, *née* Princess of Saxe-Coburg-*Gotha*, might find a way of making the editor-in-chief of the calendar listen to reason.

The Empress cut the audience short, and never returned to the subject of the two offending words.

ECONOMY

Alexandra Feodorovna was habitually economical down to the smallest details. I recall the incident of the allowance proposed for Mme Vyrubova.

Mme Vyrubova was in an exceptional situation at the Empress's Court. She had not, strictly speaking, any official function, and did not seek any. Every day the Empress sent for her to the Palace; the two spent hours together at music, or talking and working at their embroidery. The Empress openly called her her 'personal friend'. It was Mme Vyrubova who was Rasputin's principal advocate with the Empress, and Alexandra Feodorovna felt that some of the authority which the Staretz[1] exercised over her descended even to the devotee of so extraordinary a man.

Freedericksz knew that the Taneyev family, to which Mme Vyrubova belonged by birth, was none too well off. Her daily visits to the Palace, and the dressing and preparation for the many journeys

1 See p.126.

she made with the Empress, whom she accompanied almost everywhere, could not but be a heavy drain on her private resources.

One day, therefore, Freedericksz suggested to the Empress that a position at Court should be created for Mme Vyrubova, and asked for authority to make her a sufficient allowance to enable her to hold her own among the very rich people who made up the society at Court.

The Empress showed little interest in the idea of creating a new post:

'Am I not entitled to choose my friends where I like?'

In regard to the allowance she made no objection. Freedericksz asked what figure should be fixed. Alexandra Feodorovna replied that the amount was to be 2,000 roubles, equivalent to £200 per annum! Freedericksz pointed out the inadequacy of the allowance, but the Empress held to her decision.

She was economical even in providing for her own children. The Emperor's private office had received instructions to buy three pearls for each of the Tsar's daughters each time she had a birthday, so that they might have fine necklaces when they grew up. Prince Obolensky, the head of the private office, suggested again and again that it would be better to buy four duly assorted necklaces and to give one of them to each of the four children on her birthday; odd pearls would never make satisfactory necklaces and would cost more in the end. But the Empress insisted that the necklaces would cost too much. Obolensky, however, consulted Freedericksz, and with his approval bought the four necklaces.

Still more symptomatic was an incident that occurred at the time of the state visit of King Edward to Reval in 1908.

The number of decorations awarded on this occasion was relatively small. All the important personalities in the Tsar's suite had received presents instead of decorations, presents which the King had made a point of giving personally.

We had to follow the same procedure. Soon after the arrival of the *Victoria and Albert* I had got into touch with Ponsonby (now Lord Ponsonby), who was one of our guest's principal aides-de-camp. We agreed to go together to choose gifts suitable to the situation and the tastes of each of the intended recipients.

Ponsonby showed the most perfect tact; it had been a delicate task, but we felt that we had got through it with credit.

I sought an audience of the Tsar in order to deliver the gifts to him, and suggested that he should hand them personally to the various officials of King Edward's Court. But at this stage the Empress said she wanted to see the gifts we had chosen.

She said at once, to my dismay, that she was going to change the destination of certain cigarette-cases. All my arrangements were in danger of being thrown into confusion.

'Besides,' the Empress said to me, crushingly, 'these presents are all much too expensive. Another time, please let me see them beforehand!'

The only thing I could do was to pull out of my pocket the massive gold cigarette-case which the King of England had just presented to me. It was covered with black enamel, and had the royal monogram in diamonds. This case was of greater value than any of the objects at that moment in the Tsar's hands. The Empress herself had to admit it. I took advantage of her momentary confusion to get the Tsar to proceed to the distribution.

SHE WAS NEVER POPULAR

Alexandra Feodorovna had never succeeded in winning popularity in the country of her adoption. A whole series of unlucky events had completed the work of her morbid timidity in preventing it.

She was only seventeen when she came for the first time to St. Petersburg, to see her elder sister, Grand Duchess Elizabeth Feodorovna. She met the heir to the throne, who was later to become her husband. Nicholas Alexandrovitch was then twenty-one, and the young princess made such an impression on him that people at once began talking of a love match.

Nicholas told his father before the princess left that he wanted to marry her; but Alexander III would not hear of an engagement. He considered that Nicholas was too young to marry. As for the Empress Marie Feodorovna, she showed a strong dislike of the idea of 'a German girl'. Bismarck's annexation of Schleswig-Holstein in 1864 had, of course, brought a deep estrangement between Copenhagen and Berlin.

In a Court everybody knows everybody else's business. 'Society' in St. Petersburg was impregnated with the nationalist ideas of which the Tsar himself was full; and the occasion was seized for an exhibition of the Teutophobia so fashionable at the time. The princess from Hesse was treated with undisguised contempt; industriously mocked at behind her back, and made the subject of stories busily invented and as busily passed round.

Alix Victoria Helen Louise Beatrice of Hesse-Darmstadt was old enough already to realize what was going on on all sides, and strongly resented it.

Her marriage in 1894 took place in painful and tragic circumstances, which made an unfortunate impression on the mass of the Russian people. Alexander III had fallen seriously ill. Grand Duke Michael Nicolayevitch, the oldest member of the Imperial family, had gone to see the Tsar and had broken to him the news of the dangerous nature of his malady (acute nephritis), and of the urgent need, in consequence, for Nicholas Alexandrovitch to take a wife as soon as possible. The Tsar gave his consent. The Grand Duke learned from the Cesarevitch that he would never marry any other princess than the one he had loved since 1889. The necessary formalities took a good deal of time, and it was not until four weeks after his father's death that Nicholas II went through the religious ceremony of his marriage.

Shoulders were shrugged all over Russia.

Next spring, in Moscow, at the popular merry-making organized on May 18th in honour of the coronation, there was a disaster which gave everybody in Russia, where everybody was superstitious, occasion for predicting that Alexandra Feodorovna would be dogged by misfortune.

There were to be great celebrations in the open air at Hodynka, near Moscow. The news that everybody was to receive a gift with the monogram of the young Imperial couple spread like wildfire. The police forces were insufficient to control the crowd; the barriers were broken down by the thousands of men, women, and children who had settled on the field of Hodynka since the evening before. Hundreds were trampled to death, and many unfortunates were pinned and suffocated, unable to escape from the pressure of the human torrent around them.

'Ill omen!' 'She is bringing us bad luck!' Such was the impression produced by Princess Alix of Hesse on the Russian masses.

As Empress, Alexandra Feodorovna failed equally to gain the allegiance of Court circles and of St. Petersburg society.

She was excessively timid; and she had no liking for society talk and no aptitude for that delicate art. She thus earned a reputation for hauteur.

Grand Duchess Marie Pavlovna, aunt of Nicholas II, set out to 'nurse' her, to guide her through the social labyrinth of petty rivalries and jealousies; she met with repeated rebuffs, the more violent since the Empress sought to conceal her timidity beneath a surface show of assurance and energy and strength of will. The Empress found herself faced in consequence with the hostility not only of the Court of the Empress Dowager, which was gradually outshone as the Court of the young Empress grew in importance, but of the still more important Court, from the social point of view, of the Grand Duchess Marie Pavlovna.

Aged and very respectable ladies ventured into the presence of Alexandra Feodorovna, full of good intentions, and ventured to offer a little sensible advice: they received sharp and stinging answers. They went away mumbling words that they had not dared to speak aloud; one is always full of bright ideas of what one might have said. What the old ladies did say subsequently, in the bitterness of their outraged dignity and *amour-propre*, drifted back in due course to the Court, garbled, taken out of its context, and deliberately accentuated in its malice. There followed open breaches; Alexandra Feodorovna found herself almost without a friend; and thereafter the personal humiliations suffered by the Empress were hailed as so many triumphs for 'society'.

'AS FOR MY HOSPITALS . . .'

A characteristic incident remains vivid in my memory. The war was going on and on, more and more murderously. The Tsar had invited Freedericksz, who was very ill, to go for a rest to the Crimea. I went with him, for there were fears that his state might become critical. Almost immediately after we reached the Crimea we received a telegram saying that the Grand Duchess Marie Pavlovna[1] was coming on a visit. The question arose how to arrange for the Tsar's aunt during her stay.

There could be no question of putting her up in the Palace; Freedericksz knew that the idea would be thoroughly disagreeable to the Empress. Apart from that, the Palace was undergoing its annual renovation. We decided that it would be possible to fit up for the use

1 Grandmother of Marina, Duchess of Kent.

of the Grand Duchess a set of rooms in the house occupied by the Imperial suite. We telegraphed to the Marshal of the Court, Count Benckendorff, to send us cooks, servants, and utensils. He replied that there was not time to do what we wanted.

Freedericksz showed utter astonishment at this cool reply; Count Benckendorff had always been equal to any task imposed on him. I realized at once that the telegram had been sent off with the Empress's knowledge, perhaps by her direct order.

I increased the number of workmen at the Palace, to make it more plainly uninhabitable; I had bits of scaffolding put up everywhere. Freedericksz lent me his own chef; we borrowed a sufficiency of silver from my sister-in-law, Countess Nirod; the necessary motor-cars were lent by the Transport Department. I had the quarters of the Imperial suite decorated with flower-boxes. When the Grand Duchess arrived she expressed her delight with the arrangements made for her.

Next day we visited the hospitals at Yalta and within the precincts of Livadia, a domain which the Tsar had presented to his wife; then we went on to Gourzouf, a spot visited by all who came to the Crimea.

As we got into the cars the Grand Duchess, to my astonishment, asked her maid of honour. Mile Oliv, to go in the second car, and made a sign to me to sit by her side, a thing quite against the rules of Court etiquette.

We had scarcely passed through the gates of Livadia when she took a telegram out of her bag and passed it to me with a hand that trembled. The telegram was in English:

'Am astonished that you should be at Livadia without having asked the lady of the house. As for my hospitals, I know that they are in good order. Alexandra.'

'What impertinence!' she said to me, flushed with anger. 'Anyhow, here is the answer I am sending.'

I read an endless message. Heavens! there was no mincing of words in it.

'I hope your Highness has not yet sent off this telegram?'

'No,' she answered, 'I wanted to see what you think.'

We discussed the draft, word by word, throughout the journey. I heaved a great sigh of relief when at last the Grand Duchess said to me:

'You are right — I will leave it unanswered. It would be beneath my dignity, at my age, to take any notice of a piece of tactlessness on the part of a woman, and a princess at that, who had to come to me to learn how to behave in society — '

And so on, until the moment of our arrival at Gourzouf.

THE EMPRESS'S FRIENDS

Apart from the problem of Rasputin,[1] little happened to disturb the Empress's peace. She was completely satisfied with her family life. It would have been impossible for her to find food for jealousy; her husband devoted every free moment to her.

Any time when the Tsar was not there was taken up with the care of her children — to whom she was the tenderest of mothers — or spent in conversation with her maids of honour. There was deep affection between the Empress and Princess Orbeliani, an intelligent, graceful, elegant woman with a caustic wit.

But the time came when Princess Orbeliani was struck down by the malady which brought her, after terrible sufferings, to her grave. One day at Spala, while we were waiting for Their Majesties to come to dinner, she fell to the ground for no apparent reason. Hirsch, the Court surgeon, told me that that was a very serious sign, the first symptom of creeping paralysis, which was hereditary in her mother's family.

The Princess was aware of the fate that awaited her; she faced it with great courage. One day, when talking to me, she pointed to four sorts of crutches standing in one of the corners of her room.

'So many years for this simple one,' she said, 'so many months for the next, more complicated one, and so on. My mother passed through it all, and I know exactly what I have to expect.'

The progress of the malady was very rapid. That did not prevent the Princess from accompanying Her Majesty wherever she went — on train journeys, to Livadia, to Spala, on board the yacht. The Empress went to see her every day, and told her the latest news. Her Majesty had to conceal from the Princess any new friendship that she formed. If ever the Princess suspected that the Empress had been unmindful of their long intimacy she made terrible scenes in her

1 See pp.123ff.

jealousy, with never-ending tears and reproaches. She lay helpless for eight years on her bed of suffering before death released her.

As the Princess's condition grew worse it became easier for the Empress to enjoy the society of her friend Madame Vyrubova. This admirer of Rasputin had discovered another sensitive chord in the enigmatic heart of the Empress through posing as a 'poor little orphan adrift in the world' and in need of petting and care. Vyrubova's tactics lay in alternating scenes of jealousy with despairing appeals for protection to one whom she looked upon as a second mother or as her big sister. The part was congenial to the Empress, who was always ready to act as guide and counsellor, if only to one of the ladies of her Court.

There remain to be mentioned the maids of honour less intimately associated with the Empress (Princess Obolenskaya, Mile Olenina, Countess Hendrikov), the principal Lady in Waiting to the Empress, Madame Geringer, and Fraulein Schneider, whose official title was Reader to the Court; unofficially she was in charge of the children. That exhausts the list of those who gravitated around the Empress.

I do not know of a single case of an invitation being sent by the Empress to any person outside the restricted circle of the Court and her immediate entourage. Even the Grand Duchesses only made rare visits to her, either on various anniversaries which had become regular occasions for celebration, or on actual invitation to tea or lunch. No artist, no writer, no man of learning, even of world renown, was ever admitted to the Tsarina's intimate circle. She felt that the fewer people she saw, the better!

When her husband went to G.H.Q., and she took upon herself the direction of affairs of state, the Empress proceeded by trial and error on her own initiative; instead of following steadily and intelligently along the lines indicated by her husband, she tried to co-ordinate her own ideas with those of 'our friend' (Rasputin), and made it impossible for those Ministers who took their office seriously to get anything done.

THE SPIRITS

There was a short period of close friendship with the two Montenegrin princesses, Militza and Anastasia (Stana). Sometimes the Empress would go to Dulber (the domain of Grand Duke Peter

Nicolayevitch, the husband of Princess Militza), and pass long hours there; sometimes the Montenegrin ladies would come and shut themselves up with the Empress in her apartments in Livadia.

This friendship, suddenly formed and abruptly broken off, was always an enigma to me. Their bringing-up had given the two Montenegrin ladies nothing in common with the descendant of a long line of German and British sovereigns. The two princesses were exceedingly dark, almost black, and were in striking contrast to one who admitted only one superior — the foremost lady of her epoch. Queen Victoria.

It has always been said that the friendship was based on the common interest of all three in spiritualism. Both at Dulber and at Strelna, the Grand Duke's winter residence, near St. Petersburg, there were table turnings and consultations of spirits; dead Tsars answered the call of the mediums. The Emperor himself was said to have taken part in the seances, which were carried on by two foreign occultists named Papus and Philippe. This seems to have been the first manifestation of this tendency to a morbid mysticism, which later on enabled Rasputin to gain a footing at Court.

Papus was soon expelled, on an order from the Tsar himself. Philippe lasted longer, but he too was got rid of in the end. A Paris detective, M. Ratchkovsky, was instructed to undertake an elaborate investigation of Philippe's antecedents; his report was so enlightening that Philippe was told to clear out. Immediately after Philippe's disappearance from the scene Ratchkovsky himself was relieved of his post — why? Nobody knows.

In any case, in this first crisis of occultism the Tsar had the energy to intervene effectually. What a pity that he did not do the same with regard to the man who took up on his own account the 'occult' methods of Papus, and forged for himself an unparalleled influence, seasoning the Papus dish with a sauce made up of elements of the *mujik*, the mystic, the sectary, and probably the blasphemer.

I will add only a few words concerning the people whom I found Rasputin had attracted to his side when I came back from Jassy for a short stay at Petrograd in 1917. It would be too painful to dwell on what I witnessed at the time. I was concerned to discover who these persons were, in order to establish the influences that had inspired the latest appointments. 'Which of the ladies has influence with the Empress?' I asked.

Some said 'Munia' Golovina, niece of Princess Paley. Others indicated Princess Guedroytz, the head physician of Her Majesty's hospital, an entirely masculine woman. Others said to me in a tone of surprise:

'Why, don't you know Mile So-and-so, the head sister? She dictates to the Empress who is to have every important post.'

I asked a friend who lived at Tsarskoe Selo. He knew all these people, without being 'one of them'. He told me that these ladies were sisters of charity, of good family, and were trying to make a show of possessing great influence but probably had less than they imagined.

It was an utter nightmare. I only felt safe once more when I took train again to Jassy.

HER PIETY

Alexandra Feodorovna was deeply and sincerely devout. She gained in her early youth a knowledge and love of the Orthodox service, with its wealth of symbolic ceremonial. As soon as she became engaged to our heir-apparent she was prepared for conversion to the faith of her adoption.

Sincere in all that she did, she protested vehemently against that part of the ritual of conversion to the Orthodox religion in which the neophyte had to make a theatrical renunciation of the errors of her past religion. The ritual included the act, instituted in the Middle Ages, of 'spitting thrice on the ground' in evidence of contempt for the religion formerly professed. Our clergy were asked to suppress this painful ceremony in the case of the young German princess.

On many occasions I was able to watch the Empress during the long services of the Orthodox Church, in which the congregation stands from beginning to end. She stood erect and motionless — 'like a taper', as a peasant who had seen her said. Her face was completely transfigured, and it was plain that for her the prayers were no mere formality.

Father Alexander, who became her confessor and personal chaplain, read aloud a series of prayers which, under the Orthodox rubric, priests are required to read sotto voce before the altar. Her Majesty was fond of the service as Father Alexander conducted it, and never grew weary.

Later, when she had become weak through illness, she had a private chapel installed, from which the whole of the service in the church at Livadia could be heard. It was only with reluctance that in the end she had a small sofa placed in the chapel, so that she could lie down if she grew too tired.

At Tsarskoe Selo the Empress preferred the sombre transept of the Feodor Cathedral, which had been built in accordance with her personal indications.

Rasputin's 'preaching' fell on a soil long prepared and eager to assimilate every mystical revelation.

• • • • •

The Empress's activities fell into two very different categories. When she was concerned with affairs of state she submitted herself to an occult and disastrous influence, and dissipated her energies in sterile efforts.

But when she was occupied with matters within her competence she showed herself a very efficient organizer. She showed her capacity in the installation of hospital trains, convalescent homes, and hospitals. In such matters she knew how to gather round her persons of ability and energy.

It is right that her success in that field should be acknowledged. Fate dealt hardly with this woman.

The story of the heroic courage shown by the Empress in captivity is beyond the scope of this work.

III. THE CHILDREN

THE CESAREVITCH: HIS PRECARIOUS HEALTH

The children were objects of Their Majesties' special solicitude. My duties left me little time for observation of the heir to the throne and the Grand Duchesses. They grew up almost without my noticing it. The maids of honour were not authorized to take any part in their education. (Princess Orbehani and the Mistress of the Robes were exceptions to this rule.) Thus few intimate details about the children's life could become generally known.

At first the Cesarevitch was a bright and lively boy. His terrible malady (haemophilia) only showed itself later. I well remember the way he used to put in his appearance at table, when dessert was being served, as a baby of three or four years. He would go to his parents and chatter a little to them, and then make the round of the guests, talking to them without the least sign of timidity. He used to slip under the table and catch hold of the ladies' shoes; if they started he would be greatly amused. Once he pulled off the slipper of one of the maids of honour and carried it away as a trophy to his father, who told him to put it back. He plunged under the table. Suddenly the maid of honour screamed. Before putting the slipper on her foot the Cesarevitch had put into it an enormous strawberry. The cold wet mush made the young lady jump out of her chair.

The child was scolded and sent back to his room, and for a considerable time he was forbidden to appear at the dinner-table, much to his grief.

Even after the first signs of his malady showed themselves, the Cesarevitch kept his high spirits; but if one watched him closely one could see his face cloud over; sometimes it would lose all its brightness and become sickly and lifeless.

Repeated efforts were made to find a boy of his own age who could be a playmate for the Cesarevitch. At first sailors' sons were tried; then the children and nephews of Derevenko, the Cesarevitch's attendant (*diadka* in Russian — 'little uncle' — that is to say, guardian and confidant and nurse for the boy). In the end the attempt was abandoned.

M. Gilliard, the Cesarevitch's tutor, an incomparable teacher and a man of the highest intelligence, often told me that the boy's education presented enormous difficulties. Scarcely had a course of study begun when the Cesarevitch would fall ill; the effusions of blood brought him terrible suffering; he spent whole nights groaning and begging for help that no one could give him. His malady exhausted him and set his nerves on edge; and in that state the little sufferer came back to his lessons, with everything to begin afresh.

Could this poor little unfortunate be blamed if he proved wanting in diligence and concentration?

THE TOBOGGANS OF SOLID SILVER

Two incidents that I recall show how simple and rudimentary were the amusements of the Grand Duchesses as young children, how easily they were pleased.

The first occurred while the Imperial train had stopped in the neighbourhood of Roshkovo, in Moscow county. The Tsar was inspecting the troops of the region, and his train stopped in the open country for five days.

There were long hours with nothing to do, and one day Grand Duchess Olga, the Tsar's sister, invented a new sort of sport for her nieces. The train was standing at the top of a high embankment, and advantage was taken of the slope to enable them to toboggan — in the middle of August! It would have been difficult to find sledges, but that was not allowed to stand in the way of the sport. Silver salvers were fetched from the pantry. Each of the children had her own salver; they slid down and then climbed up again with the salvers on their backs.

The children were so delighted that it was decided to go on with the tobogganing after dinner, in the presence of Their Majesties. One of the military attaches asked me, with some apprehension, whether the guests would have to engage in the new sport. I hastened to reassure him.

One of the maids of honour set off first, to act as judge at the finishing point. General Strukov, A.D.C., announced to the children that he was going to be the first to get to the bottom. When the signal was given to start he made one jump in his gala uniform, with the ribbon of Alexander Nevsky over his shoulder, his diamond-studded sword of honour (he had taken Adrianople in the 1877 campaign) in his hand; he precipitated himself down the twenty feet of the embankment, and sank up to his knees in the slipping sand. How did he manage to come unscathed out of that risky adventure?

THE LIVE SABLE

The second incident is that of the live sable which was brought straight from the depths of Siberia.

One day I had an urgent report for the Tsar to draw up, and had given orders that I would not see any one. Suddenly my senior and confidential messenger came into my office.

'What is it? Is there any need for me to be disturbed?'

'I venture to mention to Your Excellency that an old peasant and his wife have just arrived straight from Siberia. They have brought a five sable as a present for His Majesty. The man insisted that I should announce him to Your Excellency. He says he has not the means to pay for a night's lodging.'

'And you took pity on him?'

'I cannot deny it.'

'Bring him in.'

A very attractive old man came in, a woman accompanying him. He said: 'I am a hunter. One day I caught a sable alive. I have succeeded in taming it, with my wife's help. We decided to make a present of it to the Little Father Tsar. It is a wonderful sable. We got together all the money we had, and here we are.'

He produced his sable, and it jumped at once on to my desk and began sniffing at the dockets of papers concerning Court appointments. The old man gave a peculiar whistle, and the sable jumped into his arms and took refuge behind the lapel of his caftan (a sort of long frock-coat), leaving only the tip of its snout visible.

'How did you get to St. Petersburg?'

'The money we had lasted us as far as Moscow. We were just getting ready to do the rest of the journey on foot when a gentleman — may the Lord preserve him! — gave us the money for a fresh ticket. We arrived this morning and set off at once for the Winter Palace. The officer on guard sent us on to you. We haven't a kopek left: but we should like to see the Little Father Tsar!'

I decided that a live sable would delight the Grand Duchesses; they were quite children then, I gave the old man a little money and left him in charge of my messenger.

I took care, of course, to find out from the old man whom he could name in Siberia that had knowledge of him.

'Before leaving,' he said, 'I went to see the governor of the province; he told me he couldn't prevent me from going, but that I had no chance at all of being received by the Tsar. He also refused to give me a letter or write anything for me.'

I had a telegram sent to the governor, to make sure that the old man was not a revolutionary. Next day I had an entirely reassuring reply. I telephoned to Princess Orbehani and told her about the sable. An hour later a message came from the Princess telling me to send the old man and woman and their sable to the palace — 'as quickly as possible, for the children are wild with impatience'.

I sent the messenger with the couple, telling him to bring them back as soon as the audience was over. It was a very long one. The two old people remained over an hour with the children, in the presence of the Empress herself.

'We meant to bring the sable back with us,' the old man told me, 'and to take it back when a proper cage had been got ready for it. But the children would not part from it. Finally the Tsarina gave the order for the animal to be left with them. I said I absolutely must see the Tsar; I could not go back to Siberia without seeing the Tsar, They told me they would let me know.'

He added, thoughtfully:

'What I'm afraid of is that my sable may make too much of an upset in the Palace. It is not used to apartments like that.'

Next day I received instructions to send the two peasants to the Palace at 6 p.m. They came back about eight; the sable was once more under the lapel of the old man's caftan.

'It's as I said,' he told me, 'The sable couldn't behave properly. And as soon as I got there it made one leap to me.'

'Little Father Tsar,' he went on, dwelling on the words, 'Little Father Tsar came in. We threw ourselves at his feet. The sable looked at him as if it understood that it was the Tsar himself We went into the children's room. The Tsar told me to let the sable go, and the children began to play with it; when I'm there, you see, it doesn't get wild. Then the Tsar told us to sit down on chairs. He began to ask me questions — what made me think of coming to see him and how I managed to get to the Empress.'

The peasant continued, with more and more animation:

'He asked me what things are like in Siberia, how we go hunting. . . . Then the Tsarina said it was time for dinner. Little Father Tsar asked me what had to be done for the sable. When I had explained he told me to send it to the Hunters' Village of Gatchino. But I said:

' "Little Father Tsar, that won't do. All the hunters will be wanting to sell the skin of my sable. They will kill it and say the animal had an accident. I know them, those hunters. They have no pity for a live animal."

'The Tsar said:

' "I would have chosen a hunter I could trust. But perhaps after all you are right. Take it back with you to Siberia. Look after it as long as it lives. That is an order you have received from me. Go to Mossolov and tell him to give you a good present. But mind, don't forget to look well after the sable; it's my sable now. God be with you!" '

Next day, before Freedericksz had begun his report, the Tsar told him of the two hours he had had with the old Siberian hunter.

The old man was given a watch with the Imperial eagle; the old woman received a brooch; they were paid on a generous scale for the sable and given the money for their return journey.

The Grand Duchesses were inconsolable.

'There was no help for it,' they said. 'Papa had made up his mind.'

THEY HAD NO GOVERNESSES

The children were given a fairly comprehensive education; but it was so organized as not to bring them into the company of too many persons, whether teachers or fellow-pupils. At the time when I commenced my service at Court, the Grand Duchesses had no teacher. There were nurses to be seen in their apartments, but that was all. When the nurses had gone the children were virtually without supervision, except, of course, that of their mother. The Empress, however, remained almost always in an arm-chair, motionless, and never spoke to her daughters in the presence of a third party.

To save them from acquiring their mother's timidity, the Grand Duchesses had had lunch with their parents from a very early age; Marie Nicolayevna had done so since she was six. As young girls they were well-behaved at table, although they were under no supervision — their mother was often absent from lunch, and the maids of honour let the four children alone, as they had received no special instruction to teach them good manners. I must add that after meals, when they mixed with the grown-ups, the princesses did not always behave in the way that one might fairly have expected of the daughters of the Tsar.

Ultimately a teacher was found for them, though she was not officially given that description. Her name was Catherine Adolfovna Schneider. She was a niece of Dr. Hirsch, the Court surgeon, and had been engaged as Russian teacher by Grand Duchess Elizabeth

Feodorovna after her marriage with Grand Duke Serge. Subsequently she passed into the service of the Empress.

Slender, fragile, self-effacing, this young lady was active everywhere, and ready for any sacrifice. (She was shot by the Bolsheviks somewhere in Siberia.) She adored the Empress and the children. Her capacity for work was astonishing. She taught Alexandra Feodorovna Russian, and was at the same time her private secretary; she did all the shopping for Her Majesty; she accompanied the children whenever they went out. She was infinitely sweet-tempered and good-hearted. One sole shortcoming she had: the children paid not the slightest attention to anything she said.

The time came when Freedericksz, feeling that there were objections to a young girl being constantly in Their Majesties' presence without having any officially recognized function, created for her the titular position of Reader to the Court.

It was she who gave the Grand Duchesses their first lessons; at this time she was their schoolmistress for all subjects. A little later there was a division of labour; Fräulein Schneider took the children in German (the four sisters all detested the language and refused to learn it); the Empress taught them English; M. Gilliard, the tutor to the Cesarevitch, gave them lessons in French; M. Petrov, a Russian schoolmaster, was in charge of Russian literature and all remaining subjects.

I was always told that if the Grand Duchesses had been, at a public school they would all have been among the top ten in their various classes.

THEY HAD NO GIRL FRIENDS

I shall tell elsewhere[1] how the one and only attempt to give the Grand Duchesses a governess properly so-called came to an end. Mlle Tuytcheva remained only a short time at Court.

The four girls grew up surrounded by a large number of servants, but, in spite of their mother's supervision, they were left a great deal to themselves. Not one of them ever had a real girl friend of her own age.

1 See pp.135-6.

The seven children of Grand Duchess Xenia were the only ones who came to see the Grand Duchesses without ceremony; they would come for tennis and tea — but they were never sent all at one time. The children of the Grand Dukes George and Constantine, aged ten, twelve, and twenty, were never present at these intimate meetings. Countess Emma, the daughter of Count Freedericksz, and a few of the officers of the yacht *Standard*, were the only persons not related to the Romanovs who joined the Tsar's daughters at play now and then.

To the best of my belief, there was one solitary ball organized for the two eldest of the Grand Duchesses, at Livadia in 1911 or 1912. The Marshal of the Court had been put in charge of the arrangements for this ball, and the officers of the *Standard* had been invited to come to the dancing, together with some other lieutenants from the Crimean cavalry division. The children long regarded this ball as one of the greatest events in their lives.

Every year a lottery was organized; the Empress and her daughters sold tickets.

In normal times there was a cinema performance every Saturday. The covered riding-school at Livadia had been appropriated for the performances, which were one of the main subjects of conversation for the whole of the week that followed.

The choice of films was a troublesome business. The Empress had settled the programme, once for all, as follows: first, as news film, the record taken during the week by the Court photographer, Jaguelsky, of the firm of Hahn; then an instructional film or a series of attractive views; finally, something amusing for the children. How many times I had to send for Mme Naryshkin, Mistress of the Robes, to view the film! She was solely responsible for deciding what was suitable or not suitable for the children. She was a pitiless censor; again and again the brightest spots in a film would be condemned as indecorous, and Jaguelsky's scissors got to work at once on them.

One day there was a real disaster. I was very busy, and told Jaguelsky not to trouble to show me the news film. 'You are not a beginner, and I don't suppose you could go wrong with nothing to show but Tuesday's review before Her Majesty!'

Jaguelsky confirmed that the film had nothing in it but the review. At the performance we saw the Emperor's arrival; then Count Mussin Pushkin, A.D.C., the General Commanding the troops in the Odessa region, passed in front of the Sovereign, saluted with his sword, and stood on his right like a statue. Everything was in perfect order.

Then came the catastrophe.

The film went on. It should be explained that at every thirty or forty yards there were soldiers holding little flags; as the troops defiled before the Tsar they had to 'feel' on the right with their shoulders for the imaginary line formed by the 'markers' with the flags, so as to ensure good formation.

The soldiers began to get more and more out of line with the markers. Mussin Pushkin stood impeccably at attention; but he made a sign with his left arm for the markers' line to be kept better. The soldiers were unable to obey the mute order. The Count's face grew fierce. Finally he clenched his fist and shook it at them, apparently about to tell them in the plainest language what he thought of them.

The children began to laugh. The Emperor bit his lips to keep from laughing too. I was in despair, but could not help smiling; it really was a funny spectacle.

After the performance Their Majesties made not the slightest allusion to what they had seen. I tried to get away as quickly as possible. But I felt my arm seized, and none too gently. It was Coumt Mussin Pushkin himself.

'My dear chap,' he said, 'what is the meaning of it? What could induce your photographer, how could he dare to show a General in Command of a whole region — like *that*? And before Their Majesties! I never heard of such a thing!

'Besides, I tell you he is lying! D'you get me? He has some grudge and is lying. I never, never threatened with my fist.

'I take it my word is good enough, and that this damned photographer will be placed under arrest for a week at least.

'To show me in an attitude that I never struck! It's unbelievable!'

The offending section of the film was cut out at once.

THEIR LIFE WAS MONOTONOUS

So the children grew up, living simply, in a tolerable but monotonous existence. They seemed entirely satisfied with their life; it hardly occurred to them that they might agitate for other distractions.

Olga, in 1912, was already seventeen, but she still had the ways of a 'flapper'. She was a blonde; with a face typically Russian in its curve, and a charming complexion and teeth that made her very pretty. Fraulein Schneider said she was 'as good as an angel'.

Tatiana was taller, more slender, and of more distinction; she was the best-looking of all the sisters. She was very reserved and quiet, and difficult to govern.

Marie was distinguished by her muscular strength; she was bright, energetic, and determined to get her own way. She was the least studious of the sisters.

Anastasia, the youngest, had the liveliest intelligence of all four; whoever was sitting next to her had to be prepared for some unexpected question at any moment.

As they grew up, the Grand Duchesses grew more reserved; at first it had been plain that they had never been under supervision.

During the war they passed their examinations as nursing sisters, and worked with their mother in the Palace hospital. They showed a great deal of self-sacrifice and absolute devotion. In that they were but following in their mother's footsteps. The Empress easily acquired an excellent knowledge of everything connected with the organization of hospitals, hospital trains, and sanatoria. In this field she showed herself thoroughly equal to her responsibilities, which at times were very exacting; she was successful in the choice of her immediate collaborators, and gave evidence of exceptional energy.

CHAPTER II

THE RELATIVES OF NICHOLAS II

I. THE DOWAGER EMPRESS
'A charmer'

The Dowager Empress Marie Feodorovna, Princess of Denmark, was descended collaterally from a line of princes of Schleswig-Holstein. The atmosphere of Holstein was patriarchal and thoroughly 'provincial'; but she had learned there to attach no very great importance to questions of etiquette, and to show indulgence for the little failings of those around her. Marie Feodorovna considered that her chief function as Empress was to charm those who came into contact with her. She had every quality needed for doing so, and was venerated alike at Court and by the great mass of the people.

She was particularly indulgent to all her suite. I recall the incident of the coachman who had drunk so much that he fell asleep on his seat, leaving the horses to their own devices; it was only with the utmost difficulty that they were brought to a stop. Marie Feodorovna had only one concern — to treat the incident as a joke and to make sure that it did not reach her husband's ears.

She went frequently to Copenhagen, having the yacht *Pole Star* at her disposal. On these voyages her servants used to buy considerable quantities of foreign goods.

That was forbidden alike by the Customs regulations and by those of the Court, On one occasion, on the return of the yacht to Russia, Freedericksz had all the baggage searched. There were cigarettes and playing-cards and silks in profusion. But the purchasers were neither prosecuted nor even required to pay the duty on all this contraband: Marie Feodorovna, with her charming smile, declared that she wanted everything, duties and fines alike, charged to her personal account. The personal account of the Dowager Empress was in charge of Freedericksz, so that the Minister of the Court himself paid the sums due from the persons whom he had set out to catch red-handed.

Marie Feodorovna could not refuse anything to the members of her suite. And Nicholas II agreed to everything that his mother asked.

The consequence was that most of the appointments at Court were made through the channel of the Empress Dowager's Court. She had a Lady in Waiting, Mme Flotow. This lady was officially responsible for the care of her mistress's jewels and wardrobe; but she had succeeded in gaining a position of altogether extravagant influence. As soon as the name of Mme Flotow was to be found in the papers of an applicant it was a foregone conclusion that the Tsar would grant the request, even if at first he was for rejecting it.

Somehow, I do not know how, Mme Flotow would know all about the Sovereign's decisions, at times well before the writer of these pages!

LONG STAYS IN COPENHAGEN

Did the Dowager Empress intervene directly in affairs of state? As regards foreign policy, I believe that at the outset of her son's reign she gave him advice which must have influenced him, since Marie Feodorovna was the sister of Queen Alexandra. Later, I know, Nicholas II consulted his mother more and more rarely on foreign policy. In any case she was without ambition, except the ambition to be loved and admired.

In regard to home policy I can be much more definite. Even when she occupied the throne by the side of her husband, Alexander III, Marie Feodorovna never had either the occasion or the desire to delve into the delicate and complex questions of Russian internal politics. She considered that she had no concern with that; as a royal lady she occupied herself only with what came within the province of a personage in the highest society. Agrarian problems, the Duma, the country's finances — all this simply did not interest her.

The Dowager Empress soon began to make her visits to Copenhagen longer and longer; and well before the end of her son's reign her influence over him in matters of state had been reduced to nothing.

II. THE GRAND DUKES

TWENTY-NINE MEN

When I took up my duties at Court in 1900, the Imperial family was numerous and active. At that time the Tsar had a great-uncle, four uncles, ten 'uncles of the second degree', as they are called in Russia (sons of his great-uncles), a brother, four male cousins, and nine male 'cousins of the third degree' (sons of uncles of the second degree) — in all twenty-nine men; enough to form a good bodyguard who would die, if the call came, sword in hand around the threatened head of the family. Were they not all interested in defending their privileges?

I am deliberately leaving the women members of the Imperial family out of account. My purpose in this chapter is to show how far, if at all, the members of the family played any part in politics. The Tsar never discussed politics willingly with ladies; he made an exception now and again of the Grand Duchess Marie Pavlovna, of whom I shall write later, for he knew that she was well acquainted with the intentions of Emperor William II, through her German relatives. The two Montenegrin princesses, Militza and Stana, were ready to act as advisers to the throne; they were constantly putting forward political proposals, and hot discussions were frequent in their two Courts on ail the current problems. But the Tsar kept these two princesses at a distance. They were advocates of the cause of Montenegro, and that gave the principality an importance in our Balkan policy which was out of proportion to the part it was able to play. But if ever they ventured to approach the Sovereign it was most likely to be with a request, preferably by letter, for subsidies for their father, Prince Nicholas of Montenegro.

The Tsar's two sisters were entirely withdrawn from public life. Many of the Grand Duchesses had married foreign princes and lived outside Russia; they were thus entirely eliminated from the life of the Grand Court.

Of these twenty-nine men, who were bound to the head of the family by the dynastic principle and even by interest, how many rallied to the support of the Tsar at the tragic moment of his abdication? *Not one.*

In Pskov, where the abdication took place, the Tsar had no member of his family at his side. The Grand Dukes were faced with the fact of his abdication; they were not consulted either before or after the event. The Imperial family had been put in a position in which it could do nothing to alter what had been done. Nicholas II and Michael Alexandrovitch, after the Tsar's abdication, acted on their own responsibility without attempting to get into touch with their relatives, without even consulting one another. The flood of the revolution had been so sudden that it had been impossible from the first to arrange any discussion.

But on that tragic day of his abdication the Tsar was unable to consult his family not only because of practical obstacles but also for personal reasons, resulting from the relations which had gradually grown up between them. One single initialling by him cost the lives of seventeen members of his family in less than two years. (Most of the members of the Imperial family had remained in Russia for no other reason than that their flight might have aggravated the Tsar's situation.)

I shall try to explain how these relations had developed and how they stood in 1917; I shall show the personal position in which each of the Grand Dukes who come into question stood at the moment of the abdication.

Dimitri Pavlovitch had been sent to the Persian front a few weeks before as a punishment for his part in the murder of Rasputin, though he had regarded his action as a means of saving the Imperial family.

Grand Duke Cyril had gone to the revolutionary Duma at the head of the naval detachment under his command. He thought that that gesture would be sufficient to calm opinion in the capital, to restore some sort of order, and to save the dynasty. But his effort was entirely abortive.

Grand Duke Nicholas, the Tsar's representative in the Caucasus, had implored the Tsar 'on his knees', as he said in his telegram, to abdicate. Grand Duchess Marie Pavlovna, with her son Andrew, was at Kislovodsk, in the Caucasus.

The Grand Dukes at the front were passive witnesses of the revolution. And when Michael Alexandrovitch, the Tsar's brother, became Emperor through the Tsar's abdication (on his own part and on that of his son Alexis), those Grand Dukes who were in Petrograd failed to rally round him.

The people who made up 'society' in Petrograd had hastened events, and had, indeed, precipitated the abdication by their irresponsible talk. They accepted the collapse of the throne with indifference, some of them with joy. In Jassy, in my Legation, I received whole packets of enthusiastic, frenzied letters which gave me the impression that everybody in the capital had gone mad.

In the pages that follow I shall deal in turn with each of the Grand Dukes, and try to explain the personal reasons that account for their strange attitude towards the Tsar; but I must preface that analysis by some general considerations.

DISSENSIONS IN THE ROMANOV FAMILY

The first blow at the solidarity of the family of the Romanovs was struck by Tsar Alexander II.

He had contracted a morganatic marriage with the young and radiant Princess Dolgorukaya (after her marriage she became Princess Yurievskaya). This was the second morganatic marriage contracted in violation of the Statute of the Imperial family, the fundamental code of the house of Romanov; the first was the marriage of Constantine, the brother of Nicholas I. That union was indirectly the cause of the revolt of the Decabrists in 1825.

The marriage of Alexander II brought forth protests from all the members of the family; the protests were all the livelier for being made behind his back.

Two scenes remain graven on my memory. In the spring of 1877 the Emperor asked the Cesarevitch (afterwards Alexander III) to give a grand ball at Peterhof in honour of certain German princes who had come on a visit. By the Tsar's desire Princess Dolgorukaya was invited. I remember how I was struck by the majestic figure of the Emperor as he waited under the colonnade leading to the ball-room; the princess stood in her splendour a few feet away from the Sovereign. After supper a cotillion was announced. The Tsar left the room and was escorted to his carriage by the Cesarevitch. When the Cesarevitch re-entered the room — it will be remembered how headstrong, almost violent, was his character — he crossed straight through the dancers till he came below the balcony in which the band of the Preobrajensky Regiment was playing a lively air. There he shouted at the top of his voice:

'Thank you, you Preobrajensky fellows! You can go now.'

The dancers — the wife of the Cesarevitch among them — stopped abruptly. The heir to the throne left with his wife; the guests hurriedly went home.

The second scene was witnessed almost in front of the coffin of Alexander II, who had perished a few days before, a victim of Nihilist bombs. In the hall of the Saltykov entrance of the Winter Palace, at the foot of the monumental staircase, the company had assembled for attendance at a funeral mass and were waiting for Their Majesties' appearance. To the right I saw the Grand Dukes and Grand Duchesses; at the left, in a corner, stood a pitiable group. Princess Yurievskaya and her three children, two girls and a boy, all in deep mourning. On their arrival Their Majesties turned to the group on the right. Then the Tsar took a few measured, resounding steps towards Princess Yurievskaya, who had lifted her veil. The Empress also took a few steps towards her, but stopped a little way off. After a few words with the Tsar, Princess Yurievskaya turned to Marie Feodorovna. The two women remained facing one another for a few moments that seemed to me an eternity. If Marie Feodorovna had held out her hand it would have been the princess's duty to make a deep obeisance and kiss the extended hand.[1] But suddenly Her Majesty fell into the arms of her mother-in-law, and the two women burst into tears. The memory of the man who had adored his morganatic wife swept away the rules of etiquette.

It was not for long. Their Majesties left the building, followed by the Grand Dukes. Princess Yurievskaya and her three children remained in their corner of the hall, a small, deserted group. A funeral mass was to be celebrated an hour later for those who did not belong to the Imperial family!

1 I have witnessed this ceremony in my capacity of head of the escort of Prince Alexander of Bulgaria.

GRAND DUKES WHO WERE AND WERE NOT

The second blow to the Imperial family came from Alexander III. He saw that the family was growing too large, and feared for the prestige of the title of Grand Duke; accordingly he took a step which must be regarded as dictated by the circumstances, though it was not at all to the taste of the Grand Dukes.

Under the Statute of the Imperial family, each Grand Duke was entitled to an annual allowance of 280,000 roubles (£28,000 gold). This sum was paid to the holder of the title by the 'Apanages', a sort of trust administration of domains which existed purely in order to provide funds, outside the general Budget of the Empire, for the Grand Ducal pensions. The great-grandsons of an Emperor, simple princes of the blood, had the right only to a single lump sum payment, fixed once for all, of a million roubles (£100,000).

Alexander III modified the Statute by laying down that only sons and grandsons of an Emperor should benefit in future from the Apanages. It was only natural that the distant relatives of the Tsar should be aggrieved at this totally unexpected reform, the economic consequences of which were anything but negligible. But Alexander, headstrong and energetic as he was, inspired all the members of his family with veritable terror; no protest was made aloud. The resentment was none the less intense.

When Nicholas II succeeded Alexander, it was hoped that it would be possible to breathe more freely: the new Tsar was young, and his uncles ought to be able to bring pressure on him in the interest of all his relatives.

They failed, however. The family attributed their failure to the influence of the Empress. I showed above how much animosity she could entertain towards her uncles and aunts. The ideas which had been instilled into her mind in her childhood were well adopted to reinforce her inclination for stem measures. She had grown up in an Anglo-German environment in which energies were restricted by constitutional limitations and were accordingly concentrated on relatives, on the other members of each family. She was all for the application of iron discipline to all the Grand Dukes without exception.

The Grand Dukes also complained of the Tsar's attitude to decisions of the Family Council. These decisions, in accordance with the law, could only reach the Tsar through the Minister of the Court. The Tsar did not consider it necessary to confirm them all without exception, and he would not change the law, lest he should have to have personal discussions with his relatives or their representatives. The impossibility of bringing family affairs directly before the Sovereign without the intervention of Count Freedericksz wounded the amour-propre of the Grand Dukes and increased their resentment against the Tsar and his Ministers.

Finally, there was Rasputin the Sinister. The family inevitably divided into two camps — those in the coterie, and the rest. After the banishment of Grand Duke Dimitri for his part in the assassination of Rasputin, the Grand Dukes sent a collective letter to the Tsar. I know of no other such collective communication, and this one was mortifying for the Empress. Grand Duke Dimitri's action was described in the letter as 'dictated by his conscience'. The disintegration of the family could not have been more complete.

THE PATRIARCH OF THE FAMILY

In studying the disintegration of the Romanov family it will be best to take separately each of the three generations of Grand Dukes. The first is that of Alexander II, the grandfather of Nicholas II.

Alexander II, the Liberator as he was called, was a monarch of very liberal views. His principal acts were the freeing of a hundred million serfs, the creation of a justiciary independent of the administration, and the liberation of the Bulgars from the Mussulman yoke. He was assassinated on March 1st 1881, on the eve of the day on which he was to have signed a Constitution which had been drawn up by Count Loris-Melikov, the Prime Minister. Only one of his brothers was still active in 1900, Grand Duke Michael Nicolayevitch, great-uncle of Tsar Nicholas II.

Grand Duke Michael Nicolayevitch was not particularly gifted. He had nobility and equanimity of character and a courtesy such as is rarely to be seen in our day. He had passed most of his life in the Caucasus, where he had been sent as Viceroy. During the war of 1877 he was Commander-in- Chief of the Russian troops; he was promoted Marshal of Artillery and decorated with the Grand Cordon of the military order of St. George; and until his death he occupied the important post of President of the Imperial Council.

He played no part of any importance in politics; he was too old (born in 1832), and preferred his villa, 'Wenden', at Cannes to the palaces he possessed in St. Petersburg; he died on the Côte d'Azur, carrying into his tomb all the traditions of a past epoch. As the patriarch of the family he was venerated by all his relatives; none of them would ever have risen against the old man's authority; his tactful interventions smoothed away the petty jealousies between the Romanovs almost as soon as they broke out.

The death of Michael Nicolayevitch was an irreparable loss, for the unity of the dynasty no longer existed except in name; from 1910 onwards the rifts steadily widened.

IN DIRECTOIRE STYLE

Grand Duchess Alexandra Iossifovna, *neé* Princess of Saxe-Altenburg, also belonged to the generation of Alexander II. She held ultra-monarchist ideas, and kept away from St. Petersburg, where the society seemed to her too modem and advanced. She preferred her manor house at Pavlovsk, a veritable museum.

This house, a little antiquated and *démodé*, formed a setting worthy of the old lady. It is the only palace in the world in which everything is, or was, decorated entirely in the Directoire style: furniture, tapestries, chandeliers, china, everything at Pavlovsk belonged to an age that is no more. There was no difficulty in keeping up, for instance, the tapestries; towards the end of the eighteenth century the Comtesse du Nord, wife of Emperor Paul I, had ordered while in Paris such quantities of precious damask that the palace still had large stores in reserve even at the time of the 1917 revolution. Not until 1910, or perhaps even later, was electricity installed in the palace, and the electric bulbs took the place not of gas or even oil but of wax candles.

Alexandra Iossifovna was like her palace of Pavlovsk: she lived entirely in the past; her own day did not interest her.

'ONE OUGHT TO KNOW ONE'S JOB'

The second generation, that of Alexander III, the nationalist, authoritarian, reactionary Tsar, was represented in 1900 by his four brothers and ten cousins.

The four brothers of Alexander III — the four uncles of Nicholas II — were Vladimir, Alexis, Serge, and Paul. Grand Duke Vladimir Alexandrovitch and his wife. Grand Duchess Marie Pavlovna, call for the most particular consideration.

Of ruddy complexion, endowed with a voice that carried to the farthest corners of his club, a great hunter, a refined gourmet (he had a collection of menus covered with his 'annotations', and signed immediately after the meal they referred to), Vladimir was the one among the Grand Dukes who profited most from his privileged situation.

He was President of the Academy of Fine Arts, and a lover of art and literature; he surrounded himself with actors, singers, and painters. He spoke as one having authority, and would not allow any contradiction except in the privacy of a tête-à-tête. His authority was respected both in the outside world and among the Grand Dukes.

Vladimir was the eldest of the uncles of Tsar Nicholas. He was entitled to exercise an unquestioned leadership, and he could have done so. He was twenty-one years older than the Tsar and might, alongside Michael Nicolayevitch, have become the leader of the family, the guardian of its unity and traditions. But it happened otherwise.

The Grand Duke's strong personality almost struck terror into Nicholas II. His uncle felt this from the beginning of the Tsar's reign, and steadily held aloof from all affairs of state.

The final rupture came in 1905, on the occasion of the marriage of the Grand Duke Cyril, Vladimir's eldest son. On October 8th 1905 Cyril, without the Tsar's consent, married abroad Grand Duchess Victoria Melita, of Saxe-Coburg-Gotha, the divorced wife of a prince of Hesse. This marriage, contrary to the existing laws, deeply grieved the Tsar.[1]

1 The Russian law required the Tsar's consent to any marriage of a member of the Imperial family; and it prohibited marriages between cousins. (Cyril's father and Victoria's mother were brother and sister.)

Some time passed; then Cyril left for St. Petersburg. His parents felt sure that the young prince would have to listen to remonstrances from the head of the family, remonstrances which he had certainly earned, but that then he would be pardoned.

He arrived about 8 p.m. and went at once to his parents' palace. At 10 p.m. he was told that Count Freedericksz had come and wanted to speak to him 'in accordance with instructions received from the Tsar'. Freedericksz conveyed to the Grand Duke his Sovereign's decisions: he must leave Russia at once, must never set foot again on the soil of his country, and must await abroad the intimation of the further penalties that would be imposed.

That same night, at midnight, the Grand Duke left St. Petersburg by train.

This rigour revolted Grand Duke Vladimir. He was outraged at his son being given such treatment, and without any prior communication with him. He went next day to the Tsar and resigned all the positions that he held in the Russian army. That was the most vigorous protest that he was in a position to make.

The Tsar's drastic decision was attributed to the influence of the Empress. It was whispered that she wanted to be revenged on Grand Duke Cyril for daring to marry a woman who only a little while before had abandoned her husband, the Grand Duke of Hesse, the Empress's own brother.

There were other causes of friction between the Grand Court and the court of Marie Pavlovna, Vladimir's wife. I have already related how Marie Pavlovna failed to impose herself on the young Empress as her initiator into the petty social details which in the aggregate determine the success or failure of every woman, even the wife of a Tsar. When she found herself cold-shouldered, Marie Pavlovna, overbearing and irascible by nature, gave full vent to her spleen in acid comment on everything that her niece did or did not do. The Court — her Court — followed the example set to it. It was from the immediate entourage of Marie Pavlovna that the most wounding stories about the Empress emanated. This counted all the more since that Court had none of the exclusiveness of the Grand Court; all the artists in vogue at the end of the nineteenth and beginning of the twentieth century had access to the Court of the President of the Academy of Fine Arts, a post which the Grand Duchess assumed after her husband's death. Marie Pavlovna kept up a regular correspondence with many statesmen and authors in Europe and the

United States, and her views were echoed in the four quarters of the globe.

To quote only one out of a thousand instances of the Grand Duchess's capacities — Grand Duke Vladimir was sent to Bulgaria in 1907 as representative of the Emperor of Russia on the occasion of the unveiling of the monument to Alexander II at Sofia. Marie Pavlovna went with him. On the day of the grand banquet given in honour of the Russian guests, I had scarcely more than a few minutes for the necessary explanations to the Grand Duchess about the outstanding personalities in Bulgar society who would be at the banquet and at the reception that was to follow it. For three hours the Grand Duchess was the centre of animated and brilliant conversation. She was talking with persons whom she had never before met; and she did not make a single mistake.

Later in the evening I congratulated her on her diplomatic adroitness; she replied:

'One ought to know one's job. You may pass that on to the Grand Court.'

It must be admitted that she knew her job to perfection.

Her Court entirely eclipsed the Empress's. An appointment as maid of honour to Marie Pavlovna would have carried with it the best of opportunities for becoming a Beauty Queen if beauty competitions had been organized in Russia in those days. The charity bazaars which the Grand Duchess opened at Christmas in the salons of the Nobles' Assembly in St. Petersburg were the event of the season. Snobs who would have no other chance of access to this exalted realm of society crowded round the Grand Duchess's stand, adding large sums to her fund for her charitable works. If they showed sufficiently lavish generosity they would subsequently receive a gracious invitation to a reception at the Palace. Marie Pavlovna presided in St. Petersburg over everything connected with high society, every social event. Here, too, her sayings spread all over the town.

Ineradicable jealousies, constantly fed by fresh incidents, alienated the two Courts. I have already told how the Empress treated her aunt towards the end of the regime (the incident of the Livadia hospitals). In such conditions any sort of family friendliness had long become impossible between the Empress and her uncle and aunt.

GRAND DUKES ALEXIS AND SERGE

The second son of Alexander II was named Alexis Alexandrovitch. He had a fine athletic figure and gave the impression of strength, allied — that had been the special gift of some of the Romanovs of earlier generations — with infinite charm.

I recall how one day in Paris I was walking along the Grands Boulevards behind a man in civilian dress, tall and finely proportioned. Passers-by turned round and I heard some exclaim: 'What a fine man!'

Coming up with him, I recognized Grand Duke Alexis.

Alexis Alexandrovitch was the High Admiral of the Russian navy, and was one of the organizers of the circumnavigation of Africa and Asia by Rodjestvensky's armada, which ended with the attack on the Japanese fleet off Tsushima and utter disaster in a glorious but unequal combat. That enterprise destroyed the Grand Duke's career; he gave up his post and settled in Paris. He died there in 1908.

The third son, Serge, came to a tragic end: he was assassinated by a Russian terrorist in the Kremlin Square.

Smart, elegant, graceful, Serge had been the Commanding Officer of the Preobrajensky regiment, and had been adored by his officers. His private life was the talk of the town, and made his wife, Grand Duchess Elizabeth Feodorovna, very unhappy. He was reactionary as few others; and he was fond of discussing political problems with the Tsar. Nicholas II listened with visible pleasure to his uncle's exposition of his Die-hard ideas; he never contradicted his uncle and brother-in-law (they had married sisters), but had too much good sense to follow the advice of this representative of the ideas of a past age. When the Grand Duke was appointed Governor-General of Moscow — a post to which he would have been well suited a century earlier — he was pursued by the terrorists, who had marked him down as their principal victim. Elizabeth Feodorovna visited the assassin in his prison, interceded for his life with the Emperor, and then took the veil.

THE MORGANATIC MARRIAGE OF GRAND DUKE PAUL

Nicholas's fourth uncle was Paul (Alexandrovitch). The relations between Grand Duke Paul and the Emperor were broken off when the

Grand Duke contracted a marriage abroad with Mme von Pistohlkors, *née* Karnovitch, the divorced wife of one of the aides-de-camp of Grand Duke Vladimir, The marriage took place at Leghorn in 1902. I was a very old friend of Mme von Pistohlkors; I had, indeed, been her witness at her first marriage. How many times we discussed her plans! I advised her not to let the Grand Duke proceed to a legal ceremony, for I was sure that, the consequences would be terrible. Mme von Pistohlkors replied that the Tsar was very fond of his uncle and would not want to destroy his future for regularizing a situation which was no secret to anybody.

What happened was more painful than the worst I had feared. The Tsar gave the order for the maximum penalties provided by law to be applied against his uncle; that meant banishment for life, the loss of all his posts and functions, and the confiscation of his revenues. It was said, and it was the opinion of my friend Mme von Pistohlkors, that the Empress's influence had entirely overcome the sympathy which the Head of the House professed towards his uncle — who was scarcely eight years older than the Tsar himself.

Later the Grand Duke was pardoned, on condition that he returned to Russia unaccompanied by his wife. There followed a long-drawn-out correspondence between St. Petersburg and Paris, where the Grand Duke had settled. In the end the Countess of Hohenfelsen (this title had been granted to Paul's morganatic wife by the King of Bavaria) was given permission to cross the Russian frontier.

The problem of precedence remained still to be settled. Grand Duke Paul had formulated his claims on behalf of his morganatic wife in six paragraphs. The Empress intervened personally and had the principal paragraphs struck out. The Countess of Hohenfelsen received the rank of wife of a General A.D.C.; but she was granted the right of being presented to her new relatives, the Grand Duchesses, not through their Mistresses of the Robes but directly by her husband. She also received the right of not signing the books in the palace ante-rooms but leaving her card.

All this bargaining produced friction between uncle and nephew and especially the nephew's wife (the Empress). Ostensibly their relations had become normal; in actual fact resentment and injured dignity robbed them of all cordiality. Grand Duchess Marie Pavlovna seized her opportunity; she loaded her new sister-in-law with attentions and favours. Grand Duke Paul's Court quickly won distinction and popularity throughout St. Petersburg society. During the war the Countess of Hohenfelsen received the title of Princess Paley; her son Vladimir, a remarkable poet and a fascinating man, was one of the centres of attraction for all that was brilliant in the capital.

These were not circumstances that could allow of good relations between the Grand Court and the Court of Grand Duke Paul; the Grand Duke had no opportunity of giving advice to his nephew; and the part played by his son Dimitri in the assassination of Rasputin completely put an end to the friendship between the Tsar and his uncle.

I am bound to add that the two long talks that I had with Grand Duke Paul after his return from Paris produced rather a painful impression on me. Exile had brought him no well-thought-out political creed. It was impossible that he should be a useful counsellor for his nephew. And the coolness with which he was received in the Grand Court hurt and angered him.

'IF IT HAD ONLY MEANT LOOKING AFTER HORSES '

Keeping still to the generation of the father of Nicholas II, let us pass now to the sons of Nicholas's great-uncles. Strictly they were second cousins; in Russia these relations were called 'uncles of the second degree'.

There were ten of them: three sons of the late Constantine Nicolayevitch; two sons of the late Nicholas Nicolayevitch (called the Elder, to distinguish him from Nicholas Nicolayevitch the Younger, his son, the Generalissimo during the world war); and five sons of Michael Nicolayevitch (to whom reference has already been made).[1] The eldest of this group was fifty in 1900, the youngest thirty-one — one year younger than the Tsar although he was his uncle.

We will consider them one by one.

The eldest son of Constantine Nicolayevitch was named Nicholas Constantinovitch. His story may be told in very few words. A life of dissipation brought him very serious illness and he had to be put under restraint through incurable mental trouble. He passed his life at Tashkent, in Central Asia. Thus there could be no question of his influence on affairs of state.

1 See pp.64-5.

The second son was named Constantine Constantinovitch. He was a highly cultured man and a writer of verse; his poems were highly thought of by the Russian public. He signed them with the initials K.R., a pseudonym treated with great respect by Russian reviewers. His life was peaceful and patriarchal. Towards the end of it he was promoted to the modest post of head of the military schools. There he showed some directing ability. He always held aloof from the Grand Court, where he found none who shared either his outlook or his tastes.

The third son was Dimitri Constantinovitch, a man of wide sympathies, modest, and full of good sense. I can declare without fear of contradiction that he never took any active part in affairs of state — on principle, and from conviction, a conviction based on thoroughly prudent considerations.

'The Grand Dukes,' he said to me one day, when in a confidential mood, 'should begin their apprenticeship as simple lieutenants, and incognito. If they show aptitude for the Service, they can be promoted in accordance with the rules laid down for everybody. But they should never be permitted to reach positions of command or posts of great responsibility. Any mistakes they made would at once involve the Tsar, and that might diminish the Sovereign's prestige.'

'Does your brother' (Constantine Constantinovitch, see above) 'express the same opinions?'

'He does. These principles were instilled into us by our mother; our father rarely discussed things with us. My brother would admit, however, that there have been exceptions among the Grand Dukes; some of them have shown great capacity in command. For these exceptional cases he would have laid down severe rules defining penalties for neglect of duty; penalties far heavier than for plain subjects of the Tsar.'

'What penalties did he envisage?'

'Immediate dismissal for any Grand Duke who proved unworthy of the post he occupied. It is at that point that I disagree with my brother. The necessity of dismissing a near relative might be productive of very great difficulties for the Tsar; and we are all grouped round the throne in order to facilitate the tasks of its occupier.'

One day he told me of his first entry into official life. He was a lover of horses and wanted to join a cavalry regiment. His father. High Admiral of the Russian navy, gave his decision:

'You have got to represent our family in the navy.'

He was sent with cadets of the naval college to serve for a period on a warship. He proved unable to endure the sea. His sufferings were terrible. On his return he prayed for a long time in front of his icon, and then, gathering up all his courage, went to his father. He drew himself at his feet and begged to be freed from the naval service.

'Go away, and do not let me see you again,' his father answered. 'Admiral Nelson himself suffered from sea-sickness, but that did not prevent him from becoming a famous sailor!'

His mother had to intervene; in the end he was permitted to join a regiment of Horse Guards. His elder brother had ruined his health by excessive libations; and his mother made him swear that he would never drink a single glass of wine. He was conscientious in the extreme, and never let anything induce him to break the promise he had given.

Later, when he became Commanding Officer of the Grenadier Guards, he found that the 'dry' regime to which he was bound interfered with cordial relations with the officers of his regiment. In spite of his age and situation, he went to his mother and asked her to free him from the solemn promise he had made. Up to that moment he had never allowed himself to touch a bottle.

It may fairly be said that Dimitri Constantinovitch was the one among all the Grand Dukes who was most deeply imbued with the sense of his duty as a prince and a cousin of the Emperor. One day he turned over to me a very considerable sum for the maintenance of a little village church.

'If you make gifts everywhere on this scale,' I said, 'your revenues from the Apanages will not last out.'

'The Apanages,' he replied gravely, 'are not intended to enable us to have as sybarites; this money is put into our hands in order that we may augment the prestige of the Imperial family.'

In spite of all Ins qualities, this Grand Duke never played a part of any importance. His timidity was beyond imagining. When his train arrived at a station he would hide in his compartment so as not to be seen by people on the platform. But if a deputation or some officials had come to greet him, the first breath of a suggestion that it was his duty as a Grand Duke to receive them was sufficient for him to stifle his feelings and receive his visitors with the utmost amiability. Then he would go back and lower the blinds of his compartment lest he should be asked to meet anyone else.

Like so many timid people, he imposed a fixed regime on himself, a time-table to which he kept religiously; so many hours for his official duties, so many for prayer, and the rest for endless reading 'to improve his knowledge'. He even made difficulties about accepting the modest post of State Studmaster. When the post was offered to him he said to me, with touching sincerity:

'I should gladly have accepted the appointment if it had only meant looking after horses. But it means control of men as well, I think I might have been able to be of use in this field, but I am afraid I shall never get on properly with officials. In any case, I shall make one condition for my appointment: I shall reserve the right to resign the moment I feel that I am unable to be useful to my country.'

This remarkable man, educated and cultivated in the best sense of the word, never had his talents made use of in Russia. He even gave up the Studmastership, for he came to the conclusion that he ought to work at the improvement of the breeds of the equine race as a simple private individual, within the modest limits of his private stud at Dubrovka.

THE GENERALISSIMO

The two sons of Grand Duke Nicholas Nicolayevitch the Elder, Field-Marshal of the Russian army, were named Nicholas and Peter. Nicholas Nicolayevitch the Younger was probably - the only one of all the Grand Dukes who tried to play any important political part. He was also the only one who might, if circumstances had aided him, have become the leader of a movement dangerous to Nicholas II, I am bound to say that my confidence in this Grand Duke was greatly shaken, especially after the events of 1905; I never felt satisfaction in his appointment as Generalissimo of the Russian army in 1914; may God pardon him for certain of his errors which we, his contemporaries, find it hard to pardon!

His mother was descended from one of the daughters of Emperor Paul (married to a prince of Oldenburg); that Emperor's mental instability was notorious. Nicholas had inherited a nervous morbidity from both his parents. Like his mother, he was very intelligent, but excitable and violent, and liable to uncontrollable fits of temper. He was an extreme mystic; his mother had left her husband well before

1880 and had gone to Kiev, where she surrounded herself with nuns and fanatical priests; in the end she took the veil.

The first impressions that I had of this Grand Duke confirmed what I knew of his unfortunate heredity. It was in 1888, during the grand manoeuvres at Rovno.

Thirty squadrons of cavalry on either side — such was the main element in these military exercises. General Strukov was the Grand Duke's 'enemy'. I had no difficulty in securing permission to watch the final battle alongside the Grand Duke.

He was visibly worried by the importance of his task, and above all by the presence of his father, the Field-Marshal. He had about ten orderly officers, and kept sending them off right and left. They had to go at a full gallop even if there was not the slightest apparent necessity for it. If the Grand Duke thought an officer was not pushing on sufficiently he shouted after him 'On! on!' — all the time striking his own charger, which was covered with lather and foam.

The exercises proceeded in accordance with all the rules of the military art, and produced a very good impression.

At nightfall the Strukov cavalry appeared on the far side of the valley separating the forces. This was the moment of the decisive attack. Our troops deployed with spirit. The Grand Duke, however, thought they were behindhand.

'An orderly officer!' he shouted.

They had all gone off on one side or the other. I approached the Grand Duke; he said to me:

'Do you see that group? They are not deploying quickly enough. Go off and tell them to go at a full gallop.'

'Might I venture to point out that an orderly officer is already on his way to that group and another officer has gone in the same direction? But I am at Your Highness's service.'

'No, quite right, there is no use in going.'

He made a grimace that betrayed his annoyance at having lost control of himself.

'Would it not be best,' I then said, 'for me to go over to join the reserves? They hardly have time to fill up the gap that is growing in the centre of our front.'

'You're right. Quick, go along!'

After the manoeuvres were over General Strukov spoke about me to the Grand Duke. He mentioned that I had fought at his side in the Russo-Turkish war (at the capture of Adrianople). His Highness said:

'Experience of active service always shows itself. Mossolov was the only one to call my attention to the problem of the reserves. It is thanks to him that I was pronounced the victor.'

LEFT — THEN RIGHT

My own confidence in the Grand Duke was particularly shaken, as I said above, during the events of 1905.

The month of October 1905 was marked by grave disorders. There were demonstrations and rioting in the streets of the capital, and the Emperor was on the point of taking one of the gravest political decisions of his lifetime. Count Witte had been received by the Tsar on October 9th, and the rumour spread that he had recommended the Sovereign to grant a Constitution and had undertaken personally to see that it was given practical effect. Some people added that Witte had told the Tsar that there were only two possible solutions — a Parliament, or a military dictatorship.

It was learned almost at the same moment that Grand Duke Nicholas (who was then hunting on his estate of Pershin, in the Tula Government) had been asked urgently to return to Peterhof, the residence of the Imperial family.

The Die-hards were exultant; they already saw a Dictator putting an end to all the disorders. Count Freedericksz had expressed the same hope, that the Grand Duke would bring the revolutionaries to heel; after that it would be possible to think about the granting of political liberties.

I was with the Minister of the Court when the Grand Duke was announced (October 15th).

I took the Grand Duke into Freedericksz's room, and withdrew to an adjoining one. Almost at once I heard raised voices; the Grand Duke was shouting.

A little later he rushed out, jumped into his motor-car, and went off. Freedericksz followed, saying as he got into his car:

'I could not have believed it!'

He told me later what had happened.

He had been delighted at the Grand Duke's arrival, and had told him that it had been looked forward to in order that he might take the responsibility of setting up a dictatorship. At that the Grand Duke had suddenly and unaccountably lost all control of himself; he whipped out a revolver and shouted:

'If the Emperor does not accept the Witte programme, if he wants to force me to become Dictator, I shall kill myself in his presence with this revolver. I am going on to the Tsar; I only called here to let you know my intentions. You must support Witte at all costs! It is necessary for the good of Russia and of all of us!'

Then he went off like a madman.

Freedericksz added:

'He suffers more and more from the hereditary hysteria of the Oldenburgs.'

I was struck by this unusual behaviour on the part of the Grand Duke, and was curious to learn how he could have acquired his sudden sympathy for Witte. I made a few inquiries among the personages of the Grand Duke's Court.

It seems that on the day of his arrival in the capital he had had a long talk with an employee in the State printing works, a man named Ushakov. This man was regarded as the leader of those workers who had remained faithful to the monarchical principle. What he had to tell the Grand Duke had deeply impressed His Highness and had given him the idea of supporting Witte.

On October 17th 1905 Witte gained a complete victory; the manifesto granting a national representative body was published in accordance with the plan which he had elaborated.

The Grand Duke had been the decisive factor in the promulgation of the manifesto of October 17th; but he did not long remain a supporter of Witte and his liberal policy. The day came, I do not know how or why, when he came out as leader of the extreme Right, in diametrical opposition to everything that Witte did and to everything connected with the manifesto of 1905.

The extreme Right contended that the manifesto had been wrung from the Sovereign by force; for this capital reason it was null and void, and it must be so interpreted that it abated not a jot or tittle from the autocratic powers of the Tsar. The Duma must be reduced to the role of a consultative assembly, with no direct influence on the course of affairs of state. If necessary force must be resorted to in virtue of the supreme prerogative of the Sovereign.

Grand Duke Nicholas was temperamentally inclined to violence, and was the first to advise the Tsar to go counter to the Constitution which he had granted. If the Tsar had listened more to him, the abyss between the representatives of the people and the Sovereign would have grown yet more rapidly and the final collapse would have come yet sooner.

The Grand Duke was under the influence of his wife, Anastasia (Stana) Nicolayevna, the divorced wife of Duke George of Leuchtenberg. She was surrounded by clairvoyants, and believed herself to be destined to a glorious career. She made her husband share this outlook; filled him with aggressive ideas in foreign policy; and all but inveigled the Empress into a circle of shifty 'spirits'. It was under her direct influence that the Grand Duke plunged into what he called high policy.

The Grand Duchess's influence at the Grand Court was, of course, only felt through the Grand Duke. I do not know whether this ambitious princess ever intended to carry any of her plans further than simply working upon her husband.

At the time of the Tsar's abdication the Grand Duke wrote him a letter which he must have bitterly regretted after the fall of the dynasty. In exile in France, Grand Duke Nicholas was unsuccessful in gathering the Russian monarchists around himself, and was unwilling to recognize the authority of Grand Duke Cyril. His attitude did much to make the group of Russian legitimists impotent through depriving them of a common centre.

GRAND DUKE PETER NICOLAYEVITCH

The younger brother of Nicholas Nicolayevitch Junior was named Peter. He was much better balanced and less like his mother. His health was very poor — he was almost consumptive; and he lived in retirement, without showing signs of any particular ambition. He had great abilities, but was never able to take the close interest in his duties as Inspector-General of Military Engineers that his elder brother took in the cavalry, in which he held an analogous post.

Grand Duke Peter was married, as I have already mentioned, to Militza Nicolayevna, Princess of Montenegro. This lady was extremely active in everything connected with politics, but never gained the ear of her husband's nephew, the Tsar.

THE FIVE SONS OF MICHAEL

We come finally to the sons of Grand Duke Michael Nicolayevitch. There had been six, but one died at an early age. The other five had no common trait of character.

The eldest was named Nicholas Michailovitch. Fairly good-looking and very intelligent, he spun intrigues wherever he went. He began his military service in the Horse Guards, but left his regiment on the ground that his military duties prevented him from devoting his whole time to historical studies, for which he had a taste and a marked aptitude. He was always criticizing, but never did anything himself. He wrote numberless letters to the Tsar; they show that he knew how to please and to make himself amusing. But one would search in vain through the letters for a single practical idea.

Nicholas Michailovitch remained in Petrograd when the Tsar went to the front. In his club, where he was always the centre of a group, his mordant criticisms, essentially destructive, did much damage to the regime; sarcasms coming from so high a quarter affected society with a morbid tendency that helped to deprive the Sovereign of all moral authority. The Empress whole-heartedly detested him. It was this Grand Duke who was one of the protagonists of the collective letter (written after the murder of Rasputin) which made the final breach between the Tsar and his relatives.

The second of the brothers, Michael Michailovitch, was unable to play any political part. In 1891, after the failure of an attempt at morganatic marriage in Russia, he went abroad and married the Countess of Merenberg, daughter of the Duke of Nassau and granddaughter of Pushkin, our great poet. She received the title of Countess of Torby, and never showed the slightest intention of returning to Russia.

The third son, George Michailovitch, was not one who carried any weight. The Tsar entrusted him with the duty of visiting the troops to hand their decorations to them. At the last moment, I have been told, George took his stand entirely on the side of his eldest brother, Nicholas.

The fourth son, Alexander Michailovitch, married Grand Duchess Xenia Alexandrovna, the sister of Nicholas II; he thus occupied a privileged situation at Court as the Tsar's brother-in-law. He was intelligent and ambitious, but not as intelligent as his eldest brother. For a short time he held office as Minister of the Merchant Marine, a post specially created for him. During the war he devoted himself to the problem of military aviation, and had successes which were not generally acknowledged. He published a book in which he advanced a bold contention — that the Tsar of Russia ought to put his nearest relatives at the head of all the important departments of government. One of our Ministers of War often spoke to me of the incredible difficulties that were created by the pressure at the head of the military air service of a man with access to the Tsar, himself accountable to nobody.

Alexander Michailovitch was always inclined to mysticism; towards the end of his life he became the apostle of a religious theory inspired by 'divine intuition', resembling the doctrines of Count Tolstoi; this, he claimed, would serve in some occult fashion to rid Russia of the Bolsheviks. He had many women admirers. His lecture tours in the United States will be remembered.

The fifth son, Serge Michailovitch, was an enthusiastic artillery officer. The result was some serious failures in our supplies of guns and munitions. As he was at the front throughout the war he was more or less free from the disastrous influence of his brother Nicholas. He could not have been of any service to the Tsar during the critical moments of 1917, for, from what I know. His Majesty would certainly not have asked his advice.

THE THIRD GENERATION

I shall have little to say of the third generation, that of Nicholas II himself It consisted of a brother, three cousins, sons of Grand Duke Vladimir, and another cousin, son of Grand Duke Paul, and nine sons of 'second degree uncles', 'third degree cousins' as they are called in Russia. These cousins had not the title of Grand Duke, being only great-grandsons of an Emperor (Nicholas I). The eldest of them was four years old in 1900; the youngest was born on January 4th 1900. It is only necessary here to consider, from a political point of view, the five Grand Dukes.

The Tsar's brother was named Michael (Alexandrovitch). He was ten years younger than Nicholas II. His great defects were considered to be his excessive good nature and credulity. Tsar Alexander III, his further, often said that Michael believed everything he was told, without taking the trouble to consider the reasons that his interlocutor might have for deliberately deceiving him.

Witte, who hated the Tsar, sang the praises of Grand Duke Michael's 'abilities'. He gave him instruction in political economy, and never tired of praising his straightforwardness — an indirect way of attacking the Tsar. I am entirely ready to credit his uprightness, for he was very like his sister Olga.

But he had no influence at all over his brother. During the time when the Tsar had no male descendant, Michael was the heir to the throne, as the nearest relative of the reigning sovereign. His brother had not even conferred on him the title of Cesarevitch, a purely honorary title usually given to all heirs to the throne. The Empress was too impatiently awaiting the birth of a son![1]

Grand Duke Vladimir had three sons — Cyril, Boris, and Andrew. I have already told of Cyril's marriage, in explaining the causes of the final rupture between Vladimir and the Tsar.

The time came when Cyril was pardoned and allowed to return to Russia. During the Russo-Japanese war he was saved as by a miracle when the cruiser *Petropavlovsk* was torpedoed.

On his return to St. Petersburg after his escape, he presented himself to the Emperor as soon as he was able to do so.

At that time the relations between the Grand Court and the Court of Grand Duke Vladimir were rather strained, and the tension grew after Their Majesties had been informed of Ae intended marriage of Grand Duke Cyril with Princess Victoria Melita of Edinburgh. Ultimately the Emperor recognized the marriage, and after the appearance of Grand Duchess Victoria in St. Petersburg in 1909 relations became, thanks to Her Highness, more normal.

1 Grand Duke Michael was morganatically married to Natalia Sergueevna Sheremetyevskaya. Their son George was granted by the Tsar the name of Brassov, from one of His Highness's estates. Later, in emigration, the Grand Duke Cyril, in his capacity of head of the Romanov dynasty, created him Prince Brassov, and this title was recognized by the Dowager Empress Marie Feodorovna.

Prince Brassov died from injuries received in a motor-car accident, at the early age of twenty. He was a handsome and accomplished youth. He was debarred under the fundamental laws of the Empire from access to the Grown, but through his father he was one of the persons nearest to the throne of Russia.

After the tragedy of Ekaterinburg[1] and the death of Grand Duke Michael, Cyril became, under the Statute of the house of the Romanovs, head of the Russian Imperial family. A few years later he assumed the title of Emperor, but did not officially notify the Powers. In the order of primogeniture Cyril and his son Vladimir (who was born after the abdication of Nicholas) are the senior representatives of the house of the Romanovs.

Grand Duke Boris held no Court, and lived a rather dissipated life in his little cottage at Tsarskoe Selo. In the course of the war he was appointed Hetman of the Cossack troops.

Grand Duke Andrew had brilliant success in the study of law, and became the legal adviser and counsel of the young generation of Grand Dukes: lawyers are all protesters by profession. Among the émigrés he continued to take an interest in politics; of all the Grand Dukes he is the best informed in the international sphere. He is gifted and intelligent and a hard worker.

Grand Duke Dimitri was only a little older than the Tsar's eldest daughter. The Grand Court was always open to him, and the Emperor showed marked affection for this youngest of the Grand Dukes. The part he played in the assassination of Rasputin produced a particularly painful impression on the Tsar.

To resume, the only Grand Dukes who were in a position to exercise any influence over the Tsar's decisions were his great-uncle Michael, Nicholas Nicolayevitch, his brother-in-law Alexander, and his uncle Paul Alexandrovitch.

The other members of the Imperial family saw the Sovereign no more than two or three times a year, and then in conditions that made political conversation almost impossible; this was so even in the case of the Tsar's brother. Grand Duke Michael Alexandrovitch.

It remains for me to tell how I took part in the last attempt at a reconciliation between the members of the Romanov family.

On my arrival in Roumania in November 1916 as Russian Minister Plenipotentiary I had been particularly well received by the royal family. In January 1917 Queen Marie consulted me with regard to a plan for the union of her son Carol, the present King of Roumania, with one of the Grand Duchesses. After long discussions of the

1 The Tsar, the Empress, and their five children, were murdered at Ekaterinburg on the night of July 16-17, 1918.

question with the King and Queen and Grand Duchess Victoria I asked the Tsar to authorize me to go to Petrograd in order to present a highly confidential report.

On my arrival I went, of course, to see Count Freedericksz. We had a long conversation on the general situation.

Rasputin had just been assassinated; he had been buried, in accordance with the Empress's desire, at Tsarskoe Selo, and this had been particularly resented by all the Grand Dukes. Dimitri Pavlovitch, who had been sentenced to exile for the part he had played in connexion with the murder of Rasputin, was waiting in boredom in his palace, where he was 'under arrest' by His Majesty's order.

It was a little while before my arrival in Petrograd that the Grand Dukes had drawn up and sent to the Tsar their 'collective letter', a step that plainly ran counter to all the dynastic precedents.

I have not seen the text of this letter, and can only speak of it from hearsay. It appears to have revealed deep dissatisfaction, and was capable of being interpreted as bringing a charge against the Empress. It was drawn up in the form of an intercession in favour of Grand Duke Dimitri, and contained a statement that he had acted 'in accordance with his conscience' (in being present in Youssupov's house on the evening of the assassination).

I have been told that this letter carried the signatures of Grand Duchess Marie Pavlovna, of her sons, who were not at that time at G.H.Q,., and of the Grand Dukes Paul, Nicholas Michailovitch, and Alexander Michailovitch.

On receiving this extraordinary communication, the Tsar contented himself with the marginal note:

'Nobody has a right of assassination!'

The signatories took offence at the Sovereign's annotation, and broke off all non-official relations with the Tsar. The rupture was patent and dramatic. The Tsar saw the whole of the Romanovs ranged against himself and his wife.

Freedericksz told me what followed:

'On his return from the *Stavka*, the Tsar told me that he had settled all outstanding questions in agreement with the Empress. I was made personally responsible for seeing to the departure of Grand Duke Dimitri Pavlovitch for the Persian front; pending his departure he was to consider himself as "under arrest" in his palace.'

The Count added, sadly:

'Probably His Majesty did not want to go into details with me, knowing my strong objection to Rasputin. I only saw His Majesty yesterday — at Tsarskoe Selo, in the presence of the Empress. I took the opportunity to say how sorry I was to see the Imperial family completely disunited, and added that a reconciliation was essential in the interests of the dynasty and the country.

'We had a very long conversation, in which the Empress took a most active part. It was agreed that a way out must be found by hook or by crook. I ventured to say that the first thing needed was a reconciliation between Her Majesty and Grand Duchess Marie Pavlovna. The rest would be a much simpler matter and would settle itself.

'The Empress stated her conditions:

'She was quite ready to be reconciled with the Grand Duchess Marie, but the Grand Duchess must take the first step; must recognize that there had been mistakes on both sides, and must help to restore the solidarity of the Imperial family. It was too difficult a time for these family dissensions to be allowed to continue.'

The Count, who was plainly tired out (at this time he was suffering from frequent effusions of blood on the brain), continued:

'The Grand Duchess Marie is expecting me in half an hour. I am supposed to be going to see her on my own initiative, without mentioning the conversation that I have had with Their Majesties, to do my best to persuade her to accept the Empress's three conditions. But I am too ill to be able to use persuasion; I am taking the responsibility of sending you in my place; I know that you will carry out the mission better than I could.'

I was quite out of touch with everything, but in such a situation I could only agree. At the interview with the Grand Duchess I explained to her that I had found the Minister very ill and had decided to call to let her know how things stood, especially as I had to convey to her the best wishes of the Queen of Roumania and her daughter-in-law, Grand Duchess Victoria.

Marie Pavlovna received me very kindly.

'You were quite right to leave the Count at his home. An important conversation might have brought on in my presence the thing I most fear, a fresh fit of apoplexy.'

The conversation lasted more than an hour.

The Grand Duchess Marie recognized at the outset that a reconciliation was indispensable in the interests of the dynasty and of the whole country.

'But it would be necessary, Madame, for you to take the first step.'

'If that is so I am not ready even to discuss the subject with you. It is impossible.'

I insisted. In the end the Grand Duchess agreed to a compromise:

'I will go to Tsarskoe Selo, if Count Freedericksz comes to invite me in Her Majesty's name.'

That was her last word. I went to Freedericksz to let him know the result of my mission. It was decided that he should go to see the Grand Duchess the moment he was well enough, and should tell her that Alexandra Feodorovna, he hoped, would shortly be asking her to tea at Tsarskoe Selo.

I learned later that it had been impossible for this invitation to be conveyed to the Grand Duchess.

Three weeks later the revolution broke out.

CHAPTER III

THE EMPEROR NICHOLAS II
AND HIS ENTOURAGE

1. 'OKRUJENIE'

A. The Minister of the Court, 'The Old Gentleman'

This work is not concerned with the political history of Russia. Thus I cannot enter here into the general problem of the Tsar's relations with his Ministers, the men who were primarily responsible for the national policy.

I have spoken above of certain resignations of Ministers — resignations which excited disapproval and bitter comment. In order to judge the situation in his Empire, the Tsar received reports from his Ministers. But where could he get the necessary material for judging his Ministers? It has been said over and over again that it was the Tsar's entourage (in Russian, *Okrujenie*) that furnished the Tsar with the material for forming his personal opinion. The influence of the *Okrujenie* has often been grossly exaggerated. To show the true situation, I shall follow the same plan as with the Grand Dukes, in the preceding chapter, and shall try to delineate each of the men who surrounded the Tsar.

I must begin with Count Freedericksz, Minister of the Court, 'the old gentleman', as the Imperial couple called him. They knew his devotion in the performance of his exacting duties. Some of his tasks, such as that of watching over the relations between the Tsar and the members of the Imperial family, were of a peculiarly difficult and delicate nature.

THE APPOINTMENT OF BARON FREEDERICKSZ

Count Freedericksz was descended from a Swedish officer who had been taken prisoner by Russian troops and interned at Archangel. One of his ancestors had won distinction as banker to Catherine II, and had been ennobled with the title of Baron. The Count's father, a soldier, went through many campaigns: he was present at the capture of Paris, and was for a long time Officer Commanding the 13th Regiment at Erivan, in the Caucasus, at the beginning of the nineteenth century. He ended his career as General A.D.C. to Alexander II.

Freedericksz — then Baron Vladimir Borisovitch Freedericksz — began his career as an officer in the Horse Guards. Alexander III appointed him first Master of the Horse and later assistant to the Minister of the Court. The Minister was then Count Vorontzov. After the disaster at Hodynka[1] Count Vorontzov sent in his resignation: he had been charged with making insufficient provision for the public safety. The Tsar considered the Minister entirely free from responsibility for the disaster, and asked him to remain at his post.

But Vorontzov made one great mistake. He had known Nicholas II since he was a baby, and took up a protective attitude towards him, the attitude, as it were, of an older relation. Nicholas himself regarded this as entirely natural; but the young Empress did not. She could not permit a Count Vorontzov to be on familiar terms with her husband. One day, when nothing could have been farther from the Count's mind, he was notified that his resignation, which had 'so often been offered to His Majesty', was accepted; later on he was sent as Viceroy to the Caucasus.

Freedericksz took his brother officer's place, at first as Acting Minister and afterwards as Minister. The appointment created a great sensation at the Court. Freedericksz did not belong to the highest ranks of the nobility, and none of his family had ever been in close association with the Throne, except his father, as General A.D.G. It was plain that the Tsar had known how to appreciate his simplicity,

1 See p.40.

his tact, and his unsullied integrity. Freedericksz retained his post until the final catastrophe.

Count Freedericksz (he had received the title of Count from Nicholas II) was very rich, and that gave him the sense of independence that was so necessary amid the intrigues and the raging appetites that surrounded him.

Some people alleged that he was miserly. He was merely methodical in his expenditure. He certainly refused to lend money to people who were capable of making a bad use of it. But I have known him to incur expenditure, when he thought it necessary, on a scale that was out of proportion even to his nabob's fortune.

I recall the incident of Mr. E., an extremely rich man with a liking for little short-term usury deals. This gentleman had asked Count Freedericksz to admit his son into the Horse Guards as a volunteer. Freedericksz agreed, but warned Mr. E. that his son must not expect to become an officer in this very exclusive regiment. A year later young E. successfully passed his examinations for officer of the Guards. His father came again to see Count Freedericksz, and asked that his son should be admitted after all into the family of officers. Freedericksz, as Officer Commanding, refused as gently and considerately as he could. Thereupon Mr. E. announced that all the overdue bills signed by officers of the regiment and held by him would be protested next day. That meant, in default of immediate payment, the forced resignation of all the officers concerned.

Freedericksz showed Mr. E. the door. Then he sent for his officers and asked each one of them how much E. had lent him. The total, if I remember rightly, came to something like 79,000 roubles, an enormous sum at that time — about £8,000. There and then each officer received from Freedericksz's hands a cheque enabling him to free himself from his debt. Young E. went into another regiment of the Guards.

AT FREEDERICKSZ'S

I remember as well as if it were yesterday my first visit to my old fellow-officer — twenty years after I had left the regiment — in my new capacity of Head of the Chancellery.

The Count's private residence was in the Potchtamtskaya, exactly opposite the Horse Guards' barracks. These barracks occupied an enormous area in the centre of the capital, with a drill ground surrounded on three sides by yellow and white buildings.

Count Freedericksz had steadily refused to leave this house. The Countess often said that she found herself cramped for want of room, having only five small drawing-rooms for her use. She would have preferred to have a ball-room and to occupy the fine residence that the Court was supposed to place at the Minister's disposal in accordance with the law.

'Yes,' the Count would reply. 'That would have enabled us to organize grand receptions like all the other Ministers. But, on the other hand, when I am asked to resign you will not have to move out; you will go on receiving your friends in your five little salons. Don't you think it is better to have an assured future than gala receptions?'

An assured future! He did not dream that his house was to be the first to be destroyed on the morrow of the revolution, and that none of his staff would have an assured future after 1917!

The moment I entered the spacious room in which the Count had installed his desk, I saw that nothing had changed, nothing had been moved. The only new thing was a large picture on the wall — the parting present from the officers of the regiment he had commanded. It represented the drill ground that could be seen from his windows, and his regiment deployed in parade formation, with shining helmets and breast-plates; in the foreground was Count Freedericksz, on foot, talking to his officers.

The Count's big easy chair was in its old place of twenty years ago, near the window; facing it was another chair, for his visitor. In between was a small table at which Freedericksz worked. The desk itself had been kept unchanged, with all the presents and portraits of members of the Imperial family placed in position once for all.

I sat down in the second chair. From then on I was the Count's 'right arm'; he gave the title of 'left arm' to Count Heyden, head of the Emperor's military secretariat.

THE MINISTER'S WORKING DAY

Count Freedericksz began work every day about 10 a.m. It was my duty to be the first to go to his room. I began by opening the letters on his desk. Usually they were requests for grants. The Count wanted to know at once why this widow or that orphan needed help; often I was able to secure the passing of these applications through the regular official channels, but not without some difficulty: the Count was thoroughly humane and kind-hearted, and insisted on learning every possible detail of each case; he was very methodical.

The conversation continued unhurriedly. Sometimes the Minister would interrupt me:

'Look! There they are exercising in the square' (the Horse Guards' drill ground, as I have mentioned, was just in front of the Count's house). 'The third man from the left is tugging at the bit and irritating his horse for nothing. His fool of an N.C.O. doesn't notice anything. . . . Well, let us get back to work. I know you, too, are a keen cavalry officer.'

The Count would light his enormous morning cigar, and we went on to important matters, above all the report to be presented to His Majesty. Freedericksz had a special gift for drawing up the reports in a form which could not annoy His Majesty; I too learned this difficult art before long.

The Minister made a practice of letting me know everything His Majesty had said during the presentation of the report; this enabled me to get a good knowledge of the Sovereign's wishes. The Minister knew that he could count implicitly on my discretion. For his part, he asked me never to retail to him any of the little stories or bits of gossip current in town and at Court.

'I am as transparent as a crystal,' he said; 'you can see through me. I can never keep back anything. I am full of discretion so far as affairs of state are concerned, but little bits of scandal are always liable to slip out of my mouth; it is better for me to know nothing about them.'

Another of my tasks was to transmit the Count's criticisms to the staff; he was afraid of going too far, of saying more than he had intended. He reserved for himself the cases that called for his approval or congratulation, a task which he performed with a tact that excited my admiration.

Soon the cigar would be finished and the report completed. We went on to the signature of the papers that I had brought in. The Count considered that those of his Ministerial colleagues who scrawled almost illegible initials had no manners. For him the affixing of his signature was a ritual practice. He wrote his name with an ordinary pen, and then underlined it with a fine flourish made with a quill. Whatever carried his signature became an important document, and it was also important that future generations should be able to admire the perfection of calligraphy. On the days on which there were new appointments to be made there might be a hundred letters to sign; it was, need I say, no small trial of secretarial patience!

My morning's duty with the Count usually ended about I p.m. After lunch with his family the Count went to his barber, 'Pierre', in the Bolshaya Morskaya; this visit to the Figaro of Petrograd was part of the invariable programme of every day; the Count made a point of being shaved at Pierre's and nowhere else.

The rest of the day was marked out with an equally unvarying routine. At 3 p.m. the Minister saw one by one the heads of departments of the Court, and those people who had been granted interviews with him. The evenings, if there was no urgent business, were devoted to his family; if there was business Freedericksz sent for me about 10 p.m., and we worked together, sometimes late into the night, refreshed with a bottle of good Bordeaux and some biscuits. Towards the end of his life the doctors had the cruelty to forbid the Count this innocent little pleasure!

THE MINISTER AND THE TSAR

The Minister 'reported' to the Tsar twice a week. The first audience was on Saturday mornings, and lasted an hour; the second, of about half an hour, was on Thursdays.

But the Minister saw Their Majesties much more often than this. When the Emperor was at Tsarskoe Selo he would receive an invitation every two or three days, either to lunch or to be present at a reception or a review of some regiment. Freedericksz was also regularly invited to all the intimate festivals of the Imperial family, children's birthdays, Christmas trees, and so on.

As soon as he returned from the Palace, the Minister sent for me to give me all His Majesty's orders. It was touching to hear him tell of the many kindnesses which the Tsar and the Empress showered on him.

If the Minister was prevented by illness from going to Tsarskoe Selo, the Empress would send him little presents — something that she had made herself. They would be accompanied by a little note saying that Their Majesties hoped that he would soon be well again. Nobody else was made much of in this way by the Imperial couple, and I am sure that no one else would have appreciated these attentions so much as Freedericksz did.

The little gifts and notes were the subject of conversation with the friends of the family for weeks afterwards.

The Tsar was fond of a talk with his Minister of the Court. The Minister was the only man to whom the Emperor confided his difficulties in dealing with Ministers and Grand Dukes. The Count had a special flair for the discovery of a good solution which brought all concerned into agreement with one another. The Tsar, timid and reserved, also entrusted Freedericksz with the duty of conveying his dissatisfaction to those who had incurred it. That was the most trying of the Count's duties.

The Tsar knew his Minister of the Court to be a man of high character, of noble ideals, and of absolute integrity. He knew the depth of his Minister's devotion to him. He also appreciated the delicacy with which Freedericksz put the truth, even the disagreeable truth, before him. The Count had a special gift for always avoiding any injury to his master's feelings. And he never interfered in matters that were not connected with his duties as Minister, unless the Tsar expressly asked his opinion.

For myself, I always had a veneration for the Count, as a chief full of delicacy and charm. In him I have lost my best friend.

THE MINISTER'S POLITICS

With his ideals of order and discipline and his monarchist principles, Freedericksz considered that Russia ought to maintain the best possible relations with Germany. Prussia, in his view, was the last stronghold of the monarchical idea: we needed her just as she needed us. He admitted that Berlin's activities had made a Russo-French rapprochement necessary, in order to recall the Kaiser to the realities of foreign policy. But he considered that no alliance with republican France ought to entail any permanent weakening of the dynastic relations between Berlin and St. Petersburg.

'Neither France nor Britain,' he said to me one day, 'would come to the assistance of our dynasty. They would be very glad to see Russia turned into a republic. They know what happened to Samson when Delilah caused the seven locks to be shaven off his head.'

When Isvolsky was trying to induce His Majesty to go to Cowes, Freedericksz pointed out to the Tsar that the visit might embroil us irremediably with the Kaiser and bring a war which would be equally dangerous for both dynasties. When the voyage was definitely decided on, he talked to me for a long time of the danger which might threaten Russia; he considered that Britain would never be a loyal ally, and he predicted the worst perils for our country.

'I am not a professional diplomat,' he said to me again and again. 'I have not the necessary material for combating Isvolsky's arguments. Nor is this within my province. But instinct and reason alike make me think this voyage exceedingly dangerous. Isvolsky will get himself into difficulties through his Anglomania. One day, when I am no longer alive, you will find that your old friend was right. We shall have a war, and that war will bring us face to face with Germany.'

Up to the last moment before the declaration of war Freedericksz supported the Tsar in his efforts to remain at peace with Germany and Austria. But as soon as military operations began he submitted to his monarch's will. His chivalrous character rejected any idea of a separate peace. He was the first to protest against the methods of warfare employed by our enemies when they infringed international law.

HIS MALADY

From 1913 onwards Freedericksz was subject to effusions of blood on the brain. At times he completely lost his memory, sometimes for hours, sometimes for whole days. Those who had seen him only during these attacks of haemorrhage were liable to gain an entirely mistaken idea of the mental capacity of the Minister of the Court.

He was bound, of course, to send in his resignation. He did so several times. But the Tsar was unwilling to hurt the old man by letting him resign. It must be added that the Sovereign was quite unable to find a successor worthy to take the place of Freedericksz; he had long talks on the subject with 'the old gentleman'. The Count put the matter to Prince Kotchubey, and the Prince would certainly have been given the post, but he definitely refused it.

Thus it was as a complete invalid, greatly enfeebled by repeated attacks, that Freedericksz witnessed the collapse of the dynasty. I had a long conversation with him in Petrograd at the beginning of November 1917; he told me the part he had played during the tragic days of March 1917:

'You were not there; there was only Voyeikov to describe the situation to me, and I did not trust him. I was unable to meet Orlov' (the former head of the Tsar's military secretariat). 'I did not expect revolution to break out immediately after the abdication; like the Tsar himself, I thought the Imperial family would be allowed to leave for Livadia. But I said again and again that I was instinctively in revolt against any idea of abdication. I pointed out that abdication would bring bloodshed, bloodshed on a scale no less than would be entailed by a forcible suppression of revolution. I implored the Tsar not to abdicate.'

B. The Head of the Chancellery

'A WEALTH OF MUSICAL RHYTHM'

It was in March 1900 that I entered on my new duties as Head of the Court Chancellery. The post, I can aver, was no sinecure.

My first task was to subject the whole of my staff to a severe testing. Most of them were sons of Grand Ducal servants. It was almost a tradition that the lackey brushing the boots of his Grand Duke, and ambitious to send his son a few steps farther up the social ladder, should get him into the Chancellery. There the young man would begin as a copyist and ultimately become an official. These young fellows, destitute alike of education and social training, worked in with one another; each of them was fortified by the backing of his Grand Duke (a backing that never failed to be forthcoming at the desired moment), and they regarded themselves as virtually intangible!

It would be too long a story to tell of all the tricks of which I was made the victim by these persons. I need only say that I had to 'sack' several of them for submitting to me for signature official documents in the diametrically opposite sense of the instructions which I, their chief, had given.

There were countless malpractices in connexion with appointments as 'Purveyor to His Majesty'. This title was greatly coveted by manufacturers and sellers of luxury articles, and very large gratuities were to be had by any one who procured an appointment of this sort, perhaps for persons with very doubtful credentials. I had to keep under lock and key all correspondence concerning the Purveyors to His Majesty.

Gradually, taking my time about it, I replaced the whole of these people by young men of good family who had studied at the Law School and the Imperial Alexander School (where the future diplomats and high officials were educated). The old staff were transferred, one by one, to posts in which they could do no serious harm.

There were some outbursts of Grand Ducal irritation; in fairness I must say that they were fewer than I had expected.

My deputy was a Mr. Zlobin. For a long time he could not forgive me for my appointment; he was older than I, and at one time had regarded himself as the obvious candidate for the post of Head of the Chancellery. He was a very good fellow for all that; and a good musician, perhaps too good, as the following story will show.

One day when he was reading to me a draft reply to an important communication, he delivered the concluding passage in a sort of triumphal chant.

'But, Zlobin,' I objected, 'that sentence surely contradicts all that you said before?'

'Quite so. Your Excellency,' he replied without turning a hair, 'quite so; but did you perceive the wealth of musical rhythm in the phraseology?'

I was driven at last to the conclusion that the rhythmical phrasing of urgent papers was taking up too much of his time. Zlobin was a favourite of Freedericksz; the Count was flattered by the respect that my deputy showed him: as soon as he came into the Count's presence he seemed to be in danger of swooning, such was his awe of 'the old gentleman'! I profited by Freedericksz's interest in Zlobin to get him transferred to a most distinguished position, that of Head of the Imperial Decorations Office. He filled this post with dignity and success, convinced that he was in charge of state business of the utmost importance. When the revolution came he was the most decorated man in all the Empire.

VISITORS

The most disagreeable of my duties was the reception of visitors. Freedericksz hated to have anything to do with strangers; he did not like refusing favours — he was too good-hearted — and he did not like promising to grant them, for they might prove later on to be contrary to the law and so produce endless difficulties. Accordingly he issued a standing instruction that nobody was to be admitted to the Minister's presence without having first been received by the Head of the Chancellery, who would go into their case. This enabled me to get rid of the majority of the visitors, and to prepare the Minister as necessary whenever one of them had to be admitted to his presence.

Most of them — such is the general impression that I got after talks with thousands and thousands of applicants for favours of every sort — most of them wanted something which was not authorized by law or, still more often, was flatly against the law. To this day I can hear the constantly repeated phrase;

'If it had been permissible under the law I should not have come to trouble His Majesty.'

My day for receiving visitors was Saturday. But highly placed personages considered that I ought to receive them on days other than those fixed for the common crowd! It will easily be imagined how much useless waste of time this cost me. It should be mentioned that the Grand Dukes were not the only ones to consider themselves entitled to treatment as highly placed personages. This privilege belonged, it appeared, to all the Court dignitaries — and, God knows, there were plenty of them! — to members of the Imperial Council (our Upper Chamber), and, I am not too clear why, to the members of the Imperial Yacht Club.

These distinguished visitors never opened up at once with the object of their visit. One might have supposed that they thought it bad form to fail to waste at least twenty minutes of my time on preliminary gossip about society and the Court. The older personages had a litany of their own to recite; the same litany in every case. They told me at length of the infirmities with which they were afflicted; they recommended me their family doctor; and they described to me die methods of cure that they had had the good fortune to discover, infallible methods against troubles which fortunately I had been spared.

It was useless to try to cut short these therapeutical confidences — the story would only grow longer still, and the sufferer would go away ill-humoured into the bargain. Once the litany had been completed, the visitor would suddenly remember what he had called about; he would begin to sing the praises of some relative. That was all — but what a plague in the midst of my work!

For that matter, requests for promotions and appointments dogged me wherever I went. One day, at the New Club, the Head of the Prisons Department sat down next to me, and said, for once without any beating about the bush:

'A splendid man! Young! Rich! with a fine education! Put him into Court dress and he will be an ornament of your balls. My word, he will be better than that baboon X whom you allowed into the last promotion list — that man's Court dress sits on him like a strait waistcoat on a cow.'

'Well, what is the name of your protégé?'

'Name? His name? Here, steward, what's the name of that young man who lost to me three times yesterday at billiards?'

'Prince Karageorgevitch, Your Excellency.'

'No, no. I know Prince Karageorgevitch well. Besides, the Prince beats me, and this other fellow lost three games. How can you be ignorant of the name of a member of the club?'

'My dear chap,' I said, 'send me a little note and tell me who the young man is.'

'Yes, yes. Don't forget what I've been telling you!'

THE CROWN OF THE PRINCESS OF GEORGIA

The industry that was expended at times on waylaying the Head of the Chancellery, as the officer in charge of the distribution of Imperial favours, is almost beyond belief. The story of the princess of Georgia is worth telling.

Mile Bezobrazova had married a prince of Georgia, a subaltern in a regiment of the Guards. She attached an altogether undue importance to her husband's title. She claimed to be considered as a 'reigning' princess (her husband's great-grandfather had been King of Georgia), which would have given her the right to go in processions alongside the Imperial family.

Year after year she complained of Masters of Ceremonies who failed in her opinion to show her due reverence. An old law of sixty years before, completely forgotten, had to be unearthed in the end to dispose of her claim: descendants of reigning princes from the third degree onwards are entitled to precedence only if it is justified by the functions with which they are entrusted by the Russian Government. The prince was a subaltern; there could, then, be no question of his being placed alongside the Grand Dukes.

The princess had recourse then to another stratagem. She sent in a request that the Tsar should be godfather to her second child. Freedericksz reported; the Tsar did not refuse — he considered it his duty to show favour to large families.

To have the Tsar as godfather brought certain privileges: there was a grant for the boy's education; the mother was entitled to a present from Court funds; on attaining his majority the young man could claim a post in the Ministry of the Court, and there were certain other grants in case of need. The Georgian princess knew how to make the most of this manna, by repeatedly declaring that she was destitute.

It was the present that ultimately brought disaster to the writer of these lines.

The value of the present was determined by the lady's 'rank'. One day I said to the keeper of Imperial presents:

'Fix up something to please her; the grant is 600 roubles; you can go a bit beyond that if necessary, but not beyond 1,000.'

A few days later I was informed that the princess wanted a 'diadem'. It was impossible to get one for so small a sum.

'Explain that to her,' I said.

'I have done, but do you think she is going to give way? She says she agrees to have Ural stones in the diadem.' (Ural stones are semi-precious coloured gems.)

'If that will please her, get her a diadem with Ural stones.'

That was all she wanted.

Count Pourtalès, the German Ambassador, was giving a ball. The princess telephoned to him and pointed out that as a reigning princess she was entitled to an invitation. 'The Tsar himself has just sent me my crown.' A crown! Pourtalès was profuse in apologies, and sent the invitation demanded of him.

The princess telephoned to the Court Stables office:

'Count Pourtalès has invited me to his ball as a reigning princess. Please send me one of the Court carriages.'

The request was refused.

The princess telephoned again to Pourtalès and explained to him why the Embassy must put a car at her disposal. That made the Ambassador suspicious. He telephoned to the Master of Ceremonies, and the cat was out of the bag.

The Tsar asked Freedericksz for explanations. The rumour was going about that I was 'distributing crowns'.

I had to have the unlucky diadem photographed and to draw up a report several pages long to explain the case of the Georgian princess.

NO SINECURE

I may end this section as I began it: my post was no sinecure. A good part of my day was taken up by conversations with the Minister; the rest of the time was largely spent in receiving visitors; and every day there was a steady flow into my office of reports from my staff. In the evenings I worked on the most important of the reports, and read the printed matter sent to the Minister in his capacity of member of the Imperial Council, in order to keep him constantly in touch with what was going on in our Upper House; the Tsar was in the habit of asking him for information on this subject. I brought my day to an end by signing papers and going through my correspondence.

It took me a good many years to master my duties. Some of the 'tricks of the trade' could only be acquired in the course of experience and professional training. Shall I give an example? The Imperial family was, let us say, expecting what the newspapers call 'a happy event'. The Chancellery had to prepare in advance the manifesto which the Tsar would sign (writing in himself, in a space left blank, the name decided on for the baby), to inform the country of what had happened.

A manifesto? Surely two, the careful reader may say: one for a boy and the other for a girl. The careful reader will still be far from the truth. Under the law Freedericksz had to be present in the next room at the happy event; and every time he went off for that purpose he took in his dispatch-case five — I say five— different manifestos: one for a boy, one for a girl, one for two boys, one for two girls, and one for a boy and a girl. This last case has not occurred, so far as I am aware, in any reigning family since the world began.

In sixteen years I scarcely had one free night. The work came in unendingly, like the water for the mill-wheel. If friends came to see me and I spent a few hours in their company I had to start the next day's work without having closed my eyes for one moment. My nerves stood this infernal grind fairly well.

MY DEPARTURE FROM PETROGRAD

I left my post of Head of the Court Chancellery against the will of Coxmt Freedericksz. To satisfy him the Tsar had signed a decree sending me to Jassy as Minister Plenipotentiary while retaining me nominally in the position which I had held for more than sixteen years. In 1913 Freedericksz had expressed the desire that I should be given the rank of Deputy Minister of the Court, but another person was appointed. From that moment I knew that the Rasputin clique would end by 'downing' me. My authority progressively declined, and his illness made it impossible for Freedericksz to support me with the necessary energy.

In December 1916, when I was in Petrograd, the Empress offered me the post of Deputy Minister of the Interior. She said to me on that occasion:

'Everybody is criticizing; nobody is ready to give any help.'

I shall tell of this incident later, in the chapter dealing specially with Rasputin. At that moment my appointment might have meant one of two things: either an attempt to cover the activities of the Rasputin clique, or the offer of the opportunity to assist in righting the helm of State. If in talking to me the Empress had touched on the problem of Rasputin, and if I had had the least hope that it was not already too late to combat her mysticism (and ail that it involved), I should have accepted; I should even have asked for another audience, in order to offer my services.

I did not do so. I had not the heroic quality such a step would have called for. I left for Jassy; I do not know whether history will justify me.

When I first entered on my duties at Court I had set before myself the purpose of restoring the pedestal on which the Tsar ought to stand; of assisting the Tsar in making justice and order prevail; of seeing to it that the Tsar's subjects should enjoy all the blessings that can be showered upon them from a throne. My chief collaborated with me in that purpose, himself entirely imbued with these same ideals. I was surrounded, moreover, with members of the suite who were thoroughly honourable men and ready, as I was, to worship the Tsar and to die for the dynasty. Each one of these men did his duty. But every one of us felt that we had never succeeded in inspiring in the

Sovereign the confidence without which the difficulties of our task inevitably became more than mortal man can overcome.

C. The Tsar's Immediate Suite

IT WAS OF NO GREAT SIZE

The Tsar's immediate suite was composed of a small number of dignitaries holding definite posts.

First of all I must mention the Marshal of the Court, Count P.C. Benckendorff. He was an old officer of the Horse Guards, and had become the supreme arbiter of all that concerned the traditions of the Russian Court. Thoroughly well-up in his job, even-tempered and hard-working, he was most punctual in the execution of his rather complicated duties.

Their Majesties treated him with great respect and entirely as a personal friend. He could also boast the friendship of the Grand Dukes and of all the sovereigns who came on visits to the Russian Court. (His brother was for a long time our Ambassador in London.)

Count Benckendorff was a man of principle. He abstained from any sort of political activity and would not even discuss politics. It was a matter of tactics, and there was much to be said for it.

He did not follow the Tsar to Siberia, for at that time he was confined to his bed, seriously ill. His place was filled by his son-in-law. Prince Vassily Dolgorukov, formerly of the Horse Guards. Dolgorukov was too young and too modest to venture to offer political advice to the Tsar. He preferred to go into exile and die with his master under the fire of the Bolsheviks.

Next came the Commander of the Palace, head of the Court police. This post was held first by General Hesse, A.D.G., and later, after various changes, by General Voyeihov.

The first of these two dignitaries kept rigidly to his specific duties. The second tried to play an important part at the Tsar's side.

Voyeikov, who had married the daughter of Count Freedericksz, was friendly with Mme Vyrubova, Rasputin's great admirer. It was on her recommendation that the Empress proposed the General for the post of Commander of the Palace after the death of General Dediulin. Freedericksz felt that it would be entirely impossible for him to work in harmony with his son-in-law; their temperaments were utterly dissimilar. He begged Alexandra Feodorovna to put forward another candidate, but his resistance was broken down. Voyeikov obtained the post he had coveted. He was very ambitious, and his tactics consisted in gradually alienating from the Tsar everybody who could interfere with his (Voyeikov's) plans. There was a time when I thought that Voyeikov and I would be able to work together in entire agreement; but a thing happened that made our collaboration impossible. Voyeikov presented to Freedericksz a report addressed to the Tsar which the Tsar sent back to the Minister, because the proposals made in the report ran counter to the existing laws. Freedericksz, greatly alarmed, said that in future all reports from Voyeikov must first be passed by me; and that, naturally, was enough to make Voyeikov hate me.

At the moment of the Tsar's abdication Voyeikov, owing to a succession of unfortunate circumstances, was at the head of the Tsar's suite, which at that time included only four other persons. Admiral Nilov, Prince Dolgorukov, Count Grabbe, and Naryshkin (Freedericksz being ill). What I have here to relate suflaces to show that these people were incapable of giving proper advice to the Tsar. Among the Tsar's immediate suite, Voyeikov bears the chief responsibility for what happened after the arrival of the deputies from the Duma on their baneful mission.

There is little to say of Admiral Nilov, His Majesty's Flag Captain, who represented the Imperial navy, and who accompanied the Tsar on all his journeys. The Admiral owed his appointment to the intervention of Grand Duke Alexis, whose A.D.C. he had been for many years. Nilov had habits of intemperance which made him incapable of efficient work. He was very devoted to the Tsar, and after the revolution he remained at the *Stavka* until summoned away by the Tsar's express order.

The post of Head of the Emperor's military secretariat was held successively by Count Heyden, Prince Orlov, and, finally, Naryshkin. The Count had been in a privileged situation because he had been a friend of Nicholas II in their childhood; he sacrificed his post, his wife, and his children to a transient passion.

Prince Vladimir Orlov, a former officer of the Horse Guards, and an exceedingly rich man, soon became one of the intimates of the Imperial family. He was a highly cultivated man, sarcastic, with a dry humour, and enjoyed great social prestige. In 1915 he advocated the formation of a Ministry 'that could inspire public confidence', as the phrase went at the time. His whole policy was directed primarily to enabling Russia to escape from the disaster that he could see approaching; he was able to appreciate its premonitory symptoms at their true import. With no thought whatever for his personal career, he was devoted to the Tsar and to the cause of the Russian monarchy, devoted in the highest sense in which the word can be used. He was in regular correspondence with certain leading statesmen; he was the only one among the members of the suite who had any real political ability. Unfortunately he was no admirer of the Empress, and showed his feelings towards her in the presence alike of adherents and opponents of Rasputin, and even in audiences with the Empress herself.

I shall tell later, with all necessary detail, how this remarkable man's career was broken the very day the Empress decided to get rid of him. The Tsar had to take his wife's side (probably against his will, for he had a great regard for Prince Orlov); otherwise he would have been publicly sacrificing her prestige.

Orlov's place was taken, towards the end of the regime, by Naryshkin, a son of the Mistress of the Robes. Naryshkin made no attempt to share the captivity of Their Majesties after the revolution.

Three officers were attached to the military secretariat, Drenteln, Sablin, and Count Vorontzov Dashkov. They were the only officers attached to the person of the Tsar who were constantly at the Palace; they were regarded as assistants to the Head of the military secretariat. The rest of the officers (aides-de-camp, Generals 'in the suite', and even Generals A.D.C.) could only present themselves to the Tsar after obtaining authorization firom Count Ereedericksz.

Drenteln was a straightforward and intelligent man with a strong personality, and a man of culture. I found him thoroughly well qualified to be in the immediate and intimate entourage of the Tsar. He was a courtier in the good sense of the word, a man of good judgment and full of tact; apart from Freedericksz he was probably the only man to whom the Tsar was attached. The Sovereign greatly appreciated his company, and in the course of time Drenteln might have been able to render very valuable service through his good judgment of character and his ability to recognize straightforward people who were honestly devoted to His Majesty: he would not have been one to try to lure them away from his master!

Then, however, came the Orlov incident. Drenteln had been Orlov's right hand, and his position was badly shaken. To fill the cup to overflowing, there came one more incident: Djunkowsky, the officer in command of the gendarmerie, felt impelled to seek out the Tsar and tell him the whole truth about Rasputin. The whole truth! He was at once relieved of his office, and fell into disgrace. But he had belonged to the same regiment as Drenteln, on whom some of his disgrace fell accordingly. Drenteln was put in command of the Preobrajensky regiment. It was a promotion; but it meant leaving the Court.

Sablin, the Empress's protégé, was not of sufficient calibre to be able to give political advice to the Tsar. He would have been unable to impose his point of view.

Count Vorontzov Dashkov played no part of any importance.

Finally, there was the commander of His Majesty's personal escort, Count Grabbe. This officer failed to arouse in the soldiers forming the escort the indispensable sentiment of fidelity to the Sovereign, and proved personally unequal to his task when the final catastrophe came.

There was one more member of the Tsar's immediate suite, his physician — first Hirsch, afterwards Botkin and Feodorov.

Botkin was notoriously cautious in the extreme. Nobody in the suite had ever been able to get him to say what was the matter with the Empress or what treatment the Cesarevitch and his mother were being given. Feodorov was a man of great intelligence. He watched particularly over the health of the Cesarevitch; at the *Stavka* he was considered to have a great deal of influence with the Tsar. It was on the strength of his final diagnosis that the Tsar abdicated the throne in his son's name as well as his own: Feodorov had said definitely that Alexis would always be an invalid.

These were the principal personages in the Tsar's immediate suite. The aides-de-camp went on duty only for twenty-four hours at a time, in rotation; they would never have dreamed of submitting memoranda on general policy to His Majesty. Freedericksz, moreover, was jealous of his own function of adviser, and would never have tolerated such an abuse of influence. And it was well known that the Tsar himself detested those who attempted to discuss matters that did not come directly within their province.

The Head of the Apanages, the Grand Masters of Ceremonies, the Head Librarian and the Director of the Imperial Theatres only presented themselves in order to report on their respective spheres of duty.

I will say little on the subject of the Tsar's entourage at the time when he was at the *Stavka*, his headquarters, as Generalissimo. Persons who were there for many months have often told me that these officers (I deliberately say nothing whatever about them in their military capacity) produced an impression of lifelessness and apathy, of people drifting and resigned in advance to whatever catastrophe might be approaching: 'petty bureaucrats in the service of a sovereign faced with an unexampled crisis'. All the new appointments seemed to have been dictated by some malignancy of fate: good men went, and their places were taken by careerists. The cleavage between the Tsar and the rest of the country continued to grow while he was at headquarters. Ministers rarely came, and when they did they showed no solidarity with their colleagues in the Cabinet. There was a total lack of unity in action and policy alike in the Cabinet and between Government and G.H.Q.: 'We were living on another planet'.

The Tsar saw only what the Empress allowed him to gather from her personal letters; and these letters were, of course, neither objective nor even informative.

The 'wall' of which I write in the next section suddenly grew and converged above the Tsar's head, turning into a cavern without air or light.

Here I will allow myself one single quotation, the only one in this work. On page 537 of the 1928 volume of the *Revue des Deux Monies* there is this passage in the article 'Mémoires du comte Benkendorf', dated March 21st 1917:

'It was on this day that our detention in the Alexander Palace began. Our company consisted of Mme Naryshkin, my wife. Baroness Buxhoewden, Countess Hendrikov, Drs. Botkin and Derevenko, Count Apraxin (who left us at the end of a week), and myself. Next day, in the Emperor's train, my son-in-law Prince Dolgorukov arrived. We were also expecting General Naryshkin, Head of His Majesty's military secretariat; Count Alexander Grabbe, commanding the Cossack escort, and Colonel Mordvinov, A.D.C. to the Emperor; but they did not come. In addition, Mme Vyrubova, an invalid, and Mme Denn were in the Palace, but apart from the rest.'

In all, six women and five men, one of whom left on March 25th.

THE SUITE PLAYED NO POLITICAL PART

It is clear from what I have written that the Tsar's immediate suite could have had no part in determining His Majesty's policy. It was made up of specialized officials who kept to the tasks for which they were responsible.

Their principal concern was to maintain their position amid the whirlwind that surrounded them. The best policy for each one of them was to confine himself to his own restricted province, not to go beyond his orders, and on no account to embark on any political adventure, for fear of the exceedingly unpleasant results that it might bring. 'Keep out of trouble' became the general motto, 'lie low', 'do nothing on your own responsibility if you can help it'.

Moreover, these officials were quite unfitted for playing any political part. Almost all the important members of the suite owed their positions to earlier service in the Horse Guards. Count Freedericksz, a former Commanding Officer of that distinguished regiment, felt it his duty to seek candidates for any vacancy that he had from among its officers, that big family to which he belonged and which provided the indispensable guarantees of correctness, tact, and perfect training. There was a very close solidarity between all those who had worn the white and gold uniform; that solidarity also constituted an important guarantee.

But none of the ex-officers of the Horse Guards had had any sort of preparation for playing any important political part. They all belonged to the high Russian nobility, a category of Russians who had kept a little apart from the other classes; they came to the Palace with a military education acquired in the schools for pages or cadets and completed by ten years or so passed in an elegant and socially brilliant regiment. Among them there were some very well-educated men; but most of them were without the special training through which it is necessary to pass, by one means or another, before having anything to do with affairs of state.

II. 'SREDOSTENIE'

'THE WALL'

The Tsar's immediate suite was incapable of bringing him fresh ideas concerning what was going on in his country, of suggesting political ideas independently of the reports from his Ministers. But an autocrat can only exercise his sovereign functions if he has the means of personal judgment, investigation, and supervision. In order to be an autocratic sovereign, Nicholas II required independent sources of information as a check on his Ministers.

We touch here on the problem which was the origin of the great tragedy of the last of the Romanovs; it is best described by its Russian name, *Sredostenie*. Throughout the reign of Nicholas II the *Sredostenie* was the principal subject of political discussions.

Sredostenie means literally a wall. It was virtually a technical term in Russian politics. The explanation that follows will indicate the theory underlying the term.

At the head of all stands the Sovereign, the autocrat. Below him, teeming and inchoate, is the struggling mass of his subjects. In order that Russia may live in entire tranquillity and content, all that is necessary is that there shall be direct relations between the Sovereign and his subjects.

The Tsar can do no wrong; he stands above classes, party politics, and personal rivalries. He desires the good of his people, and has practically unlimited means for assuring it. He seeks nothing for himself; he has a profound love of all those whom God has confided to his supreme care. There is no reason why he should not be the benefactor of each and all. *All that is wanted is that he should know exactly what his people need.*

The subjects love the Tsar, for he is the source of all their well-being. They cannot fail to love the Sovereign, for no other feeling is possible toward Beneficence personified. The subjects are not always happy, for the resources of the State are not unlimited and not everybody can be wealthy. But they have the consolation of knowing that the Sovereign does all that he can and everything that his essentially good heart dictates, in order that each one of them may have his share of well-being. Does not the idea of being constantly the object of the solicitude of an almost all-powerful being constitute the greatest possible consolation?

I repeat: in order that this idyllic picture may be complete, the sole link needed to complete the chain is this — *The Tsar must be in possession of sound information.*

Where is this information, indispensable for the proper working of any system of autocracy, to be sought?

Two political elements are interested in keeping the Tsar in more or less complete ignorance of what is passing in the minds of his subjects. The bureaucracy (including the Ministers) forms one of the sections of the 'wall' which surrounds the Sovereign. The bureaucracy is a caste with its own interests, interests that are not necessarily the same as those of the Tsar. In an empire with a hundred and fifty millions of inhabitants, an empire stretching from Warsaw in the west to Vladivostok in the east, it is impossible to do without a bureaucracy. It is essential to appoint supervising and executive agents. But these agents tend to substitute their own influence for that of the Tsar. How many times have certain Ministers represented the rigours of their administration as proceeding from the pitiless severity of the Sovereign, and any mitigation of those rigours as the fruit of pressure put upon the Tsar by themselves, the Ministers! The bureaucracy is interested, moreover, in keeping the Tsar in ignorance of what is going on: it is in this way that it makes itself more and more indispensable.

The second part of the 'wall' is formed by the fomenters of disturbances, the Intelligentsia (intellectuals), a name which the Russians borrowed from the French language and which subsequently spread back over Europe with a special connotation. The intellectuals are those who are not the bureaucracy that is at work and would like to become the bureaucracy of a different régime, a régime that can only be introduced into Russia at the cost of revolutionary convulsions.

The intellectuals are interested in attacking the bureaucracy and the Tsar whenever and wherever they can, blaming both for all the mistakes of the Ministers. The tactics of the intellectuals, the 'Third Estate' (in a slightly changed sense), are to misrepresent the relations between Beneficence personified and the mass of the people. With their newspapers, their pamphlets, their lectures, their teaching in the universities, their doubtful foreign connexions, their money, the intellectuals are tireless in weaving a fabric of venomous lies. They tell the people the opposite of what ought to be told them in order to prevent them from becoming too agitated; they declare that the Tsar has no love for his subjects and no concern for their fate. Knowing how false all this is, the Tsar detests the intellectuals, the agitators, the disturbers, the revolutionaries.

Bureaucracy — intellectuals: those who had arrived and those who wanted to take their places. Two enemies, working together in one respect — in their tendency to reduce the personal prestige of the Tsar. Brick by brick, lie by lie, between them they built up a veritable prison wall around him, confining him to his palace and preventing him from leaving it to speak directly to his good subjects and to tell them as man to man how he loved them. That wall was equally effective in concealing the extent to which the true subjects of the Tsar, those whose natural sentiments had not been perverted by propaganda, those simple subjects with open hearts ready to accept his beneficence and grateful for it, loved their Little Father Tsar.

The peasant masses loved the Tsar. The soldiers loved the Tsar. The townspeople, who crowded to see him pass and huzzaed from the moment when his motor-car came into sight, loved the Tsar. He would have been loved still more if the 'wall' had not prevented him from doing his work as autocrat.

Towards the end of his reign Nicholas II seems to have felt that he had succeeded in destroying the accursed 'wall', the *Sredostenie*. I remember a very significant conversation that I had with him on February 14th 1917, fourteen days before the end of the régime.

In discussing with the Tsar a measure that was to be adopted, I was unable to refrain from saying:

'That will do a great deal to assure the position of the dynasty!'

In spite of his reserve, the Tsar replied with heat, plainly disturbed at what I had said:

'What! You, Mossolov, are you too going to tell me of the peril that menaces the dynasty? People are continually harping on this supposed peril. Why, you have been with me and have seen how I was received by the troops and the people! Are you too, even you, panicking?'

'I have seen all that. Sire, but I also see them when they are not in Your Majesty's presence. Forgive my freedom of speech.'

The Tsar controlled himself, and went on, with a smile:

'I am not put out — far from it. Let us go in to dinner. The Empress will be waiting for us already.'

That, I repeat, was on February 14th 1917. Did the Tsar realize the danger, and was he merely trying to keep up the courage of those who were around him?

That is a possible explanation. But I think the truth is that the Tsar did not see the danger, or did not see that it was already at the Palace gates.

THE CANONIZATION OF SAINT SERAPH

What had the Tsar done to demolish the 'wall'? Two main things. It was possible to enter into relations with the mass of the people by personally appearing in the presence of the crowds, or by making use of intermediaries. The possible intermediaries were the regularly elected deputies, representatives of the nation; more or less representative delegations; and individuals in a position to tell the Tsar what their fellow-countrymen thought.

It will be observed that this list gives the sources of information in a definite order. It begins with statutorily regularized methods and ends with purely arbitrary choice, chaos.

I was a witness of one of the principal efforts associated with the first idea, that of immediate relations between the Tsar and the masses. Its setting was the neighbourhood of the monastery of Sarov; its occasion was the canonization of the Staretz[1] Seraph.

The monastery of Sarov is in the province of Tambov, near the town of Arzamas. The Staretz Seraph passed his last years there.

The Holy Synod had made certain objections to the canonization. Pressure had been put on it by the Court, and after a great deal of discussion the canonization was decreed. The Tsar took the opportunity of this ceremony to gain strength from the mounting tide of popular enthusiasm through communion with the lowly in their prayers. The Empress intended also to take part in the journey to Sarov; she wanted to be present at the 'miraculous' healing of Princess Orbeliani, an event that was considered certain to occur.[2]

1 See p.125.

2 The princess — see p.43 — was one of the Empress's favourite maids of honour; she had been attacked by creeping paralysis, and had been given up by all the doctors. She had now conceived the project of being immersed in

Sarov was not on the railway, and to get there a platform was specially built near Arzamas for Their Majesties' use. Barouches drawn hy four horses were brought for the Sovereigns and the suite. This mode of locomotion seemed to have been particularly relished by the Empress and the maids of honour.

Thousands and thousands of peasants had crowded along the whole length of the mail route to Sarov, well before the Imperial procession started. I have been told that five hundred thousand peasants, from all over Russia, had swarmed into the neighbourhood of the monastery. Barracks had been built to house them, but proved totally inadequate; most of the pilgrims spent the nights in the open.

It was a wonderful spectacle. The crowds, in their Sunday best, greeted the Tsar as he passed with unfeigned enthusiasm. It was a sight to see the radiant faces of the people who were selected to present salt and bread to the Sovereign at the halts, in accordance with the old Russian custom.

The Emperor seemed fully as pleased as his subjects; he replied to the acclamations with short sentences full of good nature. The Empress herself, normally so cold and distant, did her best to put some warmth into her response to the crowd.

The arrival at Sarov was invested with remarkable grandeur. The last rays of the setting sun gilded the vestments of the priests and the countless heads of the crowd, which held its breath to catch the words of the Tsar's address. The old monastery was covered with creepers. Vespers were sung by the choirs of the arch-diocese of Tambov, choirs such as existed only in Russia.

On the day of Their Majesties' departure things went less well. It had been decided that the Sovereign should go to visit the *skit* (hermitage) of St. Seraph, and the miraculous bath alongside it.

There was a mile to walk alongside a little stream flanked by the mountain on whose slope the monastery was built. The Governor of the province, Launitz (he was assassinated later by revolutionaries) had received definite orders not to prevent the crowd from watching the Sovereigns as they went on their way. Troops were brought up; the soldiers held hands to keep the peasants on the slopes of the mountain; every minute there seemed a danger that the 150,000 men

a 'miraculous bath' near St. Seraph's retreat. No miracle of any sort was effected; Princess Orbeliani died ten years later, reduced to complete immobility.

and women would break through the fragile barrier so formed and press on to the path.

After a mass at the *skit*, the Sovereigns started back along the path. Half-way back a short-cut goes straight up to the monastery. When he got to it the Tsar unexpectedly took this path, deliberately passing through the crowd of peasants massed on the slopes of the amphitheatre on the left.

I saw the Tsar disappear in the peasant flood; the rest of the Imperial suite was already separated from him by the crowd. 'Come!' I shouted to Launitz.

After superhuman efforts we succeeded in rejoining the Tsar, who was slowly going forward, repeating:

'Let me through, little brothers!'

They all wanted to touch a bit of his uniform! The situation at once became alarming. We were being suffocated. Some well-intentioned people, seeing the danger the Tsar was in, began to shout:

'Don't push!'

In vain! It was scarcely possible to move one's arms. I said to His Majesty:

'Sire, they all want to see you. If you would agree just to get up on our crossed hands, Launitz's and mine — '

The Tsar would not. But a few seconds later, amid another crush, he involuntarily sat down on our crossed hands. We hoisted him on to our shoulders. There was a veritable thunder of hurrahs!

To save the Tsar we kept him on our shoulders and made for a sort of footbridge that descended the slope a little farther on, joining the monastery with the river below. With the aid of a couple of specially vigorous *mujiks* we succeeded in getting the Tsar on to this footbridge.

But there was still great danger. The peasants followed on to the shaky structure, some yards high at that point, and it collapsed just behind the Tsar; I do not know how I managed to cling to the rail that had stood firm. The Tsar hurried on and reached the side door of the monastery.

'Where is my suite?' he asked.

'It was swallowed up at once. Sire, I saw Count Freedericksz fall. I am afraid he may have got into difficulties.'

'Go and find him.'

After some searching I saw the Count go into his cell. His face was covered with blood. It seems that he had been unable to get up again and had been trodden on by the peasants; his pince-nez had been smashed by a man's heel and had cut his cheek. Fortunately his injuries were not serious; an hour later the Count was able to present himself to Their Majesties, with his face bound up by a not very efficient attendant. The Empress made him let her adjust the dressings better.

This unfortunate incident (it might easily have led to a repetition of the Hodynka disaster! — see p.40) showed the immense difficulties in the way of allowing the Tsar to yield to the very human impulses of his good heart. The desire of the crowds to show their Sovereign their love for him almost brought a tragedy.

But I shall never cease to declare that the Sarov incidents are manifest evidence that the Bolsheviks are wrong when they claim that the people never manifested any other sentiments toward the dynasty than those of envy and hatred.

THE INTERMEDIARIES BETWEEN THE TSAR AND THE MASS OF THE PEOPLE

I come now to the indirect means employed in order to keep the Sovereign in touch with the mass of his subjects. The regular statutory method of delegating representatives of the people ultimately took the form of an assembly of elected deputies.

The first idea had been to create a consultative Duma, an assembly of deputies which would have the right to discuss the proposals submitted by Ministers but would not be able to impose its decisions on the Tsar. A Bill on these lines, drafted by M. Bulyguin, was promulgated; but the public reaction to it was such that it was not proceeded with.

October 17th 1905 brought a Duma with the right to reject the measures proposed by Ministers. It was a real Parliament, but with a Ministry independent of it, something like that of Germany at the time or that of the United States at present.

The Duma was intended to serve two different purposes: to keep the Tsar informed of the main trends of public opinion in Russia; and to serve at the same time as a nursery for the gradual replenishment of a bureaucracy that had degenerated and grown effete through three centuries of unchecked power.

A NURSERY FOR MINISTERS?

It must be freely admitted that we were entirely without statesmen equal to the crushing burdens of Ministerial power.

I recall the Tsar's words after one of the visits from William II:

'The German Emperor has been advising me to do as he does: it seems that each time a new Minister is appointed he writes down on a secret document the name of the man who could take the place of the new Minister if necessary.'

The Tsar added, bitterly:

'What is the good of giving me advice like that! How many times I find it impossible to discover a single suitable man for a vacant post! After superhuman efforts, I select a candidate; but it would be utterly impossible for me to find a second. Probably there are more men in Germany who are capable of filling positions of command than among us.'

I had exactly the same impression of our penury of men one day when talking with General Vannovsky, Minister of Education, and a former Minister of War. (I had been his personal A.D.C., and he had no secrets from me.) We were in the hall in which one waited before going into the presence of the Tsar.

The General said:

'Who are the people who whisper in His Majesty's ear all the rubbish that it takes so much trouble to prove baseless?'

'Your Excellency, the members of the suite are too well disciplined to dare to pass on to His Majesty unverified rumours — '

'Then it must come from the womenfolk. And that makes the struggle still harder. I should have resigned many months ago, but have to stop on because I cannot find a successor. It is impossible to discover anybody capable of holding the portfolio of Education.'

'But I am sure that you have His Majesty's full confidence.'

'Confidence or none, he is always in a state of nerves when I am making my report to him. He shivers!'

'Shivers — ?'

'Yes! Don't you remember how one day at the manoeuvres I told you to look at Nicholas Alexandrovitch? — he was then Cesarevitch. We had all been caught in drenching rain out in the field. I said to you, "Look at him shivering!" '

He added, smiling: 'Now I am the rain. I hate the part, and I should be glad to go. But where is the man to take my place?'

There was a time when it had been hoped that the Duma would produce a steady succession of politicians who would be capable of filling Ministerial posts as they fell vacant.

THE DEPUTIES IN THE WINTER PALACE

Everything possible was done to smooth the way for the first meetings between the Tsar and the deputies elected by universal suffrage. There was, especially, a formal reception of the deputies at the Winter Palace. The Masters of Ceremonies excelled themselves on that occasion.

The procession left the interior apartments and made for the throne-room. In front of the Tsar went the high dignitaries of the State, carrying the emblems of supreme power — the Imperial Standard, the Seal, the Sword, the Globe, the Sceptre, and the crowns studded with diamonds. The Palace grenadiers escorted the dignitaries, carrying their rifles and wearing their enormous bearskin kalpaks.

In the throne-room the deputies were waiting on the right, with the members of the Upper Chamber in firont. The left side was taken up by the members of the Imperial Council, the Ministers, and the high dignitaries of the Court.

The Emperor, the Empress, the Dowager Empress, and Grand Duchesses Olga and Tatiana, with the other members of the Imperial family, came to a stop in the centre of the great hall. The insignia were placed on either side of the throne, which was left half-covered by the Imperial mantle. An altar was brought, and a Te Deum was sung.

Then the Empresses and the members of the Imperial family defiled before the Tsar and took up their places on the left of the throne. The Tsar was left alone in the centre of the room. He went with measured steps towards the throne, and took his seat. He was given the text of the Speech from the Throne, which he read aloud, very distinctly, standing.

Immediately afterwards the procession formed again and withdrew to the interior apartments.

What was to be said of the deputies? I saw them then for the first time in my life. Their dress contrasted strangely with the magnificent uniforms of the Ministers and the high dignitaries. Some of them were in evening dress, others in grey lounge suits. There were some peasant kaftans to be seen, some uniforms of officers on the retired list, and the national costumes of the Caucasian deputies. The whole scene created a painful impression. The deputies' faces had no friendly look.

A few hours later the Minister of the Court and I were present at the opening session of the Duma in the Taurida Palace. On our way back the Count said to me:

'The deputies? They give one the impression of a gang of criminals who are only waiting for the signal to throw themselves upon the Ministers and cut their throats. What wicked faces! I will never again set foot among those people.'

I suppose the impression made on M. Goremykin, the Prime Minister, was not very different. It is said that at the tribune in the Duma, which was too high for him, Goremykin produced a poor impression; this head of the Government, his hands trembling with ill-controlled emotion, could not but be an unimposing figure, especially alongside M. Muromtsev, the President (Speaker) of the Duma, an accomplished orator.

I am convinced that the throne-room ceremony, with dignitaries covered with gold braid and decorations, merely filled the deputies with envy and hatred. It certainly did not succeed in restoring the prestige of the Sovereign as had been hoped. The deputies seemed to me to be incapable of collaborating with the Government; they produced the effect of enemies engaged in an internecine struggle with it for the upper hand.

As for the Tsar himself, the idea never entered his head that these few hundreds of men could be accepted as legitimate representatives of his people, the people who had accustomed him to the spectacle of delirious acclamations. One felt at once that His Majesty would not dream of expecting this Duma, these deputies, these drab nobodies, to be able to assist him in the accomplishment of his duties as Tsar.

The Tsar had signed a manifesto granting political liberties. But he had no sooner done so than the representatives of reaction set themselves to insinuate to him that the manifesto had been extracted by force, and, a still more effective argument, that the Tsar of Russia had not the right to renounce the autocratic power bequeathed to him by his ancestors.

That theory found zealous partisans especially in the entourage of the Empress. Even after the abdication in 1917, the Empress continually repeated that her husband might renounce his throne but could not renounce his autocratic power, for on ascending the throne he had sworn to transmit the power to his successors as he had received it, that is to say, unfettered by any constitution.

The reactionary groups who claimed autocratic power for the Tsar (subject to the proviso that the autocrat must comply with their own demands) soon had the upper hand; and they determined the fate of the first Duma.

The second Duma was even more violent than the first; and the question of receiving it in the Winter Palace was not even considered.

REVOLUTION FROM ABOVE

At the time of the dissolution of the second Duma it had become clear that there was no way out through fresh elections: they would do nothing to facilitate collaboration between deputies and Government, the purpose which had been aimed at.

Two tendencies showed themselves among the leaders. One was represented by my brother-in-law, D. Trepov. It was in favour of entirely constitutional procedure. Trepov declared that, once the experiment had been entered on, it should be pushed to its logical conclusion: a 'homogeneous' (Parliamentary) Ministry must be formed, and the attempt made through this Ministry to procure the indispensable modification of the electoral law.

The protagonist of the second tendency was Stolypin, a courageous and very popular man, but with insufficient breadth of political views. Stolypin held that the first elections had caught our administration napping. In Western countries, he said, the officials had learnt decades ago the difficult art of influencing the electorate; here in Russia we had made no attempt to give the governors of provinces the opportunity to bring into play their moral ascendancy over voters, who had been worked upon only by 'Left-wing propaganda'. Consequently there must be a new electoral law, and it must give the administration the necessary means for countering 'propaganda'.

Stolypin considered that it would be impossible to get this law passed by the Duma. He induced the Tsar to dispense with the Duma; this was the proposed *coup d'état* from above. It was a dangerous step, one which was bound to shake the authority of the Tsar. No more than two years after the promulgation of the Constitution, one of its principal provisions was to be infringed.

The Tsar adopted the Stolypin policy. I do not know how far he realized the political results that might follow from it. Revolutions from above are apt to provoke revolutions from below.

The third Duma entirely justified Stolypin's diagnosis; it became a docile instrument in his hands.

The fourth Duma was almost exactly similar to the third. The irony of history willed it that such a body should develop into an instrument of revolution; two members of the Right wing were sent by this fourth Duma to extract an abdication from the Tsar.

By then the original theory of the purpose of the Duma had been forgotten for many years — the theory that it was to become a nursery for Ministers and a source of information for the Tsar.

THE DELEGATIONS

Since the duly elected deputies did not seem to provide the link so long sought for between the Tsar and his trusty subjects — even after the modification of the electoral law, the search was pursued elsewhere.

Delegations were the alternative expedient tried.

On the bi-centenary of Poltava[1] the administration arranged, at His Majesty's desire, a meeting between the Tsar and a delegation of peasants.

These Khokhols (the familiar term[2] used, rather slightingly, by the Great Russians for the Ukrainians) were drawn up in serried ranks in a public square. The Tsar mixed with them and chatted right and left of him; he was so keenly interested that the reception lasted more than two hours, much longer than had been proposed for this patriarchal ceremony. The delegates seemed to me to be completely spellbound by the charm of the Tsar's approach to them.

1 Peter the Great's victory over Charles XII of Sweden at Poltava (Ukraine), in 1709.

2 The word means 'top-knots', and refers to the lock of hair by which the head was carried off the battle-field where a corpse had to be left without burial.

As for the Sovereign himself, he was full of the subject afterwards, and continually referred in conversation to the knowledge that he had gained from 'those splendid, sincerely devoted *Khokhols.'*

After the promulgation of the 1905 manifesto, granting political liberties, there were attempts to group into a political party those who were declared adherents of the autocratic, rigorously nationalist regime. This party took the name of 'Union of the Russian People'. Its delegates were certainly brought on several occasions into the presence of the Tsar and the Empress.

The leader of the party was a Dr. Dubrovin. His newspaper was the *Russkoye Znamya* ('Russian Standard'). Dubrovin found means, I do not know how, of presenting himself to His Majesty not through the channel of the Master of the Ceremonies but through the simple intervention of the Tsar's valet. Dubrovin secured receptions in the same way for provincial delegations of the 'Black Hundred' — as his 'Union of the Russian People' was nicknamed by the Liberals.

The Minister of the Court only learned of the arrival and reception of these delegations through the Court harbingers' journal, a secret document that recorded the whole of the Tsar's activities from hour to hour.

Freedericksz felt it his duty to point out to His Majesty more than once that unofficial visits of this sort might involve serious political dangers. But each time the Tsar replied:

'Surely I am entitled to know what the people particularly devoted to me think of affairs!'

The newspapers of the 'Black Hundred' gave me a great deal of trouble. These reactionaries denounced the liberal reforms of which Count Witte, the Prime Minister, was the great promoter, and their attacks on him grew more and more scurrilous. Dubrovin and his staff felt that they had the Sovereign's protection. In my capacity of head of the Court censorship I had to take steps against all articles that mentioned the Tsar or members of the Imperial family unless the articles had been submitted to me before publication. Dubrovin attempted on several occasions to evade compliance with the provisions of the law. In the end I sent for him and called his attention to his neglect.

A few days later the *Russkoye Znamya* again published an account of a reception granted by the Tsar to a delegation of provincial reactionaries. Some of the Sovereign's remarks were quoted in a way that could not be permitted, and I had them struck out.

Dubrovin did not accept defeat. He came to see me and began to tell me that the accounts were 'to the Tsar's liking'. I had to recall him to a sense of realities, and energetically asserted my right to censor anything relating to the Imperial family.

On that the 'Black Hundred' began a counter-attack; and I was made to realize that Dubrovin had influence. Late at night the telephone at my bedside woke me up. I heard an unfamiliar voice.

'We are aware,' it said, 'of all your intrigues against the only people who are really devoted to the Tsar. . . . I am instructed to inform you that if you do not make an end of your insinuations we shall use our opportunity to tell the Empress some scandalous things about you.'

I hung up the receiver. It was not the first time that I had received anonymous attacks.

The threats were carried out. The Empress suddenly became very distant and avoided meeting me. The maids of honour informed me that most compromising stories, completely false, had been told her about my private life.

There were also official interventions. One day, after his report to the Tsar, Freedericksz told me that Dubrovin had complained of the 'revolting' lack of impartiality that I had been showing towards him. I had to get together a whole file of articles by Dubrovin that had been struck out by the censorship. Freedericksz took it to the Tsar, and told me afterwards that my intervention had been approved by the Sovereign.

I had occasion to speak personally to the Tsar about the matter, I told him that the Liberal newspapers gave me far less trouble than the organs of the people who were 'entirely devoted to His Majesty'. I showed His Majesty an article, manifestly a fabrication from beginning to end, concerned with the Cesarevitch and attributing certain statements to him. The Emperor said to me:

'Yes, that would have rendered ill service to the cause of the dynasty. You did well to stop it. Send me this paper; I will show it to the Empress.'

In his Memoirs Count Witte declares that the reactionary Press was subsidized by the Empress, and that it was she who inspired the tone of the *Russkoye Znamya* and similar papers (the *Moscow News*, the *Tocsin*, etc.). I do not think that is true, though the case of the newspaper projected by Prince Andronnikov[1] seemed to me a little suspicious.

1 See pp.136-8.

I can say definitely that not a kopek of the funds administered by the Minister of the Court was ever sent to the 'Black Hundred' Press. The sums of which the Tsar disposed as 'pocket money' (about £20,000 a year) served to meet the cost of the Sovereign's wardrobe and of the small presents that he gave personally. I do not think his resources would have been sufficient to enable him to subsidize newspapers. As for the Empress's expenditure, it was in charge of her secretary, Count Rostovtzev.

All the principal clubs were up in arms over rumours that the Black Press was under the special patronage of Her Majesty, and to get to the bottom of the matter Freedericksz instructed me to investigate the stories. I sent for Rostovtzev, and an hour's talk with him sufficed to establish the baselessness of the rumours.

The Tsar's meetings with the delegations of members of the Black Hundred were not arranged through official channels, and were kept rigorously secret; it may be that their true history will never be written.

UNOFFICIAL INTERVIEWS

It remains to mention the persons whom the Tsar was able to consult personally without their communications with him being sanctioned by any other authority than their own conscience.

The first place in this category belongs to Prince Vladimir Mestchersky, editor of the weekly paper *Grashdanin* ('The Citizen'). The Prince had made the acquaintance of Nicholas Alexandrovitch (elder son of Alexander II) when he was Cesarevitch;[1] he had managed to get permission to visit Alexander III informally at any time, and his paper received regular subsidies from secret funds. The Prince was a man of great intelligence. He knew that his paper was read by Alexander III and by Nicholas II, and made full use of the influence that the fact gave him. His articles often contained sensational revelations; the administration stood in fear of these pungent paragraphs, based on full knowledge of everything that was going on in the Government departments.

I do not remember the Prince ever meeting with a refusal from the Tsar. He wrote direct to him, without any intermediary, and I have

1 Nicholas Alexandrovitch died of tuberculosis at Nice.

had many of his letters in my hands, in his illegible scrawl, with the Emperor's initials and the word 'Granted' in the margin.

Some of these letters had reference to political questions. The Prince also secured two or three private audiences every year. I am unable to say in what direction he influenced the Tsar, for His Majesty never mentioned him to Freedericksz. But this reactionary prince could only have spoken in direct opposition to every liberal reform.

I may also mention the ex-Ministers Pobedonostzev and Vannovsky, who wrote to the Tsar when they wanted to see him. The Sovereign then sent them an invitation. One more name, that of General Richter, A.D.C., and the list is virtually complete of the remarkably few persons whom the Tsar was able to consult individually.

CHANCE ENCOUNTERS

Finally there come the people whom the Tsar met in casual encounters. I recall the amusing story of Alexander III told me by Mr. Heath, the English tutor to the Cesarevitch.

One day while holidaying in the Finnish fjords, Alexander III had gone out with rod and line. Seeing a Finn peacefully installed by the riverside, he sat down a little way off and cast his fly. An hour passed in unbroken silence. At last the Tsar spoke to his neighbour:

'What do you do in the world?'

A pause. Then, in a tone that betrayed his sense of dignity, the other replied:

'I am a master mariner.'

'Ah! A fine job.'

Silence fell again, perhaps for a further half-hour.

Then the sea-captain spat out his quid and said:

'And what do you do yourself?'

'I am Emperor of Russia.'

'Ah! That's a fine job too.'

There the conversation ended.

Nicholas II was always ready to catechize any plain citizens he met. The incident of the Siberian hunter with his live sable[1] is a typical one.

1 See pp.49-52.

Rasputin was a typical peasant in the Tsar's eyes. He filled a gap of which the Tsar had always felt conscious. Three main elements combined to smooth Rasputin's path:

(1) The Tsar's anxiety to be kept informed of 'what those who are particularly devoted to the Throne are saying';
(2) The morbid mysticism of the Empress. She was fascinated by the medieval methods of address of which the 'Staretz' made use in talking to her: he was a master of the art of mingling his miracle-worker's gibberish with passages intoned from the liturgy in the habitual peasant style;
(3) The despair of Tsar and Tsarina at the inability of the medical world to do anything for their son, and their readiness to place him in the hands of any quack. Rasputin had incontestable success in the field of healing; I have no idea how he managed it.

Rasputin's rise was of lightning rapidity. Once he had reached the presence of Their Majesties, he succeeded in establishing an unshakable ascendancy over them. He must have had an extraordinary gift of intuition, an instinctive sense of his interlocutor's thoughts and subconscious reactions; and he adapted himself to them instantly. He never ceased to play a part in the presence of Their Majesties — a part which, indeed, was not a difficult one to keep up. The thing that is surprising is the sureness of touch with which this rustic discovered the one and only means of asserting his influence.

He certainly had a large share of elementary common sense, that sound peasant sense that creates havoc when it breaks into the hothouse existence of the *habitués* of a palace. A show of good nature, its hollowness well concealed; an impudent familiarity, combined with a servility which fitted like a glove on this upstart, this man of utterly obscure origin; a few empty formulas, borrowed unconsciously from the criminal sects of the flagellants or the 'white doves' (castrated in mystical rites), or the 'torches' (the sect whose adepts went through fire in churches fitted up for this type of sacrifice) — such was his stock-in-trade. The famous 'Slav soul' was capable of plumbing depths in the realm of mystical perversion of which the outer world has no conception. The combination of these disparate elements produced a Tartuffe of a 'little brother', professing unbounded adoration of the 'Little Father Tsar', and able to discuss political questions without any discordant note ever disturbing the Sovereign. Rasputin brought

Nicholas II precisely the assurances which the Tsar had sought at Sarov, at Poltava, in the deliberations of the Duma. . . .

This part of my story is most painful, and I shall devote only a few words to the libidinous side of Rasputin's activities. There is a widely accepted theory that all the ecstasies may merge into one another — so that religious transports may find their climax in those of sexuality. Rasputin knew nothing of this or kindred theories; but he applied them. The Orthodox liturgy has, for instance, a few moments before Holy Communion, the words 'Let us love one another, that we may profess our faith in common'. A slight distortion sufficed to give this chant a blasphemous meaning. Sin? Rasputin disburdened himself of it with ease, declaring that the true saints 'turn to filth, in order that amid the filth their aureole may shine with double brightness'. He got drunk 'in order to show the full hideousness of vice'. He preached the life of purity 'not by means of empty phrases of admonition but by exhibiting, as food for thought, the abject state in which the sinner perishes'. According to the women who surrounded Rasputin, anything whatever was permitted to him, since his mission was to expose the ugliness of vice under every conceivable form. For those who rebelled against this abominable theory, he produced another precept, borrowed from monastical practice and enlisted in the service of his lubricity:

'You have too much vainglory; you must humiliate yourself.'

That could mean a great deal.

But there were also around Rasputin women who needed no prompting from epistemological theories to abandon all restraint. And, unfortunately, there were poor wretches who knew that there was only one way of paying a debt contracted towards Rasputin, the dispenser of so many coveted official posts.

THE HEALER

At Spala in 1912, as he came alongside in a boat, the Cesarevitch stretched his leg out too sharply; internal haemorrhage was set up in the groin.[1] The unfortunate boy suffered dreadfully. The Empress

1 The Cesarevitch suffered from haemophilia, a congenital malady transmitted only in the female line and attacking only the sons in a family. The sufferer's blood does not congeal sufficiently, and the slightest cut produces obstinate haemorrhage. Haemophilia was congenital in the ducal family of Hesse.

passed whole nights at his bedside. It was a painful spectacle. The anxiety of his father and mother was beyond description.

The doctors called in to attend on the heir to the throne were Dr. E. S. Botkin, Court Physician, Professor Feodorov, Court Surgeon, and Dr. Rauchfuss, Court Physician for children's diseases, who had been sent for from St. Petersburg.

The Empress had forbidden the publication of bulletins concerning her son's illness; the Minister of the Court insisted, therefore, that bulletins should be drawn up in his presence, in order that they might be preserved in the archives. The doctors used to meet in the room which was reserved for me, after their visits to the patient, and they discussed the situation in my presence. None of the remedies which they prescribed sufficed to arrest the bleeding, and the young sufferer's condition seemed alarming.

One day Professor Feodorov was the last to leave my room, and said to me:

'I do not agree with my colleagues. It is most urgently necessary to apply far more drastic measures; but they involve a risk. What do you think — ought I to say so to the Empress? Or would it be better to prescribe without letting her know?'

I replied that I could not possibly give an opinion on so delicate a question. The professor had scarcely gone when I informed the Minister of the Court.

It is said that a telegram had arrived just at that moment from the Staretz[1] Rasputin, in which the miracle-worker declared that the heir to the throne was recovering and would soon be out of pain, and that he must not be 'allowed to be martyred by the doctors'.

Next day, at 2 p.m., the doctors came in search of me; their first words were:

'The haemorrhage has stopped.'

---

1 Staretz means literally, in Russian, 'old man', 'greybeard', with an implication of deep respect. Certain monks to whom supernatural powers were attributed were called 'Staretz'. There is a legend that one day Alexander I simulated death and that he then took refuge in Siberia and there lived as a recluse, passing his days in meditation; in this legend he is described as 'Staretz'.

Most of the men called 'Staretz' were monks, but the title can be given to any venerable old man, whether he has taken vows or not. Rasputin has sometimes been called a monk or 'pope' (priest) by foreign writers, but he was neither.

'Did you apply the remedy you spoke of?'

As they went I detained Feodorov and asked him:

He threw up his hands and replied as he went out:

'If I had done I should not have admitted it; you can see for yourself what is going on here.'

He hurried away.

The Empress left her private apartments for dinner, for the first time since her son's illness; she was radiant in her relief from anxiety. The Cesarevitch, she said, was suffering no longer; in a week's time they would leave for St. Petersburg. The doctors, who were present, seemed in utter consternation; their advice as to the departure had not been sought.

After dinner the Empress sent for me and told me to have the road repaired, so that there should not be the slightest jolting on the way to the station.

A week later the departure took place. The Cesarevitch played peacefully in his bed, and did not seem to be feeling the slightest pain.

'It is not the first time that the Staretz has saved his life,' the Empress said to me.

Aided by the mysticism of the Empress, Rasputin had little difficulty in making his every word law. And the words of this astute peasant were fateful. In the last resort the life of Alexis Nicolayevitch, the destinies of the house of Romanov, and the whole future of Russia depended entirely on his prayers. If he died not a stone would be left standing.

Such were the whispered comments of the household staff of the Court,-when they ventured to breathe confidences.

RASPUTIN'S 'NOTES'

I do not know at what stage or by what process Rasputin began to turn to account his influence with the Empress. On several occasions I had heard of 'notes' given by Rasputin to ladies who came to him to ask for his high protection. These notes were all drawn up in the same way: a little cross at the top of the page; then one or two lines giving a recommendation from the Staretz. They opened all doors in Petrograd, almost without exception.

My turn soon came.

One day I was told that a lady insisted on being received, though it was outside the hours reserved for official visits. I disliked her the moment she came into my office.

She wore a very low-cut dress, almost a ball dress. She handed me an envelope: inside was Rasputin's calligraphy, with the erratic spelling of which it is impossible to give an idea in translation:

'My dear chap. Fix it up for her. She is all right. Gregory.'

The lady explained that what she wanted was to become a *prima donna* in the Imperial Opera at St. Petersburg. I did my utmost to explain to her clearly and patiently that the post did not depend in any way whatever on me. It became evident that she was trying to stop in my office and to make the most of all the personal charms she had left. . . .

A similar letter was brought to me one day by a deacon who was also stage-struck. He tried to explain to me that it must be possible to get him on to the stage because the Staretz Gregory had himself given him the 'needful blessing'.

A TYPICAL CASE

Rasputin's influence grew continually. He made and unmade marriages, adoptions, appointments, concessions, commissions. . . .

The Rodzianko affair, with which, by no means willingly, I found myself closely mixed up, was a fairly typical case. The story is briefly as follows.

Tamara, daughter of one of my brother officers, Novosiltzev, had married M. Rodzianko, and had gone with her husband some years later to Italy.

There he had her confined in a lunatic asylum. She succeeded in escaping, and returned to St. Petersburg to claim her children. Her husband put up strong opposition to this.

One day, at Livadia, the Mistress of the Robes asked me to write to the competent authorities to request a re-hearing of Mme Rodzianko's case. Her children's fate depended on the decision of these authorities.

The Mistress of the Robes explained to me that Tamara Rodzianko had been granted a private audience by the Empress, and that after interrogating her at length the Empress had declared that the injustice done to her ought to be remedied.

After drafting the letter to the authorities I went to see Tamara, in order to show it to her. She was so downcast that I did my best to raise her spirits. I asked her how she had managed to get the Empress to receive her. Had not Her Majesty shown some animosity towards her a few months before?

I met Rasputin at Mlle Golovina's; she is an old friend of mine, and undertook to arrange the audience. 'To-morrow,' she added with a radiant smile, 'I am going over to thank him.'

Next day Tamara rang me up on the telephone, and, in a voice choked with sobs, begged me to go to see her there and then.

I found her desolate and in utter despair.

'Do you know what happened yesterday? As soon as I entered the room the Staretz was in, all the ladies around him made obsequious bows to him and hurried away; they made no secret of their intention of leaving me alone with that man. Then Rasputin literally threw himself upon me. . . . I boxed his ears and ran away.'

Two days later I met the Mistress of the Robes.

'What has happened about my letter?'

'The Empress told me not to send it — that Rodzianko woman had been telling lies: she does not deserve help from anybody.'

From then on the Empress changed completely in her attitude toward me. Unless there was anything definite to say she never spoke to me beyond the few really unavoidable words.

I learned in the end the version of the affair that had been concocted. It was this:

It was I who had been Mme Rodzianko's protector; it was I who had almost succeeded in getting the Empress to intervene in Tamara's favour; and it was Rasputin who had unmasked the affair and had warned the Empress not do to a serious injustice to Tamara's husband.

I told Count Freedericksz of this bit of scandalmongering. He said simply:

'That fellow Rasputin — what a skunk!'

MY MEETINGS WITH RASPUTIN

It was impossible in the end for me to avoid personal contact with Rasputin. He left no stone unturned in his efforts to get into touch with me: he was trying to get received by Count Freedericksz.

It was in summer. My friends, the Mdivanis, had come to Petrograd for the season. One day, knowing that I was not well enough to go out, Mme Mdivani came to see me at my house.

The moment she entered she came straight to the purpose of her visit.

'Alexander Alexandrovitch, you have many enemies.'

'Who has not, my friend?'

'Yes, but Rasputin could do you harm. I am sure he only hates you because he does not know you. He has a fixed idea that you are constantly working on Count Freedericksz in order to obstruct him. It is essential that you should see him.'

I replied with a categorical refusal.

A few days later I was rung up by Elizabeth Victorovna (Mme Mdivani):

'I have a few friends here; come along too!'

I said I had too much work to do, but she insisted.

The Mdivanis had put up at the Hotel d' Europe. I arrived about 11 p.m., and found myself in the company of Mile Golovina and several other ladies who were well known to belong to the Rasputin clique.

'It is a trap!' I said to Mme Mdivani. 'You are expecting Rasputin.'

At that moment a bell rang. The ladies rushed excitedly towards the door. Rasputin came in, utterly drunk. He was told my name.

'Ah, Mossolov! Here you are at last! Let us be friends — do you agree?'

He was already leading me to a table loaded with bottles.

'Your old man' (Freedericksz) 'doesn't he like me? . . . I'll tell you: to-night. I'm boozed . . . boozed, dead drunk. . . . Does it upset you? I understand. . . . Don't take any notice. . . . One day, when there's more time, we'll talk more seriously. . . . But not now. Here's to your health!'

We had several glasses together. 'You must come over to see me one day . . . everybody comes to see me . . , the Ministers . . . and "Vitia" (Witte) too . . . only you and your old man make a fuss about it. That's why Mamma (the Empress) doesn't like you any longer.'

'I suppose this intrigue was your little scheme?'

'What of that? Of course it was! Love me, and Mamma will love you.'

'There now, you're the sort I like. You don't bear ill-will. Anybody who can lift it can't have any guile in him. I don't mind a bottle now and then myself.'

'Come and see me. We'll have a drink and a talk.'

'Right ho, right ho. You've got yourself into such a state that you ought to go and lie down.'

When he left he ruined my overcoat in the hall.

Some days later Mme Mdivani came again to see me. She declared that Rasputin was determined to see me at all costs.

'You will gain nothing by showing hostility to him.'

'May be, but I have no desire at all to be seen everywhere with that gentleman.'

Finally it was agreed that I should go to the house of the assistant secretary of the Holy Synod, and there I should meet Rasputin in entire secrecy.

I went to the dignitary's residence on the day fixed. He took me through many corridors and up various staircases. In his private quarters, in a room overlooking a courtyard, I found Rasputin.

This time he was sober. He spoke at length, and, I am bound to say, with a great deal of good sense. He fixed me incessantly with his bleared eyes. He spoke of 'the old chap', that is to say, Count Freedericksz. What he was after was to get on friendly terms with the Minister of the Court. He urged me to talk to the Count and to try to arrange it for him.

Next day I found myself once more in the Empress's good graces.

RASPUTIN'S INFLUENCE OVER THE GOVERNMENT

During the war Rasputin's influence over affairs of state became virtually paramount. Most of the important appointments were settled in the Empress's salons. A recommendation from Rasputin was all that was needed even for a Minister's portfolio.

The plans for the most important reforms, the very problem of a separate peace, seemed to depend on what the Staretz would say. I had myself to apply to him for enlightenment on a rumour that an armistice might be declared at any moment, and also to ascertain his view concerning a plan of administrative decentralization in which I was interested.

My idea was to divide the Empire into several 'States' which would be governed by *Namiestniks*[1] with the aid of local Dumas (Parliaments).

This reform was to be carried out, under my scheme, at the moment of the conclusion of a victorious peace; it would have democratized the local administration, while preserving autocratic power for the Tsar.

This had to be discussed with Rasputin, to see whether he was in favour of the plan and would give it his support when the time came.

The separate peace was the second problem to be dealt with. I suspected that the Staretz was playing a double game, advocating war to the bitter end only so long as he hesitated to unmask his real position.

Mme Mdivani was no longer in Petrograd, and I had recourse to the services of another woman friend, whose name I prefer to suppress, since she is still in Soviet Russia and the slightest indiscretion might get her into serious difficulties. Let us call her the Baroness.

The Baroness's flat was full of guests. On his arrival Rasputin embraced all the women present. When he caught sight of me he showed anything but pleasure.

He was taken into the dining-room, where he set to, without using knife or fork. The women's flatteries of this boor were sickening. When he got up the wine had made him more talkative; he said to the Baroness:

'Verotchka' (diminutive of Vera), 'take me and Mossolov into your bedroom. He has not come to see me eat.'

When we were alone, Rasputin said to me:

'What is it you want to see me about?'

He glared at me in his customary way.

'I am just back from the Tsar's tour of the G.H.Q., and I want to know what you think about the war.'

'You want to know whether I am working for an armistice?'

'Yes.'

1 Representatives of the Emperor; a title equivalent to that of Viceroy, which was given on some occasions to the Governors General of the Caucasus and Poland.

'And what do you think about it yourself?'

'Before the war I thought we ought to remain friends with Germany. But now that we are at war I think it is necessary to go on until we win. Otherwise the Emperor will have his work cut out.'

'Just so.'

I felt at once that that was all I should get out of him, and that he would reveal nothing of his actual views.

'There is another thing,' I said. 'I wanted to tell you that it seems impossible to govern all Russia from Petrograd. The country must be divided into a number of "States", each with its *Namiestnik* and its Duma.'

He cut me short at once.

'Duma! There's one already, curse it, and that is one too many!'

'Wait a minute. The Tsar will have no need to take any account of these other Dumas. The *Namiestniks* will deal with them themselves, in the provinces, far from Petrograd. If there is any criticism, it will be directed entirely against the *Namiestniks* and not a bit against the Tsar, All he will have to do will be to manifest his goodwill towards everybody. His popularity will become all the greater.'

Rasputin was silent for a moment.

'Then how will the Tsar administer the country?'

'As before, autocratically. It will be he that declares war, signs treaties, and is head of the army. The peasants will gain too; they will be called on to elect the local administration.'

'It may be so; but I do not fully grasp the plan.'

A message came that the guests were restive at his absence. Prince Shakhovskoy (then Minister of Commerce) had just come.

'I must go. Your plan seems interesting. Come and see me to-morrow; we will talk more about it.'

I went next day to see Rasputin about 9 p.m., and found him asleep. I waited half an hour. At last he appeared, his face bloated, his hair unkempt. We could not start our conversation at once from the point where we broke off the night before. We rested about an hour, while I told various yarns. Rasputin poured himself out some wine. As he opened a second bottle he said:

'Well, my friend, what about yesterday's conversation? Have you made up your mind not to breathe another word about it to Grishka?' (Grishka is a depreciatory diminutive of Gregory; like many peasants, Rasputin rarely spoke in the first person.)

He looked hard at me again:

132

'You ought not to treat him like that,' he said.

'I thought you had forgotten all about it,' I replied. 'Your Madeira is so good, I should have preferred to let serious matters go to-day. But as you like —'

'That's better . . . we can drink as we talk. I like you. I am at my ease with you. If you have invented something which may be useful to Papa and Mamma' (the Emperor and Empress), 'tell us all about it. Otherwise let's drink to their health.'

I set out the plan at length. At first he did not grasp my idea. Then suddenly he understood. He not only understood but rendered my idea in his own picturesque way.

'It's a pity,' he went on, 'that we cannot consult Vitia. What a devil he is. He would manipulate everything to his liking, and would so arrange that it should injure Papa. How often he has discussed plans with me that looked admirable; and then, after careful consideration, I have discovered that his idea would only have been of service to himself, to Vitia, and would have been bad for Papa.'

After the third bottle he asked me:

'Does Papa know about it?'

'He has been given a general idea of it. I don't think he had any objection to it.'

'No use, then, for me to talk to him about it?'

'When the time comes for that,' I said, 'I will let you know, so that you can talk to him about it yourself. That would help me.'

'Help you . . . help you. . . . I will tell him to let you talk to him about it, and I am sure he will. . . . He is full of intelligence. He will work out the idea himself. ... As for me, what can I do but give the idea my blessing?'

I pressed his hand. The wine was having its effect on him. He embraced me and began to snivel. When I left he said:

'Come again; we will have another drink, I like you.'

VYRUBOVA 'RESTORED TO LIFE' BY RASPUTIN

At the beginning of 1916 I was going through a difficult and critical time. Freedericksz was ill and unable to come, as he always did, to my defence.

The whole of the affairs of the Court rested on my shoulders. And I could feel that I had not the entire confidence of the Empress.

Intrigues of every sort were being hatched in all directions, shooting up like poisonous fungi. But for my devotion to Count Freedericksz, I should have sent in my resignation.

An invitation to dinner at the Mdivanis' came just at the right moment.

There were only to be three of us — Mme Mdivani, Rasputin, and I. It was an excellent opportunity for getting the Staretz to talk. Only he could say what were the charges that had been concocted against me. I accepted the invitation.

The dinner brought no help. Scarcely had soup been served when Rasputin was summoned to the telephone. He came back almost at once, white-faced and trembling. A catastrophe! 'Annushka' (Mme Vyrubova, the Empress's friend) had been seriously injured in a railway accident, and her life was despaired of. He must go at once to Tsarskoe Selo.

One of the hotel cars was put at his disposal.

It has been said that in spite of her condition Mme Vyrubova was resuscitated by Rasputin. According to some of the maids of honour, the Empress, on returning to the Palace, declared that he had performed a miracle.

THE TSAR AND RASPUTIN

I had kept Freedericksz informed of my contacts with Rasputin.

He made no objection to them. He felt, indeed, that they gave him indications of Their Majesties' attitude.

Well before this period Freedericksz had already made one effort to enlighten the Tsar about Rasputin. The Count had long had his report in preparation; he attached great importance to it. But he only had time to speak a dozen words when the Tsar cut him short:

'My dear Count, people have spoken to me several times about Rasputin. I know beforehand everything you can tell me. Let us remain friends; and never, mind you, never touch on this subject again.'

The situation, however, became more and more untenable, and Freedericksz felt it his duty to return once more to the subject. I do not know what happened at this second conversation. My impression, however, is that the Tsar replied much more energetically and still more decisively than before.

Persons of less importance than Freedericksz were paying with the loss of their posts for the least attempt at rebellion against the growing influence of the Staretz.

I need only mention the case of Prince Vladimir Orlov.

The Prince was descended from one of the favourites of Catherine II. For many years he not only occupied an important post at Court but was virtually a personal friend of the Tsar's.

He had plenty of wit and a sharp tongue, and made some stinging hits at the Staretz in talking about him. There are malicious persons at all times in every Court, and the Prince's witticisms quickly reached the Empress's ears.

That was enough. One day the Emperor and Empress were going on board the *Standard*, the Tsar's favourite yacht. Orlov had already gone down to the cabin reserved for him. The Empress sent for Freedericksz and said to him:

'Tell Prince Orlov to go ashore. I do not want to see him here.'

The order was so astonishing that Freedericksz went to the Tsar to ask his decision about it. Nicholas II took his wife's side, as always. Orlov was asked to go ashore on some pretext that I can no longer recall. A little later he lost his post at Court.

Another incident, of which several versions exist, produced the abrupt dismissal of Mile S.I. Tuytcheva, the Grand Duchesses' governess.

When she was chosen for this important post, Mile Tuytcheva was about thirty years old. She was a woman of exceptional personality and character, highly cultivated, belonging to an aristocratic Moscow family, and she had made an excellent impression on us all. As soon as she arrived at Livadia we noted how salutary was her influence over the children; their manners at once showed a great improvement.

I cannot say exactly how long the governess had held sway over her little empire when one day the news spread like wildfire that the Empress and Mile Tuytcheva had 'had words'. I was not myself a witness of the event. I know that Freedericksz went to see the Empress, and told her that the sudden departure of Mile Tuytcheva would create a bad impression in Moscow. He was told in reply that Mile Tuytcheva had meddled in things that did not concern her, and had tried to give lessons to Her Majesty on what children could and what they could not be permitted to do. Her Majesty seems to have replied that a mother was the best qualified to know what was proper for children. On that Mile Tuytcheva had said she wanted to leave and had been told that she might. It would have been impossible to retain her as a maid of honour in these circumstances.

My own belief is that the Empress regarded the Staretz as a saint and was ready to let him go into the bedrooms to give his blessing. Mile Tuytcheva's opinion was that the unsavoury *mujik* could not be allowed at night among the children.

THE 'CLIQUE'

I knew that a swarm of adventurers had joined the women admirers of the Staretz, and had succeeded in getting into the peasant's good graces. They turned his influence to account in putting pressure for their evil and criminal purposes on all the Ministries; thanks to Rasputin they were also said to be obtaining information of value to our enemies during the war, but I do not think that is likely to have been true.

It would be impossible for me to give the names and the particular departments to which one or another of them had access; I can only give an indication of the methods which these acolytes of Rasputin employed.

Prince Andronnikov was the one among them whom I met most frequently; he was, perhaps, less dangerous than the others. He was of very good family, but was not himself in good repute; he had no regular employment. I avoided him as much as I could. One day he sat next to me at a dinner given by friends of mine. A quarter of an hour's talk sufficed to show me that he was very well informed about all the proposed Court appointments. I showed my surprise; he bent his head in modesty and said;

'You know I have no official post. I might call myself the A.D.C. to the Almighty. In that capacity I have to know everything that is going on in St. Petersburg; that is my only way of showing my love of my country. I ask no other function; I follow Him who makes justice reign or, where necessary, restores its reign.'

A little while later he came into my office. He had come to tell me that he was supporting the candidature of two persons who were proposed for certain Court posts. Both were in the list of officially recommended candidates. I felt able to tell him that I would transmit his recommendation to the Minister of the Court.

But his intervention did not end there. He wanted to let me know that two other persons who were also in the official list were entirely unworthy of the honour which it was proposed to confer on them. He began to retail to me some vague gossip to their disadvantage.

'Have you any documents to prove your statements?'

'I never offer documentary evidence.'

I rose and brought the conversation abruptly to its end.

A few days passed; then I received an enormous fish, caught in the Volga; the Prince wrote that he had been given a number of these fish and felt he ought to get me to try one.

I returned his present, without a card or a word. It seems that about the same time Freedericksz had unknowingly partaken of a fish from the same quarter; his chef had found it excellent and had sent some up to the Count's table. Not until a fortnight later was the sender's name discovered.

It was too late then; the subject could hardly have been raked up.

The Prince showed no ill-feeling against me over my rejection of his present. He called to bring me a memorandum concerning a political problem, and asked me to arrange an audience for him with Count Freedericksz. The memorandum was fairly well drafted; it had many flattering remarks about the Count and the writer of these lines, but ended with a rather crude attack on one of our Ministers.

I did everything possible to prevent the Prince from seeing the Count, Reports came in from him incessantly; I passed them on to my Chief; and, to be honest, it must be admitted that Freedericksz read them with some interest, even with pleasure.

Two years later Their Majesties had gone abroad, to Wolfsgarten; their suite was housed in Frankfort. Andronnikov turned up there. He told me that he had been sent as special correspondent of one of the Russian newspapers, and in that capacity I had to receive him on various occasions in the same way as the other representatives of the Press. He wanted at all costs to be presented to Freedericksz; I found various pretexts for failing to arrange an interview.

One day I said to him:

'It is impossible. The Minister is leaving Frankfort to go with his wife to Cologne; she is taking the North Express for St. Petersburg.'

It was child's play, of course, to calculate the time of the Count's return to Frankfort after seeing his wife off.

'When we came into the station at 5 a.m.,' Freedericksz told me afterwards, 'I saw a gentleman waiting outside my compartment, with his top hat in his hands. I assumed that he was one of the railway inspectors, and went up to him to thank him briefly for the company's attentiveness. He answered: "I am not a railway employee; I am a Russian prince, and am here to express my admiration for a chevalier".

' "A chevalier?"

' "Have you not just done something worthy of the traditions of chivalry?"

' "But — excuse me, what do you mean?"

' "Taking Madame la Comtesse back to Cologne!" '

After that Andronnikov went with Count Freedericksz, who was pretty annoyed, as far as the hotel at which he was putting up; there, in spite of the Count's protests, Andronnikov took possession of his bag and carried it up to his room, continuing all the time with a string of praises that savoured of the lowest toadyism.

An introduction of that sort, Freedericksz added, would not serve to establish social relations. As to that, he was greatly mistaken; next day the Prince called on Freedericksz, had himself announced as 'a friend of the Count's', and succeeded in getting more than half an hour's conversation with him.

From then on. Countess Freedericksz received flowers and boxes of sweets at regular intervals from the Prince.

There were a few more 'memoranda'; but they were addressed direct to the Count. He passed them on to me; they had nothing to do with the Minister of the Court. I let them accumulate in my files.

One day Andronnikov came to see me.

'I am going to be the editor of a newspaper; its policy will be to foster the loyalty of the Russian masses to Their Majesties and their children. The Empress's order is that the paper shall be exempt from the Court censorship.'

'Only -the Emperor himself can give that order,' I replied. 'What is more, orders of this sort can only be transmitted to me verbally by one of the Generals A.D.G. to His Majesty. If I remember rightly, you are only A.D.C. to the Almighty; you will understand, then, that it is impossible for me to comply with this order.'

I never saw Prince Andronnikov again.

I tried with the help of friends to find out what lay behind this little incident.

I never succeeded in getting any precise information; it can only be supposed that the Prince was not telling the truth when he said that he was bringing an order from Her Majesty herself.

I think I have said enough to indicate the character of this gentleman. Rasputin was constantly to be seen at the Prince's flat, and frequently made use of it for appointments which he could not arrange at his own home.

RASPUTIN AS MAKER OF MINISTERS

I come now to the most significant incident in my relations with Rasputin. It shows the extent to which Ministerial portfolios depended on the favour of this degraded man.

Trepov had just been appointed Prime Minister. The appointment had been expected. When attending Cabinet meetings as deputy for Freedericksz, I had had frequent occasion to note that the policy suggested by my brother-in-law was almost always adopted by the other Ministers; his authority was steadily growing.

I went to see Trepov the day before he left for G.H.Q., where he was to present a report to the Tsar.

He confided to me that his report would be of capital importance, since it proposed four dismissals of Ministers. If the Tsar would agree to these four dismissals, it would be possible to constitute a Ministry; if not, Trepov would be compelled to resign. He asked me how his appointment had been received at Court. I told him all that I knew, and added that he would have to take account of Rasputin. With that he agreed.

'Do not forget that I shall never be able to have any sort of personal or friendly relations with him, whatever happens.'

After his return from the *Stavka* (G.H.Q.), he told me that things had gone 'fairly well'; he had three dismissals in his portfolio; the fourth had been signed by the Tsar, but had ultimately been deferred; this was the decree relating to Protopopov.[1] At the last moment the Tsar had said:

'Leave me this report; I will send it back to you to-night or to-morrow morning.'

1 Protopopov, a member of the Duma, was Minister of the Interior. He owed his appointment to the influence of Rasputin. He was implicated in a mysterious attempt at a separate peace with Germany. Protopopov suffered from a grave nervous malady.

If he had his way with these four Ministries, Trepov hoped that he would be able to form a Cabinet 'of public confidence', as the phrase went at the time. It would not be a Parliamentary Cabinet in the full sense of the word, but it would include several members of the Duma. This was a supreme concession in face of the rising tempest of public opinion. But the presence of Protopopov in the Cabinet would make the attempt hopeless; no leading member of the Duma would be able to co-operate with Rasputin's man.

'Can you go at once,' Trepov asked me, 'to see Rasputin?'

'Yes, but it disgusts me.'

'So it does me. And it may be very serious for me.

'But I am ready to take the risk. I must get Protopopov's resignation.'

'What shall I suggest to the man?'

'Offer him a house in Petrograd, with all his household and living expenses paid; bodyguards, which are indispensable for him; and 200,000 roubles (£20,000) down as soon as Protopopov has been dismissed. In consideration of this, I want him to refrain from meddling further in appointments of Ministers and high Government officials. As for the clergy, I leave him a free hand if he wants it. No personal interviews with me; if he wants to say anything to me he must do it through you. You know the man. Try to make him listen to reason.'

'You know that if he does not accept he will telegraph at once to the Tsar and tell him that you have been trying to bribe him? It may all come to grief.'

'If it must it must. I will risk it. In any case I am quite prepared to go. The Tsar will say nothing to me about Rasputin, but he will find a pretext that will do to get rid of me. I am putting all my stakes on this one card. So long as Protopopov is Minister of the Interior it will be impossible for me to carry on the Government.'

'And what about me?' I asked Trepov. 'What sort of a situation shall I be in if Grishka refuses? And we are almost certain to get a categorical refusal.'

'Do the best you can for yourself In any event your appointment to Roumania is practically a certainty. You will be better off there than here. Go along and come back as soon as you can.'

I took a car to the Gorokhovaya, the street in which Rasputin was living. On the way I said to myself again and again that I had made a great mistake in having anything to do with a question in which Rasputin was involved.

'Gregory Efimovitch,' I began, 'you know my friend and brother-in-law Trepov has just been made Prime Minister. I should be so glad if I could see you two on the best of terms. There is no reason why you should not be. He has nothing against you. But he does ask you not to put a spoke in his wheels; he is in a very delicate position. In return he will do nothing to interfere with you.'

'That's all right; by all means let him go ahead on these lines. But on one more condition,' Rasputin added, 'he must let my friends alone.'

'That is what I am telling you. You can have what you want for living expenses for yourself and those who depend on you. You will have a bodyguard; you cannot do without one. Take what you like and do what you like, but don't interfere in appointments of Ministers and heads of departments. You will have a free hand with ecclesiastical appointments; any one you recommend will be specially looked after.'

I did not get to the end of my offer. His eyes flamed: they showed almost nothing but the white, the iris disappearing and the pupil closing to a pin-point.

'If that's it,' he shouted, 'I'll pack my bags and go; I see I'm no longer wanted here.' I was not prepared for so violent a counter-move, and was greatly taken aback.

'Keep calm, Gregory Efimovitch. I am talking to you as a friend. Come now, keep calm; do you suppose you can govern all Russia unaided? If Trepov goes there will be someone else in his place, and who can say what he will have to offer? Perhaps nothing at all.'

His eyes flamed yet more angrily.

'You're a simple chap, you are! Do you think Papa and Mamma will let you do what you like? I don't need money: the poorest of shopkeepers will keep me supplied with enough to give to the needy. Bodyguards? You pack of fools, none of your bodyguards for me and be damned to you!'

He stopped short, as if he had just realized something startling.

'Ah! It's Protopopov he wants to get rid of.' (He gave Protopopov some nickname, as he always did, but I no longer remember it.)

I was cool again now. I had picked up my hat to go, but threw it down on a chair and said to Rasputin:

'Don't be an ass! Come along and give me a glass of Madeira — let's talk as friends, as we are.'

For almost a minute we did not speak another word. Then he smiled. The Staretz had nearly forgotten his anger.

'Come along, Sasha' (a diminutive of Alexander).

We had two or three glasses each, in unbroken silence. Then I felt that we could go on with our discussion.

'Listen, Gregory Efimovitch. After all, you don't really want Trepov to come to consult you about the Ministers to be chosen? Get it into your head that that is out of the question. Are you set on Protopopov remaining in the Ministry? He can have Shakhovskoy's portfolio (Ministry of Commerce); Shakhovskoy is a good friend of yours, and he can take over Protopopov's office. Why are you singing out like that before you know what it's all about?'

'Why does he want to dismiss him? He will never get another man so devoted to Papa.'

'Devotion is not everything! It is necessary also to be able to conduct business — '

'Business, business — there is only one business, to love Papa sincerely. Vitia was cleverer than any of the others, but he did not love Papa. He was an impossible Minister.'

We talked on for more than an hour. Our two bottles had not had the effect on him that I had been hoping for: he was still master of himself. At last I got from him a promise that he would send 'Papa' a telegram asking him to dismiss Protopopov.

He refused to draft it while I was there.

'He'll telegraph not to dismiss him,' I said to myself. But I pretended to believe him — and I realized at once that he knew I was insincere.

Rasputin had a supreme gift of reading the thoughts of his interlocutor. I have known many people to have the gift, but none in so astonishing a degree.

As I left he said:

'Let us remain friends. I will not attack your Trepov, if he will leave my friends alone. If he doesn't, I shall go back at once to Pokrovskoye' (Rasputin's native village in Siberia). 'Mamma will beg me to come back, and Trepov will have to go. One more glass. In spite of everything, I like you.'

After this fiasco I went back to Trepov. He realized that he was done for.

142

Everything happened as I had expected. The Emperor kept back the decree which he had signed and Protopopov remained at his post. Trepov had to make way for Prince N. D. Golitzin.

It was the beginning of the end.

THE 'PROTÉGÉ'

The Empress had held on to Protopopov because he was Rasputin's protege. I realized it at the time of my last talk but one with Her Majesty.

I had been appointed Minister Plenipotentiary in Roumania. One day when I had returned from Jassy I learned from one of the ladies of the Rasputin coterie that the Empress insisted that I should make the acquaintance of Protopopov before the audience which she was going to grant me.

I telephoned to the Minister to ask for an appointment, and he rephed:

'Come along at once.'

Protopopov kept me more than three hours. He wanted to explain his 'programme' to me; but he did so in an extraordinary manner, jumping from one project to another, and making me read whole pages of various files of papers that he put in front of me. I could see plainly that I had to deal with a lunatic.

Next day I was received by the Empress. She told me at once how glad she was to learn that I had met Protopopov.

'What do you think of him?'

I replied, in Russian:

'Sumburnyi tchelovek' ('A muddle-headed person'). I added, in German: 'I cannot find a word to express it in German.'

I made a few attempts to explain the sense of my Russian phrase.

'That is perfectly true,' she said; 'he does not always, perhaps, pursue his idea to the end. But his ideas are good. And, besides, he is so devoted to us! He is unable to discipline his ideas. He is not always able to carry them out, for they pursue one another in his brain. He ought to have a deputy who would be responsible for sifting out what is reasonable in his plans; in a word, a deputy who is not so erratic, and who has the energy to carry Protopopov's schemes to a successful conclusion when he has launched them.'

'I listened attentively to him yesterday for three hours, but I did not notice a single practical suggestion.'

'Quite so,' the Empress replied, 'he is extremely nervous and easily loses his thread.'

The Empress was silent for a moment; then, without any transition, she said:

'Would you not act as his deputy? If that post is not of sufficient standing for you, you could be given the right of reporting personally to His Majesty!'

I replied, in entire sincerity:

'Madame, I would accept the most insignificant of posts if I felt that I could be useful to my country in doing so. I am obliged to say that I cannot possibly work with a man whose ideas have no coherence. Apart from that, there seem to be very grave objections to the idea of letting two persons report for the same Ministry.'

'Very well — whom would you suggest as deputy for Protopopov?'

'It must be somebody well acquainted with affairs of state.'

'Yes, that is why I suggested you for the post; have you not been all these years in charge of the Court Chancellery?'

'But that,' I objected, 'has nothing to do with the Ministry of the Interior. I have not the slightest knowledge of police administration.'

We went on to other questions that I had to put before Her Majesty, On taking leave of her I said:

'Will you excuse me, Madame, if I was rather uncompromising in regard to Protopopov?'

She smiled a little dolefully:

'Not at all. I was very glad that you spoke straight out. We so rarely hear the truth from anybody! As to Protopopov, I do not feel that a man of devoted loyalty ought to be judged harshly; it would have been better to help him.'

There the audience ended; it was the last but one that I had.

I may add that Rasputin took no revenge for my intervention against Protopopov; he made no further effort to injure me with the Empress. In view of the Rodzianko incident I had had every reason to fear the worst.

This made Rasputin a more enigmatic figure to me than ever.

RASPUTIN AND THE DUMA

To end this melancholy section of my story, it remains for me to describe how Rasputin helped to make final the breach which had come between the Tsar and the body that represented the nation — the Duma. It was, of course, this breach that brought the downfall of the dynasty.

The last Duma was not of the revolutionary character of the first two. Many of its members were animated by the purest patriotism; they were genuine monarchists, and were concerned before all else to preserve Russia from revolutionary convulsions.

At this period we had Count Kokovtzov as Prime Minister; the Count considered that the country's future depended on close and whole-hearted collaboration between the Duma and the Tsar's Ministers. In accordance with this conviction he had made a change in the Cabinet over which he presided. Three of the appointments brought new men into crucial posts, men who could not be out of sympathy with the members of the Duma.

The first months of Kokovtzov's premiership, his Parliamentary honeymoon, gave reason for hope that he would succeed in his plan for rallying the Duma to the Tsar's side. The Count sincerely believed that he would be able to dispel the animosity that the Sovereigns had felt towards the first two Dumas.

But his illusions were soon dissipated.

The Press began to be full of references to Rasputin as a sinister adventurer and an indescribable curse to the country. It was continually being said that Rasputin controlled all the important appointments in the Orthodox Church; it was whispered that he had the ear of the Empress.

It is by no means easy to explain the view that Their Majesties took of the problem of the Press. They recognized freedom of speech, but not of publication. The newspapers were no more than 'tolerated' in their view, and it was never possible to get the Empress to understand that a misstatement published by the Press could not be visited there and then with penalties inflicted by administrative action — that is to say, not by the courts but by the police.

The Tsar would not understand that his will might be insufficient to prevent the appearance of 'lying' articles; and it seemed to him absurd that his Ministers should be obliged to apply to the courts for remedy, especially when it was a question of his wife's honour — as, indeed, it often was.

The censorship of all articles relating to the Court was my responsibility. What could I do? I rigorously suppressed all issues of newspapers in which Rasputin's name appeared in connexion with that of anybody belonging to the Imperial family. But articles in which no member of the Imperial family was mentioned by name were, under the very precise text of the law, not liable to be submitted at all to the censorship of the Court. That made me completely helpless.

The Empress incessantly complained that the competent authorities were neglecting to carry out His Majesty's strict orders.

News sometimes of a tendencious nature and often exaggerated by the Press circulated in Parliamentary quarters. The lobbies were full of talk that was an outrage on the Imperial family; some of it was reflected in statements made in the full publicity of the Parliamentary debates.

The Tsar sent for the Minister of the Interior, and told him that he required that discussions affecting the Empress's honour should cease both in the lobbies and in debate. Makarov could only reply that he was entirely unable to guarantee that His Majesty's order could be carried out.

The Tsar then turned to the Prime Minister, who brought all his legal knowledge to the demonstration that the law gave the Government no means of control of the Duma and its members in this particular field.

The Tsar and the Empress took great offence at this. From then on, all the declarations from Count Kokovtzov of success in maintaining cordial relations between Parliament and the Government were received merely with smiles of angry scepticism.

To the Tsar the Duma had become a rebel organization.

*Alexander III, Marie and their children, with Nicholas II,
then Tsarevich, at back, 1888*

Nicholas II and Alexandra at the time of their engagement, 1894

Nicholas II, Alexandra and their children, 1904

Nicholas II and Edward VII, 1908

Nicholas II and Count Vladimir Freedericksz

Nicholas II and his troops at the time of the Russo-Japanese War, 1905

Nicholas II and William II, 1905

PART II

CHAPTER IV

THE COURT OF NICHOLAS II

I. THE COURTIERS

'THE OFFICES'

The principal function of a sovereign's Court is to heighten his prestige. The Court is also responsible for looking after the details of the monarch's everyday life.

The Russian Court was certainly the most opulent in Europe. Great wealth had been accumulating during three hundred years in the hands of those responsible for its safe keeping. In its splendour the Russian Court came nearest to those of Louis XIV and Louis XV. In its etiquette it resembled the Court of Austria.

The credits required to meet the needs of the Court came from three main sources (apart from the personal fortunes of the Grand Dukes, which were by no means negligible):

(1) The general budget of the country, which supplied the 'civil list'; that is to say, the credits necessary for the maintenance of the Courts of Their Majesties and that of the heir to the throne.

(2) The Apanages, a fund (it would now be called 'Self-governing') created by Emperor Paul I and intended to yield for each of the Grand

Dukes and Grand Duchesses, from the day of their birth, an annual income of 280,000 roubles (about £28,000 gold). The purpose of the Apanages was to relieve the general budget of the burden of the expenditure necessary for the maintenance of the Imperial family. Their prime source of revenue was a gift of real estate made by Emperor Paul; this estate had been managed with great prudence by its successive administrators, and a little before the Revolution it constituted the greatest domain in all Russia, covering many millions of acres, and had a liquid reserve of some 60,000,000 roubles.

(3) His Majesty's private fortune, the properties belonging personally to the Tsar. It included the mining districts of Nertchinsk and Altai, rich in gold and precious stones.

Under Count Freedericksz as its head, the Russian Court consisted of persons holding 'offices'.

These 'offices' were purely titular, and were divided into two classes. The first included (in 1908) fifteen officials, with the titles of Grand Chamberlain, Grand Marshal, Master of the Imperial Hunt, and Grand Cup-bearer. In the second class came 134 offices entailing actual services and 86 'honorary' offices: the two Grand Masters of Ceremonies, the Grand Esquire Trenchant, the Huntsmen, the Marshals, the Director of the Imperial Theatres, the Director of the Hermitage Museum, and the Masters of Ceremonies (14 active and 14 honorary). This list should be completed by 287 Chamberlains, 309 Gentlemen in Waiting, no persons 'attached' to Their Majesties and to the members of the Imperial family; 22 ecclesiastics, 38 medical officers, 3 harbingers, 18 valets de chambre to Their Majesties, and 150 officers in the suite (Generals A.D.C., Generals in the suite, and aides-de-camp). The grand total, with the 240 ladies of various ranks and the 66 ladies of the Order of St. Catherine, came to the imposing figure of 1,543 persons.

The titles borne by the ladies of the Court were as follows: the Empress's Mistress of the Robes, the Mistresses of the Imperial Court and of the Grand Ducal Courts; the *Dames à portrait*[1]; the maids of honour 'of the chamber', 'of the suite', and 'of the city'. Ranked with them were the Dames of the Order of the Cross (grand and lesser) of St. Catherine, and the maids of honour who had been presented to

1 See p.166.

Their Majesties on marriage. None of the members of the Court personnel could marry without having obtained the permission of the Tsar himself.

Each office carried a uniform, with appropriate changes for various circumstances, full dress, gala dress, ordinary dress, and travelling dress. The gold embroidery grew, of course, with the person's rank. When one had become Grand Chamberlain one no longer had a strip of clothing without its covering of garlands of gold!

We may note that the appellations conferred on the high dignitaries retained a certain practical significance: when the Tsar was seated on his throne at the Coronation banquet, the dishes presented to him were escorted by the Grand Esquire Trenchant, at whose side two officers of the *Chevaliers Gardes*[1] marched with naked swords. The Grand Cup-bearer passed the golden goblet to the Tsar at this banquet and announced in a loud voice that 'His Majesty deigns to drink'. The Master of the Hunt was present at the Imperial hunting expeditions. The Equerry assisted the Tsar and the Empress when they were entering the stage coach; the Master of the Horse escorted the coach on horseback.

THE GRAND MASTER OF CEREMONIES

Everything concerned with etiquette and ceremonial came under the Grand Master of Ceremonies and the Empress's Mistress of the Robes.

The post of Grand Master of Ceremonies was held by Count B. A. Hendrikov; the second Grand Master was Baron Korff.

The Count, a man of fine presence and of extreme elegance, had a very strong sense of the importance of his duties; this, of course,

1 There were two regiments of cavalry charged with the protection of the Tsar's person, the Horse Guards and the Chevaliers Gardes, Both regiments had the same privileges, and they disputed the honour of military precedence. In point of fact, it was the Chevaliers Gardes who formed the last barrier around the person of the Sovereign; hence the particular distinction which attached to being a courtier with the privilege of 'going past the *Chevaliers Gardes*'.

2 See p.115.

facilitated matters, for a Master of Ceremonies cannot carry out his duties effectively unless he takes them seriously.

This Hendrikov certainly did. At the time of the reception that he had to organize for the members of the first Duma,[2] he considered it necessary to set up a regular committee, composed of the best specialists on his staff, together with persons in a position to give him information concerning the future deputies, and a certain number of 'experts', that is to say, officials who had had experience of similar processions in other countries.

Count Hendrikov went at the head of this committee from one room to another of the Palace; he personally marked out in chalk the positions to be reserved for the dignitaries and the representatives of the people. There were long discussions to settle whether this or the other body of State officials or group of senators should be placed on left or right, in front, or behind. Count Hendrikov grew thoroughly agitated at the idea that the deputies, unaccustomed as they were to Court ceremonial, might get out of alignment during the ceremony.

I had good reason to remember the anxieties of Count Hendrikov at the time of the arrival of the Landgrave of Hesse, a relative of the Empress. The Minister of the Court had transmitted to the Tsar a list of dignitaries from which to choose one to be attached to the person of the Landgrave. His Majesty selected Prince Ourussov for the honour.

The Landgrave was to arrive next morning at eleven o'clock. At ii p.m. I was rung up by Count Hendrikov; he was completely panic-stricken.

'There has been a catastrophe!'

'I'll bet it's the Winter Palace on fire.'

'No,really. Jules Ourussov has fallen ill; he can't go to welcome the Landgrave. Whatever can I do?'

'Select somebody else,' I answered, trying hard not to laugh.

'I can't. You told me yourself that Ourussov had been appointed by His Majesty's ukase.[1] Telephone to Freedericksz and ask him to get another ukase.'

'Right you are,' I said, and hung up the 'phone.

Five minutes later I 'phoned him to let him know that the Minister of the Court took the whole responsibility; another officer could be

1 Order given by the Tsar, which could only be modified by a further similar document.

designated by an order from the Master of Ceremonies. 'You see, we can't disturb His Majesty at this late hour.'

Needless to say I had not spoken a word to the Minister of the Court.

But Hendrikov kept me a full hour longer, suggesting every conceivable candidate. At last we agreed on an appointment. It was to be Gourko.

An hour later the 'phone rang again.

'Gourko is impossible! His full-dress uniform is at the dyer's, being cleaned, and it seems that it's all bright, as it must be for such an important meeting, down one side, but not down the other. My God, whatever can I do? It's sending me off my head.'

It was already 1 a.m., and the situation was getting a little complicated.

'See if you can telephone to the "Aquarium" ' (a *café-concert* then in the height of fashion). 'You'll be sure to find Prince Mestchersky there.'

At 3 a.m. Hendrikov considered it worth while to ring me up once more to say:

'It's all right — Prince Mestchersky's going.'

Next morning I told Count Freedericksz of the tribulations of Count Hendrikov, and we had a hearty laugh over them.

I ought to mention, in this connexion, that Nicholas II, like his father Alexander III, was completely indifferent to all questions of ceremonial.

I can imagine the anguish of the Masters of Ceremonies during the reign of Alexander II, who was rigorous in exacting every punctilio of the rules of behaviour at Court.

Hendrikov was never able to understand how anybody could, as so many did, agitate persistently for a Court appointment, and then, having got it, show complete indifference to a courtier's duties. There were frequent masses, for instance, for the souls of dead Grand Dukes, and the attendance of the Tsar's suite at these services was never anything like complete.

Hendrikov discovered in the archives of the Court a ukase of Catherine II. That Empress had had a sense of humour. She had 'presumed' that all the absent courtiers must be ill; 'they are therefore,' she commanded, 'to be required each to pay severally the sum of 25 roubles, in order that the said sum may be paid to a priest who shall be charged with the saying of a mass for the recovery of the health of the absent courtier.'

THE EMPRESS'S MISTRESS OF THE ROBES

The duty of preserving the traditions of Court life among the ladies admitted to the Court fell on the Mistress of the Robes, Princess Galitzin, *née* Pashkova.

I do not think it would have been possible to discover a lady better fitted than was Princess Galitzin to live up to the full importance attached to the high office of Mistress of the Robes. Of perfect breeding, very sure of all her movements, she had the authority needed for fending off anything that was not strictly in accordance with etiquette. She regularly dressed in 'the fashion of the year before last', and, according to a quip which went the rounds of the Court, her hats were apparently 'built at the Imperial coach-works'.

She had tactics all her own for the maintenance of discipline. If she had noticed anything that called for comment she never spoke about it to the young girls who had recently come to Court; she only attacked the ladies of maturer age, of whom the maids of honour stood in desperate fear.

On Their Majesties' way to Kiev there was a boat journey down the Dnieper. Sitting opposite the Empress was Her Most Serene Highness Princess Lopukhina-Demidova; and the princess had had the coolness to light a cigarette. The Mistress of the Robes sailed up to her, seized her cigarette, and threw it overboard, saying aloud for all to hear:

'My dear, you are forgetting that there is no smoking in Her Majesty's presence.'

The princess was furious, full of injured dignity, but said not a word. Later the Mistress of the Robes explained to her:

'You know I smoke myself like a corporal. What I said to you will be a lesson to the young ones. I don't want to have to pull them up.'

There was a similar scene later, after my appointment as Head of the Court Chancellery. I was talking to Princess Galitzin, and suddenly saw Countess Vorontzova coming up to us. The Countess hated Count Freedericksz and all his staff. I bowed low to this influential lady. She did not deign to make the sHghtest sign of recognition.

The Mistress of the Robes turned at once to her:

'This is Mossolov, the new Head of the Chancellery.'

'I have known him a long time.'

'Then why on earth did you cut him? You can behave as you like at home, but at Court you must have manners.'

I got away as quickly as I could, and I cannot say how that conversation continued.

II. THE GRAND CEREMONIES

A. Their Majesties' 'Processions'

Their Majesties' 'processions' took place on the most important anniversaries.

The processions were divided into grand and minor. All the Court staff had to attend a grand procession. A special invitation was required for participation in a minor one.

The processions were so called because Their Majesties left their private apartments and went in great pomp to church. After divine service Their Majesties returned to their private apartments amid the same ceremonies.

Half an hour before the procession, the members of the Imperial family assembled in the Malachite Room, where no one was admitted but the relatives of the Tsar. Court 'Arabs', in resplendent uniforms, guarded the entrance to this room. The courtiers gathered in other rooms of the palace, where they got ready for the procession. They were controlled by the Ceremonies Service; this might be described as the most important manifestation of its existence.

As soon as the procession had been duly formed, the Minister of the Court went into the Malachite Room and reported to His Majesty. At once the Grand Dukes, who knew exactly their degrees of proximity to the Throne, ranged themselves behind Their Majesties; the Grand Duchesses took their places in the procession according to the rank of their fathers or husbands.

The first couple in the procession was made up by the Tsar and the Dowager Empress, Alexandra Feodorovna was one of the second couple. The Minister of the Court kept on the right of the Tsar, a few steps behind the Sovereign. He was followed by the officers 'on duty' — a General A.D.C., a General in the suite, and an A.D.C. These officers were the only persons who did not go two by two.

The Sovereign regularly wore the uniform of the regiment which was celebrating its anniversary that day or which had been chosen to provide the sentinels within the Palace. Very often the Tsar changed this uniform for that of the Preobrajensky Regiment or of the Hussars, with whom he had gone through his military apprenticeship.

The officers in waiting had to be present at the processions dressed in the uniform of the Tsar's suite, and not in their regimental uniforms. The ladies of the Court were only admitted in 'Russian' dress with trains.

A 'Russian' dress is described in detail in the *Court Calendar*. It had to be of white silk, reaching only to the shoulders, weighed down with a long train of red velvet embroidered in gold (the colours were different for the Grand Ducal Courts). Each lady wore on her head a *kokoshnik*, a sort of diadem, borrowed from the usage of the Muscovite Courts; this also was of red velvet, embroidered in gold.

The ladies 'with access to the Court' might have dresses in other colours, as they liked.

The *kokoshnik* and the dress could, of course, be ornamented with jewels according to the fortune of the wearer. In this respect some families established records which it would not be easy to beat. I remember seeing Madame Zinoviev, wife of the Marshal of the Nobility of St. Petersburg, wearing nine or ten emeralds as buttons, each bigger than a pigeon's egg. The most remarkable diamonds ornamented the dresses of Countess Shouvalova, Countess Vorontzova Dashkova, Countess Sheremetyevskaya, Princess Kotchubey, and Princess Youssupova, among others.

As they came from the Malachite Room into the Concert Room, Their Majesties stopped and replied to the reverences from persons grouped in this second room, that is to say, the courtiers who had the right to 'go past the *Chevaliers Gardes*'. That expression was derived from a picket of *Chevaliers Gardes* placed at the entrance to title Concert Room. It was a special privilege to be entitled to pass this picket of honour. Hence came the two categories of people: those who went past the *Chevaliers Gardes*, and those who did not go past them.

After the Tsar's entry into the Concert Room, the procession began to form. The principal dignitaries of the Court remained facing Their Majesties until the Masters of Ceremonies indicated to them that they had to lead the procession, in the order of their 'proximity' to the Tsar.

The Sovereigns followed immediately after the principal dignitaries of the Court. They were followed by the members of the Imperial family. Then came the ladies of the Court, the other high dignitaries, the "Ministers," the Senators, and the military suite.

They went into the Nicholas Room, where the officers of the guard stood in picturesque groups. Finally the procession went through the other rooms passing in front of the *dii minores* — 'merchants with great names', and even 'newspaper correspondents' (who in most cases were admitted to galleries above these rooms).

The Sovereigns went into the church followed by the Grand Dukes, the high dignitaries, and the Mistresses of the Robes to the Courts. The rest of the procession remained in order in the adjoining rooms. This was the most delicate moment for the Masters of Ceremonies, for they were supposed to repress every attempt to speak aloud or to smoke.

The greater ones among the *habitués* of the Palace knew where they could find certain back staircases, which made improvised smoking-rooms during divine service; these were frequented especially by Grand Dukes who had quietly slipped out of church. It was, by the way, a well-established tradition that the talk on the staircases should never touch on business or official matters. The Masters of Ceremonies took care not to go near these 'smoking-rooms' or the main conservatory of the Palace, where the old Generals obstinately went to smoke in spite of all orders.

On their way back from church Their Majesties stopped in the Concert Room, and there the newly appointed maids of honour and other ladies entitled to the distinction were presented.

I have a vivid personal memory of the complications entailed for the young officers by service as 'inside' sentinels in the Palace. On great occasions like a procession or a ball, they had to wear full-dress uniform. This uniform comprised in addition to the regulation jacket a 'super- vest' (a glorified waistcoat); Wellingtons; and elk-skin breeches. The 'super-jacket' took the place of the cuirass worn on outdoor duty; for the Horse Guards it was of scarlet with large metallic eagles on front and back. The *Chevaliers Gardes* wore a large star of St. Andrew.

It was essential that the breeches should not have the slightest crease. To attain this result they were damped, smeared with soap, and put on — after taking off the pants, if I may venture to say so. The operation called for the services of a couple of vigorous soldiers, I hope my readers will pardon me for descending to a slightly vulgar detail: there is no other way of giving an exact idea of the function performed

162

by the two soldiers. Have you ever watched a miller trying to get the flour to settle in an insufficiently filled sack? He 'punches' the sack. That is just what the two soldiers had to do. They 'punched' the elk-skin breeches, and in due course the officer settled down into them.

An officer on duty as inside sentinel remained at his post for twenty-four hours on end. He had an arm-chair for his use; if all was quiet around him he had the right to undo the chain of his helmet and to take off one glove.

B. Court Balls

Of still greater importance were the ceremonies on the occasion of Court balls. As a rule the first ball of the season was arranged in the Nicholas Room, which could hold 3,000 guests. There followed a few weeks later the 'Concert' balls and the 'Hermitage' balls, with 700 and 200 guests; they were named from the rooms reserved to dancers, the Concert Room and the Hermitage Room.

Only one ball a year was organized in the Nicholas Room. In order to attend this ball it was necessary—- to belong to one of the first four 'classes' (of the fourteen classes into which the Russian officers and officials were divided); all the foreign diplomats and their families were also invited, the senior officers of the regiments of the guard (with their wives and daughters), certain young officers recognized by their chiefs as dancers, and, finally, persons invited individually by Their Majesties. The sons of personages admitted to the Court balls could not be invited with their fathers; they had to merit the favour through their own position.

The Court staffs could not know the names of all the personages present in the capital. The first thing to be done was therefore to call on the Marshal of the Court and sign a special register. Ladies who had not already been presented to the Empress had to sign the register of the Mistress of the Robes. This lady had the right to refuse admission to the ball in certain cases. The invitations were sent out a fortnight before the ball.

A ball in the Nicholas Room was thus not by any means reserved to the 'high life' of St. Petersburg. A practised eye could distinguish the men or women who did not belong to real 'society': their clothes might, for instance, be too new. Yes! too new. The persons in the authentic high society did not wear the latest Paris models for the

Nicholas Room; the great crush made it impossible adequately to display all the magnificence of the dresses. There was also the way of wearing a uniform or a ball dress, and that indefinable something that gives to the well-born the air of being 'at home everywhere'.

The time for arrival was about 8.30, not later. Everybody knew his proper entrance to the Palace. The Grand Dukes went in by the Saltykov entrance; the members of the Court had 'Their Majesties' ' entrance reserved to them; civil officials came by the 'Jurdan' entrance; officers had the privilege of using the 'Commander's' entrance.

The scene was fairy-like.

January. Intense cold. The whole of the three vast blocks of the Winter Palace inundated with light. Braziers burning around the immense Alexander Column, a granite monolith with an archangel on top of it. Carriages arriving in an unbroken line. Open sledges bringing those officers who did not fear the cold; the horses' harness covered with blue netting, to prevent accumulations of snow from being blown into the passengers' faces.

Motor-cars were regarded then as a capricious and undependable toy.

Feminine silhouettes were to be seen hurrying feverishly across the few steps that separated the arriving carriage from the entrance; some of them radiant and graceful, some bowed down with age. Furs — heavens! they were Russian furs, and that's that: sable, silver fox, arctic fox. No shawls over the heads, because of the diadems of the married ladies and the flowers worn by the girls. Police officers watched over the movement of the carriages and told the coachmen where to park.

None of the ladies had the right to bring their own footmen into the Palace, to look after their things, as was done even at the Grand Dukes'. Cloaks had to be given to the Court men-servants. Each cloak or wrap (they could not be worn in Their Majesties' presence) had to have the owner's visiting card sewn inside. The attendant (in white stockings, patent leather pumps, and a uniform bedizened with Imperial eagles in *passementerie*) indicated in a low voice the room in which it would be found after the ball. The men were well schooled in their duties! As they moved over the parquet floor their steps were inaudible.

The guests went up the grand staircases of white marble, on the soft and velvety carpets. White and scarlet uniforms; spreadeagle helmets in gold and silver; countless epaulettes; the marvellous national costumes of the Hungarian guests; the gold-embroidered *kuntusk*[1] of Marquis Veliepolski, Marquis of Gonzago-Myszkowsky; the *beshmets*[1] of the Caucasian nobles, shod in *tchuviaks* (a sort of moccasin, with supple soles, so that in dancing these mountain warriors made not the slightest sound); white dolmans bordered with precious beaver fur; finally, the Court uniforms, heavy with gold embroidery and completed by short breeches and white silk stockings —

Yes! A perfect courtier had to have legs that were neither too fat nor too bony; he had to look well in short breeches. Shall I tell? Sometimes a 'calf' would have strange fancies of its own, and one might see the courtier bend down to seize it and restore it to the normal position from which it never should have wandered — an operation performed not without embarrassment.

It may have been on account of incidents of this sort that Prince Repnin, Grand Master of the Court, a very old man and particularly troubled with gout, asked permission to attend Court balls in white trousers, though they were not authorized by the regulations. Could the Tsar be troubled with such a detail? Could permission be given without the Monarch's approval? Freedericksz was very perplexed. Finally he mentioned the matter to the Tsar apart from his weekly 'report', unofficially, as it were.

'Oh, certainly! Answer just as you think best.'

Then, on second thought:

'No, perhaps better not. These old people would be hurt to feel that the Sovereign had not himself gone into their request. You had better report to me that So-and-so still goes about but is troubled with arthritis. I should be very interested to hear that, say, the venerable Marshal of the Nobility of Kiev, in spite of his advanced age, wants to come to a Court ball. A report on those lines, in any case, will not take up much time.'

The flood of guests would grow visibly. Everybody in the elegant society of the capital would be going up those wide marble staircases.

All the ladies wore 'Court' dresses, cut very low, with the shoulders bare, and with a long train. At that time ladies were more delicate about questions of 'modesty' than nowadays, and one had to attend a Palace ball in order to admire the full effect of their necks and

1 Polish and Caucasian national dress.

shoulders. At that time, too, there were none with the ambition to display backs bronzed by the sun; skins that should be white were white as Carrara marble.

On the left of the bodice the guests wore, according to their rank, a 'monogram' (the Imperial monogram ornamented with diamonds, distinctive mark of the maids of honour) or a 'portrait' framed in diamonds (a high distinction granted to ladies of special merit: they were given the title of Dames of the Portrait).

Here was a General 'in the suite', with his wife; she was already in the forties, but still slim, and her spangled dress displayed her figure wonderfully. Her light, almost chestnut hair was decorated with a diadem set with two rows of diamonds. A *ferronnière* with a single diamond of two square centimetres crossed her forehead. A diamond necklace; the neck of her dress bordered with diamonds, with a flower at the back entirely of diamonds set flat; two diamond chains leading, like enormous threads of fire, first to the front of the bodice and then to the buckle at the waist; rings and bracelets covered with diamonds. Nowadays when I see, in some sensational film, the 'ostentation' of the Russian Court as reproduced in the studios of Hollywood, I could weep — or laugh aloud — in irritation.

The long procession moved on between two lines of Cossacks of the Guard, in scarlet uniforms, and Court 'Arabs', gigantic turbaned negroes. They were 'Arabs' only by tradition; actually they were Christian Abyssinians.

The Masters of Ceremonies, grave and gracious, moved about quietly everywhere, to assist the flow of the arrivals. As they were on duty, each of them had his baton, a sort of long ebony wand surmounted by an ivory ball and a two-headed eagle, with a bow of bright blue ribbon (the St. Andrew's knot).

I will devote a page to the officers invited to the Court balls. I had the honour to be present at balls in three successive reigns, so that I am not writing without knowledge.

Officers rarely received a personal invitation. The regiment was simply informed that so many officers were to attend such and such a ball. For the Horse Guards in my time the number was fifteen. The Officer Commanding the regiment named those who were to take on the duty. The winners in this lottery had to present themselves to the senior Colonel on the eve of the ball, and he gave his orders:

'It is not an amusement. . . . You must not think about having a good time. . . .You are detached on duty, and you will be busily occupied with your duties. . . . You have got to dance with the ladies and do your best to keep them amused. ... You are strictly forbidden to keep in a compact group. . . . Scatter . . . scatter. . . . Do you understand?'

At that time our O.C.'s aunt was Mistress of the Robes. Throughout the evening she devoted herself entirely to watching over the newly arrived officers. If one was 'approved', one received a personal invitation to the Concert or Hermitage ball. If one was 'highly approved', one received the supreme honour of invitation to the private balls organized by the Mistress of the Robes in her own house. There one was royally bored.

Personally I had the good fortune to please her. I was at once enrolled on the list of officers for duty on ceremonial occasions, and thereafter personal invitations were sent to the writer of these lines as his due.

Not everybody had the same good luck. One of my friends, a very young lieutenant, got into serious trouble over Princess Dolgorukaya, who later became the morganatic wife of Alexander II.[1] The princess was divinely beautiful, and before my unfortunate friend had realized it he had spent the whole evening at the side of the belle of the ball.

This is how he was told of his offence:

'You were presented to Princess Dolgorukaya. . . . You were at liberty to invite her, and it was your duty to invite her, to a waltz. . . . Instead of that you stuck to her right through the evening. ... It is incredible! . . . Don't you know her position at Court? . . . Your conduct has given offence, it has dishonoured the regiment. . . . You may go, but remember what you have been told.'

It will be understood with what a sinking heart I went to my first ball.

But let us get back to the 'Nicholas' ball.

The great moment was approaching. Their Majesties were coming, in full procession of state, from the Malachite Room.

The orchestra plunged into a polonaise. The Masters of Ceremonies gave three taps with their wands; the 'Arabs' opened the doors of the room. Everybody turned toward the procession.

At that time Empress Alexandra Feodorovna was about thirty years old. She was in the full glory of her blonde beauty: tall, and imposing

1 See pp.61-2.

in the deliberation and unconcern of her movements. She was particularly fond of fine pearls; one of her necklaces went down to her knees.

Her sister Grand Duchess Elizabeth was still better-looking, and more slender, although eight years older. She decorated her golden hair with a diadem in the centre of which was a tallow-drop emerald nearly an inch and a quarter in diameter.

Each of the other Grand Duchesses wore family jewellery, with rubies or sapphires. The precious stones were chosen, of course, to go with the colour of the dress; pearls and diamonds or rubies and diamonds with pink material; sapphires and diamonds or pearls with blue.

The Court 'polonaise' was a regular affair of state. The Tsar began by giving his arm to the wife of the doyen of the diplomatic corps. The Grand Dukes similarly invited the wives of the other members of the diplomatic corps, while the Ambassadors went with Ae Grand Duchesses; The Grand Marshal, surrounded by Masters of Ceremonies, all armed with their wands, preceded the Tsar, with an air of clearing a way for him through the crowd of guests. After once going round the room there was a change of lady partners, with strict observance of their 'seniority'. The number of turns round the hall depended on the number of ladies whom His Majesty considered it necessary to take as partner in this way. None of the guests, save those whom I have just enumerated, were entitled to the high honour of taking part in this dance.

Immediately after the polonaise a waltz was started. It was not danced in the modern fashion; that was called a two-step. One of the best dancers in the Guards opened the ball with a young lady designated in advance. The room was immense, but there were a great number of guests, and such was their desire to see Their Majesties that the space free for dancers gradually closed in. During the reign of Alexander II Baron Meyendorf, of the Horse Guards, was responsible for 'directing' the ball; he took me as his assistant. He made a practice of telling me to 'open out' the space reserved for dancers. In order to do this elegantly I took Mile Mary Vasiltchikova, a maid of honour not without *embonpoint*, and she was very helpful in making the spectators retreat. There was also Mile Gourko, a great adept in this particular sport. The wallflowers were pushed back toward the frescoes.

168

I must mention that if a Grand Duchess wanted to dance she sent her 'Court Cavalier' to fetch the dancer whom she had chosen. But the Grand Duchesses rarely joined in the 'light' dances. There was only one exception, the lovely and gracious Hélène Vladimirovna,[1] daughter of Grand Duke Vladimir, a passionate waltzer; officers were permitted to invite her to dance instead of waiting for her to send for some particular one. I am sure they were all desperately in love with this princess.

All the time lackeys went up and down with dishes of sweets, refreshments, and ices. In the adjoining rooms enormous blocks of ice were to be seen, shaped to hold tubs filled with champagne. It would be impossible to give any idea of the magnificence of the array of cakes and petits fours, fruits and other delicacies, which the Court pastrycooks had spread over buffets decorated with palms and flowers.

At a Concert or Hermitage ball certain rooms in the Winter Palace would be left empty. The time would come to offer one's arm to a lady and lead her far from the dancers, through countless suites of rooms. Suddenly one would find oneself far from the musicians, the society chatter, the hothouse temperature. . . . These endless, half-lit rooms seemed more homely and inviting. Here and there were to be seen sentinels and orderly officers. It was possible to stroll about in this way for a good half-hour. Outside, seen through windows as high as those of a cathedral, the Neva scintillated from every floe. One felt an element of mystery in this fairy-tale come true. How many more times, one asked oneself, shall we see it?[2]

During the mazurka the Empress would stand beneath the portrait of Nicholas I and talk with her partner, one of the senior officers of the Guard, not too old; and when it was over the Sovereigns went toward the supper-room. Masters of Ceremonies preceded them in the regular way.

For the supper the Sovereigns' table was placed on a slightly raised platform; the company at this table were ranged along one side only of the table, against the wall. Thus the guests in passing along the room could glance from one to another of the distinguished persons

1 Mother of Marina, Duchess of Kent.

2 The description of the Nicholas ball has been written in part by Princess Lobanova Rostovskaya, to whom the author owes grateful acknowledgment.

at the table. The doyen of the diplomatic corps sat on the right of the Empress, and the Grand Duke Michael, heir presumptive to the throne, on her left. The rest of the Grand Dukes and Grand Duchesses took their seats in order of rank, with the Ambassadors and some of the high dignitaries of the Court, the army, and the civil service next to them. It was necessary, of course, to have the ribbon of St. Andrew in order to be able to lay claim to the honour of a seat at this table.

A number of round tables, decorated[1] with palms and flowers, were placed in the Sovereigns' room. Twelve persons, designated in advance, took their seats at each of these round tables. In the other rooms the guests had to find a place where they could.

The Tsar did not take part in the supper. He went from one to another of the guests, and sat down from time to time to talk to the person whom he wanted so to honour. That, of course, was settled in advance. It was impossible to let the Tsar remain standing by the table, and equally impossible for all the guests at supper to rise and stand at attention throughout the conversation. The procedure was as follows:

A seat remained free at all the tables at which the Tsar intended to 'have a little chat'. A *skorokhod* stood by this seat to show its purpose. (The *skorokhod*, literally 'runner', was a Court domestic who, in the sixteenth century, ran ahead of the sovereign's coach and made way for it in the tortuous streets.) The Tsar sat down in the seat so reserved, making a sign to the guests not to trouble to rise. The members of the suite accompanying the Sovereign retired to a respectful distance, and the conversation began. As soon as it was over the *skorokhod* made a sign to the suite, who returned to the Sovereign's side.

The Tsar had a surprisingly good memory for faces. If he asked the name of the young lady on some officer's right, one might be almost certain that she was a debutante, and that the Masters of Ceremonies would have the utmost difficulty in saying who she was, seeing her themselves for the first time.

Toward the end of the supper the Tsar would go over to the Empress and take her back to the Nicholas Room, where a cotillion would be started at once. The august hosts chose that moment to retire to their inner apartments, unobserved by their guests. At the

---

1 They had a hole in the centre, through which came a palm-tree, the table being placed over the cask containing the palm.

entrance to the Malachite Room Their Majesties would take leave of their suite.

Not until then did the Minister of the Court, the suite, the Masters of Ceremonies, and the Marshal of the Court go up to the next floor, where their supper awaited them.

The great Court ball was over.

C. The Sovereigns' Visits

It is not intended in this work to give a list of the visits made by the Russian sovereigns or to describe in detail everything that went on during the meetings between Their Majesties and their 'cousins' in the various countries of Europe. I shall confine myself here, as everywhere else, to saying something of the 'human' side of those meetings at which I was present.

I shall carefully avoid all reference to any political conversations that may have taken place during the visits; others than I will concern themselves — or have done already — with the exposition of the political ends pursued in these meetings, the results they achieved, or the setbacks they met with.

THE GERMAN EMPEROR

The visits most frequently made were those to William II, and he was Their Majesties' most frequent visitor.

The Kaiser was highly excitable — he gave me the impression of a sufferer from hysteria — and he had a special gift of upsetting everybody who came near him. I remember how once at Wolfsgarten he held Nicholas II 'captive' for over two hours. After the conversation the Tsar showed plain signs of the trial that it had been to him. But every interview that he had with the German Emperor unmistakably got on his nerves.

We were thoroughly used to that. Here is one example out of a hundred. It will be remembered how, after one of these interviews, William II had his signal made from the *Hohenzollern*:

'The Grand Admiral of the Atlantic salutes the Grand Admiral of the Pacific.'

On the express order of Nicholas II, Admiral Nilov signalled this curt reply:

'Pleasant voyage!'

But to the best of my belief nobody has so far revealed the Tsar's muttered comment when the Admiral gave him the decoded German signal. His actual words were:

'He's raving mad!'

As for the Empress, she had an innate aversion to her cousin. She could not even hide her antipathy; every time she was due to lunch or dine in his company she pretended to have a bad head. I believe she only once went on board the Kaiser's yacht. She could scarcely maintain ordinary civility at their personal meetings; she confined herself to the barest compliance with good form.

When William II was joking with the children or took the heir to the throne in his arms, nobody with the slightest acquaintance with Alexandra Feodorovna could fail to see that she was literally undergoing torture.

For members of the suite, interviews with the German Emperor were a thorough martyrdom. All the time one had to be on one's guard; William II was sure to burst out with some astonishing and particularly embarrassing question. When he was in a good humour it was worse still. He permitted himself to play schoolboy tricks with the most aged and venerable of his Generals A.D.C. I myself saw him give friendly smacks to Generals like Schlieffen, on the back — and elsewhere.

One day, at lunch during a hunting expedition, William II had me placed next to him: he explained that he wanted to ask me about the Imperial ballets. But I had only time to reply to one or two questions; William II suddenly took charge and set to work to teach me the whole art of choreography. At the end of the lunch he said solemnly to me that he would have further questions to ask me later on. I am still awaiting them.

Then there was the sermon that he gave us on board the *Hohenzollern*! The Tsar had been invited to lunch; his suite had been convened an hour earlier, and found themselves in front of an altar, with William II as the officiating priest. The Kaiser had thrown over his uniform a Protestant pastor's surplice, and kept us standing for an hour while he expounded to us from every point of view a Biblical text which he had chosen for our edification.

Freedericksz, for all his experience and his even temper, admitted that every interview he had with the German Emperor left him a complete wreck.

The members of the Kaiser's suite seemed to have got used to their master's eccentricities. At Swinemunde, replying to a toast from the Tsar, William II made a fiery speech which the stenographers were able to take down word for word. What was my astonishment when I received from the Germans a text of the speech that differed vastly from the imprudent harangue which their Emperor had delivered. Chancellor von Bulow asked Isvolsky to give Reuter the text which he had prepared, as this was what William II 'was to have said' if he had not allowed himself to be carried away. Isvolsky demurred, but gave way in the end:

'The speech that the German Emperor actually made was finer, but this is more discreet; let us rest content with the official version — for the Press.'

I shall never forget the reception that William II gave to Count Lamsdorff, our Minister of Foreign Affairs, at the time of the Danzig interview. Count Lamsdorff had never left the Pevtchesky Most, our Foreign Ministry. He was a highly cultivated man, ambitious, but very timid, a defect often found in persons who have passed their whole fife in offices shut off from the outer world. To make the best of his short stature the Count wore heels high enough for the most elegant of ladies, and in addition a hat of unwonted elevation. All this was ill-suited to the swell that greeted us in the Danzig roads.

I have no idea of the reason, but the Emperor William took a manifest dislike to our Minister from the moment they met. Did he want to show his contempt for a 'landlubber' who was visibly upset by the pitching of the yacht? In any case, all through the lunch Lamsdorff was chosen as the one and only butt for the stream of sarcasms that the German Emperor was pleased to pour out. Prince von Bülow sat gloomily through it all, uneasily watching this ill-treatment of his colleague, but unable to do anything to restrain his master's tasteless exuberance.

The departure brought fresh torture for the Count. The picket-boat that was to take us ashore was dancing like a cork alongside the accommodation steps. Boarding the boat was, of course, child's play for a seaman used to such exercises, but for Lamsdorff it was a desperate problem. Twice running he missed his chance to jump; at the third lurch of the yacht he was half pushed by the people behind him and half caught in mid-air by the boat's crew. At that moment a roar of laughter was heard from above: it came from William II, who shouted down in a voice half-choked with amusement:

'You haven't found your sea legs yet, Herr Minister!'

A few hours later a decoration was brought to Lamsdorff. It was not the Black Eagle to which he considered himself entitled, but the ribbon of some unknown order that William II had just created. Prince von Bülow had to go himself to console his colleague.

There was no discoverable rhyme or reason about all these idiosyncrasies; the explanation lay simply in the fact that the German Emperor had his own peculiar ways of enjoying himself.

On one occasion I had personally to endure this irritating chaff. William II suddenly took a fancy to calling me 'Molossov'. There was no getting him to pronounce my name correctly, though it offers no special difficulty to a foreigner. Finally he sent me his portrait, with its dedication correctly spelt; but the envelope containing the present bore in large letters in His Majesty's writing the words: 'General Molossov.'

What was the point of this jest?

I think I know the particular moment at which the ruler of Germany forgot my exact name.

It is rather a curious story. The Viborg regiment, of which William II was honorary Colonel, was carrying out landing manoeuvres on the island of Carlos, in the Finnish fjords. The Kaiser expressed the desire to put himself at the head of a detachment and to lead it to the 'attack' on the imaginary enemy. The Tsar felt that this manifestation of the German Emperor's warlike tastes was thoroughly out of place, but he had to give way before his 'cousin's' persistence.

Thus we were presented with the strange spectacle of Russian soldiers led by the German Emperor.

The manoeuvres on Carlos Island were being photographed by General Nesvetevitch, a fine old officer who had gone on pension after the war of 1877, and had since become a successful photographer for the Russian newspapers. He continued to wear military uniform, and that enabled him to work with his camera in places where his pressmen colleagues were not admitted on any terms.

In order to get a good photograph of the German Emperor, General Nesvetevitch rushed off ahead of him — and lost one of his galoshes. Galoshes were, it need hardly be said, not permitted articles of military dress.

As ill-luck would have it, William II came right on the heels of the photographer. He stuck his sword through the *corpus delicti*, and bore it off in triumph to the Tsar. General Nesvetevitch was not the man to miss so good an opportunity for a snapshot.

The horror of the general staff may be imagined. Who was the soldier or officer who had dared to put on galoshes? Finally, some one mentioned the photographer Nesvetevitch. He was hurriedly sent for and came up wearing only one galosh. William II deliberately kept up a long and very friendly conversation with the photographer, and told him that he particularly wanted to have the photographs of the attack — and of the galosh.

That same evening I was instructed by the Minister of the Court to ask the General to destroy the ridiculous photo at once. The artist was disconsolate, but the loyal subject of the Tsar could only obey His Majesty's express order — protesting all the time that it was just this photo that he had promised the Kaiser. We sent to Berlin another photo, a decent one.

William II knew how to show his annoyance even to persons in very high places. I will only mention here the incidents at the entrance to the Kiel Canal after the Cowes interview, which had been very unwelcome to Germany.

We proceeded slowly along this strategic artery of modern Germany. The Kaiser had not deigned to announce beforehand his intention to pay a visit to the *Standard*. At one of the last of the locks he appeared as though by chance. He came on board the Imperial yacht, saluted Their Majesties with the most frigid formality, and asked the Tsar when he intended to proceed on his voyage. Nicholas II replied that he would be leaving Kiel very soon, having to be back in St. Petersburg for an official ceremony. After a few minutes' talk, the Kaiser took his leave, and went ashore. Their Majesties did nothing on their side to impart to this strange interview the slightest element of cordiality.

Scarcely had we anchored at Kiel when the Tsar received a message from the Kaiser, scrawled on a scrap of paper torn out of a note-book. It asked the Tsar to delay his departure from Kiel until 8 a.m., so that on leaving he might pass through the German Fleet assembled in the roads. Nicholas II replied with one or two friendly words: he wrote, in English, that he would be pleased to admire his cousin's fine fleet.

A few hours later, for no apparent reason, there came a message cancelling the arrangement: there was to be no review. What made it worse (the Tsar himself spoke of it afterwards) was that the message contained not the slightest indication of the reason for the Kaiser's fresh decision. The review would not take place. That was all. We steamed out, needless to say, at 5 a.m.

For all that, some of the officers of the suite got up to catch a glimpse, even if only an unofficial one, of the famous German units. A thick fog spoilt the morning for them.

At lunch the Tsar chaffed them for their keenness. He told them that their indiscretion had been punished.

'William II was not going to let us compare the German and British ships, and had his fleet dressed in a fog to measure.'

The painful impression produced by these incidents was more or less obliterated at our last visit to Berlin, on the occasion of the marriage of the daughter of William II with Duke Ernest of Brunswick-Luneburg. With a much larger number of courtiers around him, the Kaiser seemed to adapt himself better to the atmosphere which should surround a monarch.

I will end my recollections of the reigning house of Germany with an incident that occurred at Spala. It goes to show that Their Majesties' relations with their German relatives were always tinged with a measure of latent and almost instinctive animosity.

Prince Henry of Prussia had arrived at Spala with his wife, Princess Irene, our Empress's sister. (These visits occurred regularly and were apparently meant to keep William II informed concerning the views of the Tsar and of governing circles.)

On the day of the Prince's arrival, the Tsar suggested a ride on horseback. We rode a dozen miles or so through a wood of magical loveliness. On the way back the Prince said to the Tsar:

'It has been an interesting ride, but surely this was not the *Distanzritt*' (a test of endurance) 'of which you wrote in your letter?'

'This was only by way of preparation,' the Tsar replied; 'to-morrow I will show you some forests farther off.'

The Tsar came over to my side, and said in a low voice:

'Prince Henry wants us to take him on a *Distanzritt*. Send the cook to the place we spoke about a few days ago. I will make him do fifty miles to begin the day with. On the way back he will not boast so much of his military training.'

He added, with a significant smile:

'Tell them to saddle my "zain".'

The Tsar's zain was a cross between an English thoroughbred and a Russian trotter; it had so long a trot that the suite had continually to change from gallop to trot and from trot to gallop. That, of course, is particularly fatiguing. The whole suite was accustomed to this form of exercise. The Prince, however, seemed tired after twenty-five miles, and began to complain of his horse. On the way back he was offered whichever of the horses of the suite he fancied. He made his choice, but was hardly able to get back. His legs were covered with blood, and he was unable to get into the saddle for five days.

The Tsar consoled him by telling him that he would get used to it, but added aside, whispering in my ear:

'He will sing a little more softly now; he won't want another *Distanzritt*. It's a funny thing, but all sailors think themselves finished horsemen.'

THE KING OF ENGLAND

What a contrast there was between the visits of William II and the reception of the King and Queen of England at Reval! How entirely at ease everybody was in their company!

On a lovely June morning, sunny and fresh, the yacht *Victoria and Albert* made her appearance in the open sea beyond the roads. Our whole squadron, preceded by the Imperial yacht, went out to meet the British Sovereigns. After the usual ceremonies, King Edward, Queen Alexandra, and their daughter Princess Victoria went on board the yacht *Pole Star*, in which the Dowager Empress had come; the state lunch began at once. The Tsar received the King of England in the uniform of the Scots Greys, with the famous bearskin busby. Nicholas II was forthwith appointed Admiral of the Fleet, and at once put on his new uniform.

After visiting H.M.S. *Minotaur*, one of the cruisers of the British escort, the Tsar asked me whether I had in my trunks any suitable present for the officers' mess. I happened to have a big *zhban* (large bowl) of chased silver, in pure Russian style. It was at once sent over to the Minotaur as the first present from the new 'Admiral' of the British Navy. The *zhban* had travelled with me for many years, waiting for the appropriate moment for its appearance.

Everything was done perfectly quietly and with much dignity. The etiquette of the English Court was very different from ours. Our princes were accustomed from their earliest childhood to standing for hours and hours; after meals they formed a 'circle', dead-tired. On board the *Victoria and Albert* things were done differently. After dinner the King and his august guests sat down in comfortable arm-chairs; cigars and liqueurs were served; an arm-chair was left vacant alongside each person of high rank, and the officers with whom the King wanted to talk were invited to sit down in one of these chairs; after a fairly long conversation the King would nod and his interlocutor would retire for somebody else to take his place.

The whole of the two suites stayed in the room. There was no need at all to remain standing; those who preferred could sit down whenever they chose. Except when on duty, no account was taken of rank or social position.

I recall how Sir John Fisher (as he was then) marched up and down the room and asked me some question each time he came near me. I felt it my duty to rise each time to answer him. At last he said:

'I can't sit down — I have been fifty years going to and fro on deck; but that is no reason why people who have not my habits should be put out. We are not on duty; this is a sitting-room.'

At tea-time the band struck up, to the great pleasure of our ladies, young and old. Sir John was one of the first to carry one of the Grand Duchesses off to the dance.

The whole of the Imperial family retained the pleasantest memories of tins visit, during which every sort of constraint or nervousness was dispelled by the tact and good feeling of our guests.

THE FRENCH

The visits made by our allies also left a very pleasant impression. I shall never forget the success that attended the meeting with President Fallières and the hearty way we all greeted his son, not unmeaningly, as 'Dauphin'.

It is only in my capacity of historian of everyday trifles that I shall mention certain little happenings of the sort that stick in one's memory; there is a place for humorous anecdote, even about friends. Will it be credited if I say that it is the most idiotic story among my memories that jumps to my mind the most readily?

When the French sailors came to St. Petersburg a grand gala performance was organized in their honour in the immense People's Hall, a building that might have been specially erected for such monster entertainments. It was my part, of course, to inform the foreign correspondents of what had been going on. Had one of these gentlemen of the Press been, perhaps, a little inattentive? His newspaper, at all events, had as one of its big cross-heads:

'RECEPTION IN THE PUBLIC HOUSE
IN ST. PETERSBURG'

and the French 'public house' is not an establishment of the innocent respectability of the British. This inventive gentleman can certainly have had no idea of the chaffing that I had to endure on account of his slip of the pen, which I suppose must have been involuntary. It was the joke of the day in every club in the capital! Countess Freedericksz rebuked me sharply for not 'censoring' the foreign newspapers.

Here is another detail, now so insignificant, which kept us amused for many weeks.

On our way back from the review at Compiegne the Empress (who had at her side the Mistress of the Robes, Mme Naryshkin) found her carriage surrounded by an enormous crowd; it was almost impossible to move. Shouts of 'Vive l'Empereur!' 'Vive l'impératrice!' surged round the procession like the waves of a choppy sea. Suddenly a little man just in front of Mme Naryshkin who evidently wanted to please everybody gave a shout that carried over all the noise of the crowd:

'Three cheers for the lady on the left!'

He drew a round of applause, and thereafter Mme Naryshkin was known at Court as 'the lady on the left'.

The arrival of a foreign Court often sets pitfalls in etiquette which it is impossible to avoid with the best of good intentions. Shall I give an example?

At Vitry, during the French Army manoeuvres, the Tsar mounted a horse from his own stables, as was his habit (and also that of William II). The members of the suite had, of course, to content themselves with horses provided on the spot. Just as I was getting into the saddle an officer belonging to the President's suite came up to me and was kind enough to say:

'Your Excellency, we know you are an accomplished rider, and we have reserved a thoroughbred for you.'

So long as we were going at walking pace all was well. But the moment arrived when an echelon came into view at a distance, and the Tsar set off at a gallop. The suite did the same. Then my tribulations began. There was no holding the animal back; its paces were worthy of a Derby winner. I could see that I was going to be carried ahead of the Tsar, the worst thing possible, so I made my mount turn outwards. But the turn had no sooner been completed than it had to be begun again, for my courser took his duties with the utmost seriousness. Shall I confess it? The whole of that nm was made in successive, progressively widening circles.

As I dismounted I said to the officer in the President's suite who had been so kind;

'This animal has come from a racing stable?'

'Yes, your Excellency. She has just carried off a number of prizes at Longchamps.'

'I can believe it. It was all I could do not to beat the Tsar by five hundred lengths.'

It was during the same visit that the incident occurred of the christening of a grandson of the Marquis de Montebello, French Ambassador in St. Petersburg. Some time before the Tsar's departure, the Marquis had asked the Sovereign to be godfather at the christening. The Tsar had seen no reason to refuse this favour to the Ambassador. It happened that we had arrived at Compiègne at the time when the struggle between the Waldeck-Rousseau Cabinet and the Clericals was at its height. There were long discussions with our ceremonial staff; the French Ministry wanted at all costs to prevent the Tsar from going to the chapel in which the ceremony was to take place. Nicholas II insisted that a promise given by the Tsar of Russia must be kept. I believe that this cost the Marquis de Montebello his post; shortly afterwards he was recalled from St. Petersburg.

Both sides were right.

During our visit to Compiègne some little incidents happened which I think were due to the very praiseworthy desire to place us all in an atmosphere recalling the memories of this fine old chateau.

Here is an example. To reach Compiègne we had been put into a train which had belonged to Napoleon III. The coaches were foil of gilded furniture, and of every sort of decoration in the style of the Second Empire. It looked very fine, but what uncomfortable coaches they were! How huddled up we were! To crown our misfortunes, they had forgotten to change the springs: Second Empire springs were ill able to stand the speeds to which we are used in the twentieth century. The Empress was afflicted with nausea, and the strongest of us left these cages dead tired and aching all over.

The chateau itself is marvellous — for a picnic. When I reached the room reserved for me I found that there was no water, that razors and bottles of eau-de-Cologne had to be placed on little tables about the room, and that certain 'amenities' indispensable to the traveller's comfort were a hundred miles from my bedroom. In short, this chateau was all too thoroughly in Empire style!

For the state banquet the French ladies, full of anxiety to show every attention to the Russian Sovereigns, all dressed with one accord in Empire dresses (were these not shown in the pictures of the chateau that illustrated the memoirs of Napoleon I and Napoleon III?), and powdered themselves with a very dark lilac powder. The result was curious, but our maids of honour were none the less distracted at having neither dresses with exceedingly high waists nor this famous powder of — purplish blue.

It is undeniable that when two different mentalities come into contact the result is often a series of awkward misunderstandings.

What a desperate problem, for instance, was that of decorations! The list given me in France was three times the length of the one that had been drawn up in St. Petersburg in agreement with the Ambassador and the military attaché. When I asked what part this or the other person mentioned in the new fist had played during the Tsar's visit, I was unfailingly told:

'He wasn't there, but he has a great deal of influence.'

Long discussions had to follow to determine the decoration that should be given to this influential citizen. For some reason, I cannot say what, the French were anxious at all costs to escape from getting the order of St. Stanislas. They even refused the star of St. Stanislas.

'No, not Stanislas; say Anne, even if it ranks lower.'

Yet it was obviously impossible to give everybody the same decoration.

I will end the tale of these small trials — of which, after all, the importance must not be exaggerated — with the incident that occurred at the moment of our departure from Compiègne. I recognize that both sides were right from their own standpoint.

Everybody had gone off to attend the review, but I wanted to supervise the final preparations for our departure, and had remained in the chateau. I might have saved myself the trouble; I discovered almost at once that everybody, the commanding officer, the servants, the civil officials, the officers, had rushed off to see the manoeuvres, leaving the Tsar's luggage lying about the floor, abandoned to its fate.

I had to go in search of the Commandant of the town gendarmerie. He told me that it was nothing to do with him.

'But,' I protested, 'it will be an unheard-of scandal! Just think what it would mean if the train had to bring the Tsar back to Compiègne because the luggage had been left behind!'

Finally the Commandant put at my disposal an officer and a squad of soldiers. But I soon found that the mentality of the French Tommies was a whole world apart from that of our infantrymen:

'Sorry,' they said, 'but we are not the Tsar's porters!'

Once more, both sides were right.

I had all the trouble in the world to get them to see reason, and by the time I had got the last piece of the Imperial luggage loaded on to the lorry, the Tsar was on his way to the train.

EMPEROR FRANCIS JOSEPH

The visit to Vienna and Mürzsteg has remained vividly in my memory through a conversation that I had with Emperor Francis Joseph.

We had gone off to a hunting-box high up in the Alps, near Karlsgraben. I had been posted in a sort of eyrie at the top of the debris of an enormous moraine. I had the good luck to kill three chamois; one was hit in full flight as it jumped from one crag to another. As I descended the moraine to take possession of my quarry, I was astonished to find standing close to it the Emperor Francis Joseph.

'That was a fine shot of yours {*Das war ein Meisterschuss*),' he said very kindly.

I wanted to apologize, and to explain that I did not know that the chamois had been going towards the Sovereign.

Francis Joseph put me at my ease by telling me that in any case he 'could not possibly' kill more than three chamois that day. Otherwise he would have reached a total of three thousand chamois fallen to his gun, and that would have brought him ovations from the huntsmen which he was anxious to avoid in the presence of the Tsar of Russia.

The Emperor made me sit down on a folding chair; his attendant had gone to fetch his horse, and we had a few minutes together.

In spite of his great age, the Emperor seemed to have an excellent memory.

'Was it not you,' he said suddenly, 'who were presented to me at the time of "Sandro" Battenberg's visit to Vienna?'

I said that it was.

'I think,' the Emperor went on, 'you were one of the few of your compatriots who remained faithful to Sandro. Did I not hear that you had to give an explanation on your return to Russia? Tell me all about it. I had such a liking for Sandro.'

I told the Emperor in a few words what had happened, mentioning that Tsar Alexander III saved me from the disgrace with which I was threatened; he remembered in the nick of time that his father, Alexander II, had told me to 'serve Sandro as though he were the Tsar himself'.

Francis Joseph replied:

'The time came when the Tsar was sorry for what had been done to Sandro. Sandro's enforced departure from Bulgaria ran counter to the aims that Russia had been pursuing in the Principality. The Generals and diplomats then in Sofia had been badly chosen.'

He added that in his view Sandro was a very capable man; 'perhaps better able to lead soldiers to the attack than to reign in so young a State as Bulgaria was then'.

Many years had passed since this conversation when I found myself once more in Vienna, having been selected to accompany Grand Duke Andrew Vladimirovitch on a mission to Bulgaria. After the dinner in honour of His Highness, the Emperor came to me and said:

'Now you are in Vienna, don't forget to call on Sandro's widow. I am very fond of her.'

PRINCE FERDINAND OF BULGARIA

It would be easy to fill many pages with my conversations with the Bulgarians.

As one of those who fought in the Bulgarian war of liberation, I have been present at many Russo-Bulgarian demonstrations, some of which were of great magnificence. I may have occasion later on to devote a special work to these fine pages of Russo-Bulgarian history. Here I am confined to sketches with no sort of political character, and I shall be very brief.

As a former A.D.C. to Prince Alexander of Battenberg, it seemed impossible that I should be persona grata with Prince Ferdinand, his successor. It was for that reason that I declined the honour of being attached to his person during his first visit to St. Petersburg. Subsequent events proved, however, that I was mistaken; Prince Ferdinand showed me the greatest friendship, and invited me to Sofia as his personal guest after the Shipka ceremonies.[1]

It was during this visit that the Prince honoured me by taking me round the zoological garden which he had installed in Sofia, and of which he was particularly proud. He told me that he had there the most complete collection of the serpents that are to be found in Bulgaria.'

Would you like to see them?'

I have an innate and instinctive aversion from every sort of reptile. But politeness demanded the answer 'Yes'.

He took me over to some glass cases filled with these repulsive creatures. Suddenly, to my horror, I saw him put on a sort of green glove and pull out the serpents one by one; they twisted and reared and coiled round his arm. Finally he brought one of the abominable creatures close to me, and told me I might caress it. With all the surface imperturbability of a Spartan, I went through the necessary performance. Needless to say I was thoroughly relieved when we were able to get away from this home of horrors and go to see the greenhouses, where the Prince stopped before the most interesting of the plants and told me their Latin names. Savants have their manias, even when they are princes.

The visit to the garden and the palace lasted so long that the Orient Express which was to carry me away had to delay its departure, by the Prince's command, for more than an hour.

THE SHAH OF PERSIA

The visits of the Shah of Persia have left only two anecdotes in my memory. I think they are worth telling.

The first relates to a reception at Court. A long Court procession filed before the Oriental Sovereign. After being greeted by one of the ladies he said aloud, in his broken French:

'Why — old? ugly? naked?'

1 The commemoration of the battle of the Shipka Pass, fought in 1877.

184

It must be inferred that the etiquette of his Court was not as that of the Courts of other sovereigns.

During the manoeuvres at Kursk the Shah had seen an imposing number of soldiers paraded in front of the pavilion in which he was seated. He had been told that 100,000 men had taken part in the march past. At one moment the Shah made a sign to one of his aides-de-camp and whispered something in his ear. My brother officer Bellegarde, a former instructor of the Persian cavalry, noticed that the officer stopped near the entrance to the pavilion in obvious perplexity. He went up to him. It seems that the Shah had told his A.D.C. to go and see for himself that the same battalions were not being brought back somewhere in order to march past a second time. The poor Persian officer was at a loss to acquit himself of his delicate mission.

Bellegarde took him to the place where the battalions dispersed. He was able to verify that our generals were playing no tricks.

III. EVERYDAY LIFE

MEALS

We come now to Their Majesties' daily life. I shall write first of the daily bread.

It was the Marshal of the Court, Count Benckendorff, who ruled over everything that had to do with meals and with formalities at table. He was assisted by Colonels Prince Putiatin and von Bode, the two 'Cutlet Colonels', as they were always called.

Count Benckendorff considered himself absolute lord over everything that concerned his department; he kept watch over it with jealous care, and nobody interfered in the great problems that came under his supervision. He had, of course, to keep within his budget; but he disposed of the money entirely at his own discretion. And, supreme honour, he had the right to make oral and written 'reports' himself; which means, in plain language, that he received his orders directly from the Tsar. He referred to the Minister of the Court only in exceptional cases.

Meals at the Russian Court were divided into three categories or classes:

(1) The service of Their Majesties and their immediate suite, known as the Sovereigns' table;

(2) The Marshal's service, for the remaining members of the suite, and for dignitaries invited to Court;

(3) The domestics' service, in two subdivisions, according to rank.

The first service was reserved to persons whom Their Majesties had deigned to invite to join them. If the guest, after being presented to the Sovereigns, had not received a personal invitation, he sat at the Marshal's table.

Breakfast was served in the guest's own room. Tea, coffee, or chocolate could be had as preferred, and bread and butter were brought — household bread, rolls, and sweetened bread. Ham, eggs, and bacon could also be called for.

Then came the 'kalatch'. The 'kalatch' was an age-long tradition, kept up the more rigorously because the Empress was very fond of this sort of Muscovite bread. It is rather difficult to explain to foreigners what a *kalatch* was. Outwardly, it was a little white loaf, made with hardly any yeast, and it looked for all the world like a lady's oval handbag, with the flap turned back half-way up, and on top of it a semi-circular strip; a hundred years ago the *kalatchy* used to be hung on sticks by these strips for convenience of transport. The *kalatch* was an essentially Muscovite product, and the bakers had created a legend that it was impossible to make the dough for it without the water of the Moscow River. Consequently a service from Moscow had to be organized. Tanks filled with this miracle-working water were sent to the Court, wherever it might be. The *kalatch* was served with special ceremony. It was supposed to be eaten very hot, and was brought in a warm napkin.

Such was the breakfast. It would have been interesting to discover how this food figured in the budget of the Court (though this was a delicate subject which would have had to be approached with prudence). I will content myself with one anecdote; it may serve to illustrate a matter that went beyond my ken.

Tsar Alexander III had appointed one of his aides-de-camp to the post of Marshal of the Court.

'They are spending too much money on my meals,' he said; 'try to get a little order into the buying.'

The young Marshal of the Court set to work, full of enthusiasm. The first detail that came to his notice made him jump. Five pounds of Gruyère cheese was bought *every day* 'for His Majesty's personal table'. He made inquiries: how much Gruyère did the Tsar take for breakfast? A few days of discreet observation showed the quantity to be two or three tiny pieces. He sent for the steward concerned:

'This five pounds of Gruyère has got to stop.'

'As you wish, your Excellency.'

A few days later the Tsar took an opportunity to say to him:

'Is it you who gave the order to serve me with three little bits of cheese? Why are they shrivelled up and oily, and quite uneatable?'

There was a further interview with the steward:

'Put on the table a big piece of Gruyère; but I think it ought to last several days.'

'As you wish, your Excellency.'

After the second day the big piece of cheese had such a look about it that the Tsar sent it away in disgust.

The end of it was that the Marshal gave way. He also sent in his resignation.

I might mention an incident that occurred at the Hofburg, in Vienna, during one of our visits to Francis Joseph. It was not an incident of any great importance, but it was significant.

During dinner I had noticed some sweets wrapped up very artistically in covers which had on them photographs of members of the Imperial family. It occurred to me to take away a few in order to show them to our Marshal of the Court, but I did not have time to arrange for it. What was my astonishment when, on leaving, I was handed a box of these very sweets.

I suggested to Count Benckendorff that we might be able to do something of the sort ourselves, but he replied that it was out of the question. It was a tradition of our Court that all the sweets put out for guests and not consumed at table became the property of the domestics.

'It is quite impossible to depart from the tradition. There would be too much discontent, and in the end the guests would not get what had been prepared for them.'

Such was the confession of one of the strictest of Marshals of the Court, a Marshal in whom the Tsar had implicit confidence.

Lunch was served at noon. At Livadia and in the hunting-boxes the whole suite had the right to sit down to meals at the Sovereigns' table. Every one had to be in the dining-room five minutes before lunch time. The Emperor came in, greeted his guests, and went to the *zakusky* table, at which everybody helped himself. The *zakusky* (hors-d'œuvre) would be caviare, smoked fish, pickled herrings, of course, and tiny snacks on fried bread. Two or three dishes of hot *zakusky* were also served: sausages in tomato *purée*, hot knuckle of ham, *gruau à la Dragomiroff*, and so on. The Emperor would take two glasses of vodka and very small portions of *zakusky*. The Empress considered this way of eating before sitting down to table to be unhealthy, and did not go near the hors-d'œuvre table. This preliminary lasted about a quarter of an hour; meanwhile the maids of honour came up in turn to the Empress, who said a few words to each of them.

After the *zakusky* we took the seats assigned to us. It would not have done to be hunting for our seats in Their Majesties' presence, so that everybody made a point of finding where his seat was before they had come in.

At ordinary lunches the Empress sat by the side of the Tsar, on his right; the Minister of the Court sat facing Their Majesties. If there were guests, they sat by the side of the Sovereigns or of the Minister of the Court; otherwise the members of the suite arranged themselves according to rank and seniority. There was only one exception: the seat on the Empress's right was taken in turn by each of the members of the suite without exception, even by the youngest invited.

Before leaving the subject of *zakusky*, I should mention the picturesque ceremony of the present. The Russian language has several words for 'present'; the ceremony that I am about to describe was a tradition dating from the eighteenth century, and the gift bore the French name of *présent*.

This *présent* was a gift that the Ural Cossacks brought every spring to their Sovereign, and was made up of the finest fish caught in the first and most important haul of the year, and with it several barrels of fresh caviare.

The *présent* had been introduced as a spontaneous manifestation of filial reverence to the Tsar; subsequently it was regulated by laws duly promulgated. The *gramota* (decree) of the Sovereign which reserved to the Ural Cossacks the exclusive right of fishing in the waters of the Ural River and its tributaries, laid down that the whole product of the first catch, hereafter called the Tsar's haul, belonged to the Imperial house.

The Tsar's haul was no small matter. The fishing began at a time when the river was still covered by a thick layer of ice, and its technique had, if I may say so, a character of its own. Holes were cut in the ice, and suitable nets were dropped through them.

The Governor-General himself attended the Tsar's haul. The authorities were all there to a man. A Te Deum was sung, and the priests walked past the ice-holes, sprinkling them with holy water.

The caviare and the fish were prepared on the spot and sent off the same day in waggons that went direct to St. Petersburg. A deputation of bearded Cossacks, conscious of the honour done to them by the voters who had chosen them for the duty, left for the capital at the same time as the consignment. I want to emphasize the detail that the Cossacks had been chosen by their electors. The Cossacks have never ceased to live under a thoroughly democratic régime, with a Krug (an electoral assembly like the Agora in Athens) for each regiment. The Krug made its choice, entirely, of course, from among men of high repute who had at least a St. George's cross, a decoration which could only be obtained on the field of battle.

The delegation was received by the Tsar in the great dining-room of the Palace. The Cossacks came in with specimens of their fish and of caviare 'of pearl grey turning to amber'. The *présent* was placed near the *zakusky* table, and the Tsar and the Empress tasted the 'flower' of the Ural fishing. A glass of vodka was then drunk to the prosperity of the Ural Cossacks, and watches with the Tsar's monogram were given as presents to the delegation.

Thereafter the Cossacks went on to the Minister of the Court, the writer of these lines, the Grand Dukes, and the high dignitaries of the Court. The Tsar's haul must have been abundant. My share of it amounted to close on forty pounds of superb caviare and five or six fish, each a yard long. Did the Ural ultimately become less well stocked, or did the Cossacks' zeal abate? Whatever the explanation, the fact remained that in the end the *présent* diminished greatly, to about half For all that, there was caviare enough even for certain foreign Courts.

At lunch there were two courses, one of eggs or fish, and one of white or red meat. Those who had good appetites had time to attack four different dishes. The second course included vegetables; these, in order not to encumber the tables, were put on smaller plates, crescent-shaped. Lunch ended with a compote of fruit, and cheese.

The servant who carried the dish had to place the guest's portion on his plate; this made it unnecessary for the men guests to serve their lady neighbours. The Emperor was the only one who served himself.

Ultimately his example was followed and the old custom fell into disuse.

When there were no guests, coffee was served at the dining- table. The Tsar lit a cigarette, saying that the Empress had given permission. If there were guests the company rose from the table after dessert; Their Majesties replied to the obeisances of the guests and went into another room or into the garden; coffee was then taken standing, the Sovereigns conversing with their entourage. Smoking was allowed as soon as the Tsar had lit his cigarette.

Five o'clock tea was served in our rooms. Sometimes we would go for tea to the room of the nearest maid of honour, according to the 'geography' of the Palace. Tea was only taken with Their Majesties on a personal invitation.

Dinner was at eight. Their Majesties greeted those persons whom they had not seen during the day; I always wondered what device they could employ to make sure, as they did, of never making a mistake. At Livadia there were no *zakusky* for dinner; on days spent in hunting they were served twice.

Dinner began with a thick or clear soup, *vol-au-vent, pirozhky* (little Russian cakes), or cheese on hot rusks. The *vol-au-vent* were served with the soup and not after it as abroad. Then came fish, roast (fowl or game), vegetables and a sweet, followed by fruit. Coffee was taken in the dining-room. At ceremonial dinners the number of courses was, of course, increased, as everywhere on the Continent and in America.

The wines were: Madeira and white and red wine at lunch; beer for those who asked for it. At dinners, a series of wines in accordance with the general custom; liqueurs with the coffee.

Each meal had to last fifty minutes, not one more and not one less. The Marshal of the Court saw to the rigid observance of this tradition. Why? I am quite unable to say. But I do know that we all paid dearly for Count Benckendorff's obstinacy; the Tsar's guests benefited little from the efforts of all the master cooks in the Imperial kitchens.

The tradition dated from the reign of Alexander II. This Tsar liked to change the room used as dining-room from time to time, and there were times when he made use of a room at a great distance from the kitchens. He insisted, at the same time, that the courses should be served one after another without interruption; as soon as he had finished the fish he expected the roast to be brought in, at once. The Marshal was reduced to sacrificing gastronomy to speed. Enormous heaters were invented, using boiling water; the course was brought up twenty minutes in advance, on a silver dish; this dish had a silver cover, and was placed on the heater until the moment came for serving. Thanks to this subterfuge, Count Benckendorff was able to maintain the fifty-minute meals. True gourmets will agree with me that no sauce could retain its full flavour in such conditions.

Freedericksz protested all his life against this system of massacring good dishes, but his authority was not sufficient to make an end of this gastronomic scandal, as we called it. He made a gallant attempt to quash it at Livadia. He sent for the engineers and asked them to construct a railway and a lift: the railway was to carry the dishes to a point just below the pantry, and the lift would do the rest; the dish would arrive at its destination in all its succulence. But the Minister had neither consulted nor even told the cooks about the plan, and they were full of wrath over the installation, which robbed of their employment the young novices who carried the dishes from kitchen to pantry. It was claimed in the circles of these successors of Brillat-Savarin that the electric train did not move smoothly enough for the sauces and the chicken croquettes; nothing but the feline tread of a cook's apprentice could save them from being shaken up. Freedericksz insisted; the cooks went on a ca'canny strike; they sent the electric carriages along in a slow motion that reduced everything to an uneatable condition. Ultimately Freedericksz gave way, and the railway functioned no more. The battery of boiling water heaters made its reappearance in triumph in the pantry, and remained there to the end.

As for the Empress, she was always on a diet prescribed by her doctors, and had her food prepared in the pantry itself, on oil stoves of a well-known Swedish make.

The only place in which we really fed well was the Imperial train. The kitchen-car was next to the dining-car, which would not accommodate more than sixteen persons. Consequently it was possible to bring in the dishes as soon as they came out of the oven. I noticed that the train was the only place in which the Tsar regularly sent for the chef to congratulate him on a particularly successful dish.

The Marshal's table differed little from that of the Sovereigns. There was perhaps not quite so much of the cream of the early vegetables, and not quite such an abundance of fruit. The meals at this table were served to the Marshal himself, to the Minister of the Court when he was at Peterhof, to the Mistress of the Robes, and to the maids of honour in the suite. Generals A.D.C. and officers commanding the detachment on guard at the palace were also entitled to feed at the Marshal's table, and I have already mentioned that persons presenting themselves to Their Majesties who had not been invited to the Sovereigns' table lunched at the Marshal's; he made a point of presiding over it himself.

The domestics' table must have been particularly well loaded, if I may judge by my own servant, who was continually obliged to change his belt for an ampler one.

When the Tsar became Commander-in-Chief of the Russian armies, he completely broke with all the customs of the Court, and had dishes of the utmost simplicity served up. He said to me one day:

Thanks to the war, I have learnt that simple dishes are infinitely nicer and healthier than all the Marshal's spiced cookery.'

As to the wines — at lunch the Emperor drank nothing but Madeira: a large glass of a specially chosen vintage. A bottle of this wine was placed in front of his plate. He hated to have the wine poured out by a servant, who 'always made too much of a business of it'; he served himself. The guests' glasses were filled by servants; they had Madeira or white or red wine as in other countries. At dinner the wines were a little more varied.

All these wines were excellent, but they did not belong to the famous cellar which contained the real 'jewels'. This cellar — we all sighed for its contents — was guarded by Count Benckendorff.

In order to get anything out of it, it was necessary to have recourse to a regular stratagem. Nobody but the Minister of the Court could put forward any suggestion concerning this cellar. And it was necessary that he should have sufficient ground. We searched the saints' calendar accordingly for patrons and patronesses to be honoured; as soon as a suitable name was discovered we went in search of Count Freedericksz and put the position to him. Usually he would send for Benckendorff and say:

'I have a family festival to-day. You must let us have a glass of old wine all round.'

'But you know perfectly well that these wines are reserved for very great occasions, state banquets — '

The case would be pressed, and at length the Count would have glasses laid for the vintage that had been chosen. When the Emperor saw them he would smile:

'Have you another niece coming of age to-day? I wonder who remembered it! I'll bet it was Nilov or Troubetzkoy...

Freedericksz was fond above all of a certain Chateau Yquem, which had been nicknamed Nectar. It was no good hoping for a glass of Nectar if the Empress was going to be at dinner.

The 'jewels' were destroyed on the day of the October revolution. The immense cellars of the Winter Palace were sacked by the revolutionaries. The wine that was not drunk was poured over the Palace square; it is said that in the evening the square looked for all the world like a field of battle; the people lying about it dead drunk would have made a good subject for a photographer in search of a picture showing how the assailants had despised death.

But, after all, wine had ceased to play in the Russian Court the part which it played among our ancestors. Only one custom remained inviolable; cynics seized on it to draw certain amusing deductions.

It was the tradition of the 'golden Coronation goblet'. At one point in the course of the state banquet given after the Tsar's coronation, the Grand Cup-bearer of the Court presented a golden goblet filled with wine, and proclaimed in a loud voice so that all should hear:

'His Majesty deigns to drink.'

At that cry the 'foreign guests' (not excluding the diplomats) had to leave the Granovitaya Palata ('bevelled room'). At the last coronation this curious toast was not heralded; but the Masters of Ceremonies invited the 'foreigners' to go into another room where tables had been laid. Only the trusty subjects of the Tsar could join in the feast in the Granovitaya Palata.

The reader will have guessed the reasons that may have led the Machiavellis of the Muscovite Court of the sixteenth century to introduce this precautionary measure.

During the reign of Alexander II, only foreign wines were served. Alexander III gave a decision which made history in Russian vine-growing: foreign wines were in future only to be served when foreign sovereigns or diplomats were present. At other times Russian wines must be made to do. All the regiments of the guards followed suit. I remember that there were many officers who considered that this vinicultural nationalism was being carried too far; they abandoned their messes and went to the big restaurants, in order to get the wines they preferred. At that time it needed some resolution to rest content with the produce of the Crimea.

But that did not last long. Under the capable management of Prince Kotchubey, the Apanages brought their output of wine to an astonishing degree of perfection. Soon those people who laid in stocks of foreign wine did so only in pure snobbishness. It was impossible to distinguish champagnes from the domain of Abrau from those of the Rheims vineyards. Dessert wines became the speciality of the domain of Massandra; unfortunately its production was very limited. Specialists claimed that it was in no way inferior to the best foreign vintages.

The pioneer in this advance of Russian vine-growing was Prince Leo Galitzin. He was considered one of the best tasters in the world. He was elected president of the wine jury in the International Exhibition of 1900. He declared that he would never accept any official position: he was content to be 'a Russian vine-grower'.

His vineyards were about twenty miles from Yalta; in the Crimea. The domain was called the 'New World'. Alexander III was interested in this great enterprise, and offered Galitzin the post of director of Massandra. The Prince made difficulties; he stated his conditions:

'Never to have to put on a uniform; never to receive honours or official posts; to be free to do whatever he thought fit at Massandra.'

The Tsar was astonished, but agreed. For some time Galitzin administered Massandra with great success. Then he fell out with the Head of the Apanages; the Tsar sent for him; the Prince refused to give way, and resigned.

He returned to his domain and devoted himself exclusively to its development. Towards the end of the reign of Nicholas II, Galitzin offered his property to the Tsar as a present. Knowing the Prince's eccentricities, the Tsar asked him to state in writing the conditions of this gift. The conditions were decidedly onerous: the State must undertake to create an 'Academy of Viticulture' at the 'New World', with Galitzin as its permanent president, and he must have the right to spend the rest of his life there. Calculations were made, and it was found that the Academy would cost the Apanages much more than the whole revenue of the domain. But the Prince was a man of forceful personality. The Tsar was overborne by his eloquence, and disregarded the question of economy as a minor consideration.

I recall the visit Their Majesties made one day to the 'New World'.

The cellars were nearly two miles long. At junctions of their passages the Prince had arranged circular spaces for tasting. One of these spaces was named 'Library of Wines'; it contained, in addition to endless samples of wine, an enormous collection of old cut glass, suitable for every imaginable vintage. While we tasted the most famous 'years' the Prince went on talking incessantly.

'I should like to know,' the Empress said to me, as we returned to Livadia, 'how many hours he has been chattering without a stop.'

DAILY LIFE AT LIVADIA

As to the way Their Majesties spent the day, I can only speak of what went on during their stays in the Crimea, at Livadia, where I was constantly in touch with the Sovereigns.

The Tsar devoted the mornings to work, beginning immediately after a short walk.

His Majesty received people standing in front of his desk. As he sat down he pointed his visitor to an armchair; the visitor could arrange his papers on an extension of the desk. During the conversation the Tsar would smoke, and often he would invite his interlocutor to smoke.

The Tsar greatly appreciated those persons who were able to explain to him in the course of conversation even matters of a very complicated nature. Before listening to what the Minister bringing a report had to say, the Tsar would take the report, glance through the first few lines to discover its subject, and then carefully read its final passages, in which the Minister would have stated the conclusion at which he had arrived. If the conclusion was not sufficiently clear to him, he would read the intervening pages. The Sovereign was quick in grasping the central idea of a report. He got irritated if the papers were burdened with what he considered an excessive amount of argument. General Sukhomlinov, Minister of War, had a special gift of holding the Tsar in suspense right up to the last minute, even if his audience lasted a couple of hours.

As soon as the report was dealt with, the Tsar would go over to the window and make some remark on any subject, to bring the audience to an end.

Reports were often presented in the evening, from 4 to 6.30.

The Tsar never stayed away from a religious service, however good a pretext he could have put forward in order to escape from it. The service would not begin until after His Majesty's arrival; it would last about an hour.

The Tsar only saw his family at meals, at tea-time, and on those evenings on which he was not called to his office by urgent duties.

Before lunch was quite finished, the Empress would make a little sign to the children and they would rush into the garden, followed by Baron Meyendorf, the head of the Tsar's escort. This was a sort of special favour, and the Baron knew how to make the most of it; one could hear at once the laughing and the shouts of joy outside. Meyendorf was a past master of the art of amusing the Tsar's children.

As a 'director' of the Court balls the Baron had made himself popular with the two Empresses by his gaiety and charm. As he became older he lost nothing of his joviality, and won the close affection of the young generation.

He was an amusing figure, this poor Baron Meyendorf, whom everybody liked and nobody took seriously. But he was heavily handicapped in the presence of his wife, 'Auntie Vera', an ambitious, blundering, rather ridiculous woman.

Auntie Vera was president of the Society for the Protection of Animals; the energy with which she carried out her duties was the source of a good deal of trouble to the whole of the Crimean administration.

One day she demanded that fowls should not be carried to market with their heads down, lest they should faint. The Governor of the Crimea had to issue an order to that effect. A few days later she called on him and complained.

'Surely,' he said, 'my order has not been disregarded?'

'No, it isn't disregarded so long as these wretched peasants are going past my villa. But I have been following them to keep an eye on them. No sooner do they get round the corner of the street than the poor fowls are turned upside down again.'

There is a story of a poodle that made Auntie Vera celebrated. As ill-luck had it, this poodle ran right into her just at the moment when she was leaving her villa; and it was painted bright red!

The Baroness tried to get hold of it; a crowd of dogs of every breed, who had run up from all directions, got in her way; they went in pursuit of the scarlet bitch, and Auntie Vera ran at the tail of the procession, crying out:

'Stop him! Stop the red dog!'

A policeman succeeded in getting hold of the animal at the far end of the quay. The Baroness told him to take it at once to the Governor. The avenging woman followed close on the heels of the policeman and the red bitch. The Governor had no option but to receive her, abandoning the work he had in hand.

'What sort of an administration is this? It's a shame! The poor animal is being martyred. I hope you will have the guilty persons severely punished.'

'But, really. Baroness — where does the martyrdom come in? Ladies dye their hair, and everybody admires them!'

'But what about the poor dog's *amour-propre*?'

'Heavens, the dogs were all following her like a lady whose dress is too conspicuous.'

'I tell you that a whole rabble was in pursuit of him. You could see he was suffering, poor thing!'

'But how can you tell? It may have been flattered at attracting the attention of all the young sparks in the town.'

But Auntie Vera insisted that there should be an investigation. It turned out that the little event had been organized by one of her husband's officers. The Tsar was told all about it, and asked the Governor to inform the Baroness that it had been impossible to trace the delinquent.

.   .   .   .   .   .

At the end of lunch the Tsar would tell the company, with the utmost kindness and simplicity:

'I'm going for a ride at such and such a time. Any one who would like to go too might have his horse got ready.'

Little animals accustomed to climbing the abrupt slopes were brought along. The lovers of this very special sort of sport were not many in number. In the end I found myself the only one who still accompanied the Sovereign, except, of course, the A.D.C. on duty, who had no choice.

One day, near Massandra, in heavy rain, Nicholas II went off at a fast trot, without holding in the bit, as was his custom. The horse slipped on the wet clay; the Tsar fell and hurt his side. He was able to get back into the saddle and return to Livadia, but there his strength gave out and he only just managed to go up the few steps that led to the house.

The Empress was so terrified that she begged her husband never to ride again. Motor-cars made their appearance soon after; it became more amusing to go off to some little-known place and there to climb straight up some particularly steep escarpment. Soon Drenteln, the

A.D.C., was the only one of the whole suite who was able to keep up with Nicholas II on the forced marches that he so enjoyed. The Tsar was a very vigorous man; outside his study he rarely sat down for long, and I never saw him lean on anything for support. His endurance was surprising.

The Tsar's excursions were inevitably a source of anxiety to those who were responsible for his personal safety. It was impossible to avoid placing a number of detectives along the road that the Sovereign was going to take, especially when he meant to go through remote villages. But the Tsar hated the sight of these men — these 'lovers of the country' or 'botanizers', as he called them, for they affected to be interested in everything in the world except the august person of the Sovereign. Nothing gave him so much pleasure as to give them the slip.

Sometimes it was painful to witness the despair of the Chief of Police of the Palace. To help him a little in his work, I undertook to let him know of any changes of route that the Tsar might propose in the course of a journey. To this end I would send one of the orderlies who followed us to telephone to the police headquarters; this would enable the 'botanizers' to be re-posted. They would bring their lounging to an abrupt end and run helter-skelter for some unexpected short cut.

One day after one of these reshufflings of the detective force, the Tsar caught the Chief of Police in the act of plunging head first into a *saklia* (Tartar hut) in a little village that we had just reached. The Tsar sent for him and began to catechize him.

'I changed my mind after leaving the Palace; how have you been able to find that out and get right on to my path?'

The poor Commandant, to avoid giving me away, began a long story of premonitions and intuitions. It was all he could do.

One more formal order was then issued — as unavailingly as ever — for lovers of the country not to linger the side of roads that His Majesty might be taking.

At tea-time the Tsar often had a game of tennis. He was a good player, but his opponents, officers of the suite or maids of honour, were not good enough players for him. Hearing that the Youssupovs had their nephew. Count Nicholas Sumarokov-Elston, champion of Russia, staying with them. His Majesty had him invited to Livadia.

I have been told that Sumarokov, who was a brilliant left-handed player, won every set. After tea The Tsar asked for a revenge. After a few strokes Sumarokov had the misfortune to hit the Tsar on his ankle with a particularly hard ball. The Tsar fell down, and had to stop in bed for three or four days.

The unfortunate champion was in despair, though nobody could fairly blame him. The Youssupovs, for all that, hauled him well over the coals.

As soon as the Emperor got up, he had Sumarokov invited to Livadia. The champion played some more sets with His Majesty, but his form was not what it had been.

Few persons outside the immediate suite of Their Majesties took tea with them. Even the Grand Duchesses only came to see the Empress if they were specially invited. Neither the Tsar nor the Empress had any desire to enlarge the circle of the persons admitted to their presence.

During the whole period of my service at Court, not a single person was ever invited to go to see Their Majesties after dinner. For their part, Their Majesties never went to see anybody, except the Dowager Empress and Grand Duchess Xenia. (There was one other exception, the visits to the Montenegrin princesses — see the section on the 'Spirits', pp.44-5.)

The evenings thus passed very quietly. At first the Empress remained in the drawing-room while the Tsar played dominoes or bezique; she would sing a couple of songs. As her health grew worse, she came down more and more rarely even for dinner. She dined alone or with the Tsar, 'alone together', as the formula ran in the famous Court harbingers' journal.

The suite broke up into bridge parties. But the play did not last long, for the Empress would get up very soon. As I had a great deal to do, I was in the habit of discreetly escaping from the drawing-room, leaving someone to be responsible for letting me know when hands were being kissed for 'Good night'.

On getting that message I edged discreetly into the room, and flattered myself that nobody had noticed my stratagem. One day, however, when I happened to be the last to kiss Her Majesty's hand, I heard her remark:

'You get back very cleverly at the time to say good-bye.'

'Madame, I had a great deal of urgent work — '

'As always,' she replied.

'Madame, I could not have gone without kissing your hand.'

'I quite understand,' she said kindly.

RAILWAY JOURNEYS

Railway journeys involved a mass of complications. I had scarcely been appointed Head of the Court Chancellery when preparations had to be made for departure for the Crimea, stopping at Beloviezha for a bison (*zubr*) hunt.

What instructions there were to draw up! Palace police, for protection on the way. Railway battalion: guard of bridges and tunnels along the route. Ministry of War: sentinels on the line. Ministry of the Interior: personages to be presented to His Majesty. Marshal's office: residences to be got ready and made comfortable. Inspection of Imperial trains: route and times. Tsar's private office: presents to be taken. There was no telling who might become the recipient of an Imperial present, or when, or in what shape. I had regularly to take with me thirty-two chests filled with portraits, cups, goblets, cigarette-cases, and watches, of every sort of precious metal and of every conceivable value.

The preparations were made particularly difficult by the secrecy which surrounded Their Majesties' movements. The Tsar and the Empress hated replying to such questions as 'Where are we going? When do we start? Whom are we going to see?' Sometimes I did not know our destination at noon when we were due to leave at three. I had to get on 'friendly' terms with all the servants — messengers, footmen, court harbingers, chambermaids. They caught snatches of conversation in the passages or listened at doors and then went to the telephone to tell me what the Tsar or the Empress had said about the coming journey. Needless to say, these services had their drawbacks: the least of the lackeys had it in his power to betray me or to put me into an inextricable situation.

The Tsar's journeys were made in two trains. Externally the trains were identical: eight coaches, painted blue, with coats of arms and monograms. The Sovereigns travelled in one train, while the other served, as we have learnt to say since the war, as camouflage; it went off empty either before or after the real Imperial train. Not even the heads of the passenger department were in a position to know which was the train containing the Imperial family.

The first coach in the train conveyed the escort; the moment the train stopped, sentinels ran to take up position at the doors of Their Majesties' coach. The second coach contained the kitchen and some compartments for the chief steward and the cooks. The third, panelled in mahogany, served as dining-car: one-third of this coach was taken up by a drawing-room, heavily curtained and with furniture upholstered in damask velour. There was a piano in this compartment. The dining compartment had room for laying sixteen places.

The fourth coach, with a corridor along one side, was reserved to Their Majesties. The first compartment, a little bigger than the rest, formed the Tsar's study: it contained a desk, a couple of arm-chairs, and a small bookcase. Next came a bathroom. Then Their Majesties' bedroom, of the size of three ordinary compartments. I am unable to give a description of this room, for I never entered it. Last came the Empress's sitting-room, again about the size of three ordinary compartments; it was upholstered in grey and lilac. If the Empress was not travelling, this room was locked.

The fifth coach contained the nursery; it was upholstered in bright cretonne, with white painted furniture. The maids of honour travelled in this coach.

The sixth was reserved to the Tsar's suite. It was divided into nine compartments, the centre one, for the Minister of the Court, being a double compartment. Our compartments were much larger than those of the International Sleeping Car Company. They were thoroughly comfortable. On the door was a place for the owner's visiting card. One compartment was always kept free for persons presenting themselves to Their Majesties in the course of the journey.

Finally there came a seventh coach for the luggage and an eighth for the Inspector of Imperial Trains, the Commandant of the train, the domestics in the suite, the physician and the dispensary. The Chancellery staff and the military secretariat were accommodated in the luggage coach.

The first day that I passed in the train will always remain in my memory.

On the day before we were to start, the servants came to collect our clothes and the things we wanted on the journey and to arrange them in our respective compartments. Everything not actually wanted during the journey was put into the luggage coach, which was kept open day and night.

We assembled at the Imperial station half an hour before Their Majesties' arrival. They came with their children a few minutes before the train was due to leave. It started off the moment the Tsar had got in.

At five o'clock a 'Court runner' came down the corridors to tell us that Their Majesties invited us to tea. We gathered in the drawing-room. The Empress came up and said a few words to me, plainly in order to give courage to the new arrival. Then we all went into the dining compartment, where we sat down in order of seniority. The Tsar and the Empress were at the centre of the table, facing one another.

My rank was then only that of Colonel, and I had to content myself with a seat at the very end of the table. The two eldest among the maids of honour sat on the right and left of the Tsar. The Empress had next to her Count Freedericksz and General Hesse, A.D.C. When the Empress was not there, the seat opposite the Tsar belonged to the Minister of the Court. General conversation began at once among the persons around Their Majesties. The rest of the company talked to one another in subdued tones.

I soon discovered that the presence of the Empress created an atmosphere of constraint; we were all much more lively and talkative when she was not there.

The most picturesque of the persons present was certainly the Court Surgeon, Doctor Hirsch. At the time of my appointment he was at least eighty years old; he had begun his service in the reign of Alexander II and held his post during three reigns. His medical knowledge could not have been very up to date, and the suite did not treat him with exaggerated deference; but the Empress thought very highly of him, so that Hirsch seemed like one of the Imperial family. He was even consulted on questions of the children's education. He was forgiven all his eccentricities.

For instance, he was never without a cigar; when one was getting towards the end he lit another from it. But the Empress could not endure the smell of a cigar. There were continual little altercations on the subject between the Empress and her doctor, but it was old Hirsch who emerged from them as victor. One day I heard the Empress say to Hirsch:

'Get away from me a bit, I'm suffocating.'

'But Madame, I've only been smoking quite a little cigar to-day.'

'I should like to have seen your quite little cigar. The smoke was coming out under the door of your compartment like a tobacco store on fire.'

Sometimes Hirsch was asked:

'Is nicotine a poison?'

His answer was:

'Nicotine is a poison, but only a slow poison. I have been taking it in for fifty years and it hasn't killed me yet.'

The servants brought tea. The table was covered with cakes and fruit. There was no alcohol, except when Nilov, 'His Majesty's Flag Captain', was present; he could not do without rum or brandy and asked the servant for it.

Tea lasted about an hour. Often the Tsar would bring in the latest telegrams, if he had not had time to read them. After running through them he would pass them to his neighbours, leaving out the maids of honour, who manifested the utmost indifference to these bits of paper.

After tea we returned to our own coaches; there we talked in the corridors or read a novel.

Dinner was served at eight and lasted sixty minutes. At the end of it the Tsar got up and the rest of us saluted him with a low obeisance.

The Tsar rarely came out for the evening cup of tea, and the Empress never. We could go to the dining compartment when we pleased for this cup of tea; that is to say, there was no definite time for it as for breakfast. If we preferred, we could have it served in our compartments.

On my first morning in the train I went to my corner of the table for breakfast exactly at eight. Almost at once the Tsar came in. He told me to sit next to him, and said:

'Are you in the habit of getting up so early?'

'Sire,' I replied, 'if I got up later I should be working under pressure all day long.'

'You are quite right. I too get up in good time. Your chief is the man who doesn't. He has never finished dressing until the moment comes for going in to lunch.'

I mentioned that in St. Petersburg I regularly reported to the Count at half-past ten.

'I don't mind it a bit,' the Tsar replied. 'He is a splendid man. It will be a real pleasure for you to work with him.'

He added, after a pause:

'Were you not in the same regiment as the Count? They say that he shows too marked favour to the Horse Guards. . . . I can understand it; it is pleasanter to be surrounded with people whom one knows and can trust.'

The train stopped at the principal stations. The Minister of the Court told the Tsar beforehand who were the personages who were being admitted to the platform. The Tsar would get out on to the platform, surrounded by his suite, and enter into conversation with the members of the local administration. The provincial governors were invited to come into the train and to travel as far as the frontier of their province. This honour was often granted also to certain officers, who made their reports to the Tsar in the train; they then passed the night in the compartment reserved for visitors.

The Tsar worked in his study throughout the journey. If he took his evening cup of tea in the dining compartment, he would sometimes remain with his suite; he would then play dominoes, and if he lost he would send his servant to get the money. The Tsar never had money in his pocket. He hardly knew, indeed, the value of money. I recall the incident of his troika at Skernevitzy. The horses took Bright, and were only brought to a stop through the presence of mind of a Cossack in the escort, who jumped on to the middle horse and seized the bridle, at the risk of his life; he did not succeed in stopping it until he had been dragged a considerable distance along the ground. The Tsar told me to reward the Cossack:

'Give him a gold watch, or twenty-five roubles, whichever he prefers.'

I gave the good fellow a gold watch, and reported to the Tsar that I had done so, mentioning at the same time that twenty-five roubles (£2 10s.) was scarcely an equivalent of the value of the gift.

'It is one of the big gaps in my education,' the Tsar said to me, smiling; 'I don't know the price of things; I have never had occasion to pay for anything myself.'

THE TSAR'S YACHT

The Tsar's favourite yacht was the *Standard*. She was built in Denmark, and was considered the most perfect ship of her type in the world. Her displacement was 4,500 tons; she was painted black, with bowsprit and stern gilded; she was a splendid seagoing ship, and fitted up with every possible comfort. When we went to Cowes, King Edward asked for plans of the yacht, for his constructors to study in case a new one should be built for him.

The yacht was commanded by Rear-Admiral Lomen, the Tsar's 'Flag Captain'.[1] The whole of the naval administration stood in mortal fear of the Admiral. It is true that he asked a great deal, and if he was annoyed he could be extremely rude. He claimed that on board the yacht the Tsar himself was under his orders. Off duty he was pleasant and sociable.

The actual Commanding Officer of the *Standard* was Captain Tchaguin, and the second in command Commander Sablin. Both had the satisfaction of being thought very highly of by Their Majesties. In the letters which she wrote to the Tsar when he was at G.H.Q., the Empress frequently mentioned Sablin.

Tchaguin came to a tragic end. He committed suicide; one version given of the reason is that he had as mistress a lady who belonged to the terrorist group of the Russian Social Revolutionaries. I am unable to confirm this; Tchaguin died a bachelor.

When the Imperial family went on board the *Standard*, each of the children was assigned a *diadka*, a sailor charged to watch over the child's personal safety. The children played with these *diadkas*, played tricks on them and teased them. Gradually the younger officers of the Standard joined in the children's games. As the Grand Duchesses grew older, the games changed into a series of flirtations, all very innocent. I do not, of course, use the word 'flirtation' quite in the ordinary sense of the term; the young officers could better be compared with the pages or squires of dames of the Middle Ages. Many a time the whole of the young people dashed past me, but I never heard the slightest word suggestive of the modern flirtation. Moreover, the whole of these officers were polished to perfection by one of their superiors, who was regarded as the Empress's squire of dames. As for the Grand Duchesses, even when the two eldest had grown up into real young women one might hear them talking like little girls of ten or twelve.

The Empress herself grew gay and communicative on board the *Standard*. She joined in the children's games, and had long talks with the officers.

The officers were certainly in an exceptional situation. Every day a group were invited to meals. In return the Imperial family accepted invitations to tea with the mess.

Had the officers of the *Standard* become too much of mere society men? That charge was often levelled against them, especially in naval

1 His Majesty's 'Flag Captain' was responsible for the Sovereign's safety from the moment when the Monarch set foot in any vessel, whether a yacht, a Dreadnought, or a launch. In this last case, the Flag Captain himself took the helm.

quarters (but was this simple jealousy?), after the unfortunate incident known as the wreck of the *Standard*.

On a fine day in the Finnish fjords the *Standard* was shaken by a tragic jolt at a moment when there was not the slightest reason for expecting anything of the sort. Immediately afterwards the yacht heeled over. It was impossible to tell what might be coming next. The Empress rushed over to her children. She found them all except the Cesarevitch, who was nowhere to be seen. The anguish of the two parents may be imagined; they were both beside themselves. It proved impossible to move the yacht. Motor-boats started off towards her from every direction.

The Emperor hurried up and down the yacht, and gave the order for everybody to go in search of the Cesarevitch. It was only after some time that he was discovered safe and sound. At the first alarm his *diadka*, Derevenko, had taken him in his arms and very sensibly rushed to the hawse-pipes, as offering the best chance of saving the boy if the vessel should be a total loss.

The panic subsided, and all on board descended into the boats.

An inquiry followed. The whole responsibility fell on the pilot, an old Finnish sea-dog, who was in charge of the navigation of the vessel at the moment of the disaster, Charts were hurriedly consulted and showed beyond any possible question that the rock on which the yacht had grounded was entirely uncharted.

There remained His Majesty's Flag Captain, who was responsible in principle for the safety of the Imperial family. At the time the post was held by Admiral Nilov, the only master, under God, of the fate of the yacht.

He was in such a state of mind after the disaster that the Tsar felt bound to go to him in his cabin. Entering without knocking, the Tsar saw the Admiral bending over a chart, with a revolver in his hand. The Emperor tried to calm him. He reminded the Admiral that under the naval regulations he would have to go before a court of inquiry; but, the Tsar added, there could not be a shadow of doubt that he would be acquitted, for the disaster had been entirely unforseeable. His Majesty carried away the Admiral's revolver.

All who took part in this drama are now dead. Why should I not record that the incident of the revolver created a touching friendship between the Tsar and the Admiral, a friendship that was an enigma to all who were unfamiliar with the details of this tragedy, since the character, education, and culture of the Tsar and the Admiral were so dissimilar.

There was an immediate conspiracy of silence at Court about the wreck of the *Standard*. Everybody knew that the slightest criticism of the officers of the yacht would have brought down punishment on the head of any one who ventured to utter it.

The officers were chosen for their social gifts; their task was to create on board the atmosphere of a fairy-tale, a charming idyll. It may be that in technical knowledge they were not absolutely up to date.

THE TSAR'S MOTOR-CARS

The first motor-cars, Serpollets, made their appearance in St. Petersburg in 1901 or 1902; one was bought by Count Freedericksz and the other by Grand Duke Dimitri Constantinovitch. (This first adept of the new sport was, it may be mentioned, a great breeder of horses.) But motor-cars were not then perfected; breakdowns were constantly occurring.

One day the Count asked the Tsar's permission to take his car to Spala, for the hunt. We had no sooner started than we had to get out and push the car out of the way between us; it had stopped dead, in the middle of the road, barring the way for the Tsar himself. Thus the whole Court passed by us, and jeers were fired at us from all sides. In the end the Count sent for another mechanic, and we were able to make two further trips without any great trouble. The Count then proposed to the Tsar — it was one Sunday, after lunch — to take him for a run in the car. His Majesty agreed, without enthusiasm. We had no sooner started than the car broke down. We had to send for horses to remove the unlucky vehicle. Under a rain of chaff from the suite, the Count definitely abandoned his efforts.

Next year an ex-officer of the Horse Guards, Kvitko-Osnovianenko, brought to Yalta another car, in much better running order. The police forbade him to use it, as it frightened the horses, and that might have produced tragedies on the mountain roads of the Crimea, M. Kvitko applied to Count Freedericksz to get the prohibition lifted. He pointed out that the roads were free for drivers of cars all over Europe, even in Tyrol. The matter had to be submitted to the Tsar. His Majesty probably had not forgotten the Spala experience. His reply was brief and decisive:

'My dear Count, so long as I live at Livadia, no car shall be allowed in the Crimea.'

In the following year the Tsar had the opportunity to take several rides in a car put at his disposal at Darmstadt by the Grand Duke. The Empress was also persuaded to have a ride in this terrifying machine, which resembled an omnibus without horses. After braving these risks, it seems that the Tsar changed his opinion.

On our return to Tsarskoe Selo, we were surprised to see a car come up, a Delaunay-Belleville, driven by Prince Vladimir Orlov. After lunch His Majesty asked the Prince whether he would not give him a ride in his motor vehicle. They went round the park, and at the end of the run the Tsar at once asked the Empress to come with him for another 'excursion'.

Prince Orlov pressed the services of his car on the Sovereigns; their rides became almost a daily event, especially when the Prince brought to his garage a new car of a still more perfected type. From then on the Prince never left the driver's seat. He took Their Majesties on short journeys in every direction; but for fear of an attack on the car, or any oversight, he did not allow his chauffeur to take his place.

About six months later, Freedericksz asked the Tsar whether he would not like to become the owner of a car. The Tsar started:

'Yes, you are right. It has been too bad of us to abuse Orlov's kindness. Give an order for two or three cars, and entrust Orlov with the purchase; he knows all about it better than a professional.'

By the end of the year the Imperial garage was well stocked. It contained ten cars, and later twenty, with a school of chauffeurs. Orlov continued to drive for the Tsar and the Empress. Only when the works sent a chauffeur especially recommended by his firm (he was a Frenchman) did the Prince agree to entrust the precious lives of the Sovereigns to his care. Even with this chauffeur he took every precaution, sitting next to him for more than a month.

A few years later the Tsar's park of cars was one of the finest in Europe.

THE TSAR'S HUNTS

The Tsar's principal hunting-ground was at Beloviezha, a forest reserve of more than a quarter of a million acres in the Government of Grodno. It was at Beloviezha that the kings of Poland had hunted for centuries. In 1888 the forest was made the private property of the Tsars.

This forest was known for the variety of the trees in it. And in this forest was the only herd of bison remaining in Europe (*zubr* — very similar to the American bison). This herd, numbering about 800, was carefully preserved. Even when taking part in an Imperial hunt it was only permissible to shoot at a bison detached from the herd; these solitary beasts were particularly vicious and would attack the rest of the herd.

The hunting at Beloviezha was a great attraction for all the crowned heads of Europe. William II was dying to be allowed to fire a few shots there, but the Tsar would never offer his cousin an opportunity to join in this royal hunt.

Frequently after the two had met the Tsar would say to Freedericksz:

'He has been trying again to get invited to Beloviezha; but I turned a deaf ear to him.'

During the war, when Beloviezha was occupied by German troops, a German soldier who was captured was found to be in possession of orders concerning this forest. The orders included a prohibition of all slaughter of bison or other big game, on pain of death.[1]

At half-past seven one morning all the huntsmen assembled in hunting dress in front of the Tsar's palace. The Tsar came out, accompanied by the Empress and two maids of honour.

We took our places in *troikas*, two by two, followed by keepers. When we reached the forest we had to keep to the long straight *layons* — avenues specially maintained to enable the huntsmen to move about the forest. I may mention that wood-cutting was strictly prohibited throughout Beloviezha; the underwood had become almost impenetrable. As the wind could not pass through anywhere, the oak and beech trees grew as straight as candles. The grass underfoot along the *layons* was so well kept that we moved along as smoothly as over a carpet.

On our arrival at the shooting stands, we were received by the master of the hunt, who made us draw lots. This little lottery was a point of honour with the Tsar; he submitted with a good grace to the chance of the throw on equal terms with all his guests. In some countries it is a familiar thing for the sovereigns to receive the best

1 Unfortunately the herd was almost exterminated during the revolution.

stands as a matter of course, so that persons of lower rank run the risk of not catching sight of a single animal.

There were twelve of us, and twelve stands had been prepared in advance. We took up our places in accordance with the numbers that we had drawn.

At each stand the huntsman was protected up to his chest. Behind him stood a keeper, whose duty it was to reload the guns. The Tsar had the assistance of two keepers; they were furnished with great forks for holding off the wounded animal if the necessity should arise. The Empress shared her husband's stand. She showed astonishing coolness. It was impossible to say as much for the maids of honour who were placed in the stands of less important members of the suite; they gave little inopportune cries, which baulked the game.

I had one of these ladies in my company, but that did not prevent me from killing a very large bison. My first shot wounded it in the shoulder. It stopped short, and then charged. The second shot brought it down at once; it was then scarcely twenty paces from my stand.

It weighed 525 kilogrammes, over half a ton; a fine specimen of this almost extinct species.

In the evening, after dinner, everybody went out on to the great terrace. Below were set out the whole of the day's trophies; the keepers lit up the picture with their torches. The hunting-horns sounded a clarion in honour of the Tsar, and the head keeper unsheathed his poniard in order to point to the animals killed by the Sovereign. After that the successes of the other huntsmen were similarly saluted in order of merit.

One day Grand Duke Nicholas Nicolayevitch and Prince Kotchubey simultaneously shot and killed a fine stag with antlers of thirty-two tines. Both of the huntsmen laid claim to these exceptional antlers. They began to quarrel. The Tsar intervened and said:

'I am master here. I shall take the antlers myself.'

He had two exact copies of these antlers, the finest in the whole of the Beloviezha collection, made abroad and these copies were sent to the two rivals.

The Tsar was himself a very good shot. But he only fired when he was sure of his quarry. He was sensitive about his reputation and hated missing.

At the end of the hunting, each of the guests received a printed list of his personal exploits, as well as his trophies, specially mounted, with the date and place of shooting recorded.

EPILOGUE

JULY 1914

After the departure of the President of the French Republic, we thought that the political clouds would gradually pass away. On returning from one of his audiences with His Majesty, Freedericksz told me that the Tsar had no fears in regard to the Serajevo assassination, and had given him the impression that 'everything would be settled all right'. The Minister of War, whom I saw on the same day, held the opposite view. In his opinion, and, indeed, I agreed with him, the very cordiality of the Kronstadt meeting would itself lead William II to give his support to Austria if she formulated unacceptable conditions.

My son was on leave in Switzerland, and I telegraphed to him to return to Russia.

In the evening Freedericksz was again with the Tsar. This time His Majesty showed great anxiety. William II had just sent a telegram to say that any intervention on the part of a third Power in the Austro-Serbian conflict would endanger peace. His Majesty had replied that while he wanted peace he had been obliged to instruct the Minister of War to take certain preparatory measures in case a mobilization should prove necessary. These measures could be stopped if direct negotiations with Austria should become possible.

Next day the Austrian ultimatum to Serbia was published. The Tsar went with Freedericksz to Krasnoye Selo, where a Cabinet meeting was held.

In the evening I put before Freedericksz a plan for the partial mobilization of the office of the Marshal of the Court in the event of the Tsar proceeding to the front. The Count replied:

'No, no. I cannot ask His Majesty to give these orders; he feels sure that there will be no war.'

On July 30th Sazonov came to Peterhof and had a very long audience with His Majesty. On leaving he went to see the Minister of the Court, and told him that he had transmitted the order for mobilization to the Chief of Staff. Later I learned that General Yanushkevitch lifted the receiver off his telephone as soon as he had received the order, lest a later message should countermand it. He considered that it would be impossible to stop the mobilization once it had begun.

Next day I went to St. Petersburg on urgent business. On getting into the train on my way back I saw Count Pourtales, the German Ambassador, enter the Court coach, followed by one of his secretaries. As soon as the train started I went into the Count's compartment. He stood up at once, took both my hands, and exclaimed:

'It must be stopped, stopped at all costs, this mobilization. Otherwise it means war.'

I replied:

'It is impossible. The mobilization is pursuing its' normal course. You can't suddenly stop a car that is going at sixty miles an hour. It would inevitably capsize.'

The Count said:

'I have asked for an audience with the Emperor; I have got to ask him to stop the mobilization. It was only placarded this morning.'

The Ambassador was in a remarkable state of agitation. I did my best to tranquillize him, asking him to go to see Count Freedericksz immediately after the audience. I felt sure that my Minister would be able to persuade the Tsar to telegraph to William II to explain to him that mobilization did not in the least mean war, and that demobilization would be ordered as soon as direct negotiations had been begun.

'Above all,' I said, 'don't ask the Emperor for what is impossible.'

'No, no,' the Count exclaimed, 'if he does not demobilize at once there is no preventing war!'

I noticed the young secretary trying to catch the Count's eye in order to stop him from saying this; the Ambassador gave the impression of having lost his balance.

I went straight to Freedericksz to tell him what the Ambassador had said. Pourtalès arrived half an hour later, looking very dejected. He begged the Minister to go to the Tsar and suggest to him some telegram to William II — anything to explain the reasons for the mobilization. Freedericksz set out for the Palace.

On his return he told me that the Emperor had drawn up an excellent telegram, which had been sent off at once. He added:

'You will see — this telegram will make sure of peace.'

He had hardly finished speaking when the telephone rang. I took up the receiver. It was Sazonov speaking. I handed the receiver to Freedericksz.

I saw him grow pale. He replied:

'Yes, yes, I will arrange it.'

Sazonov had just told Freedericksz that Pourtafos had transmitted to him the declaration of war. Sazonov asked for an audience with His Majesty.

The reply to the Tsar's last telegram had been received at the moment when the movement of troops had already begun — on both sides of the frontier. The telegram from William II remained on His Majesty's desk, and it was not possible to publish it with the other documents concerning the declaration of war. I only learned of it through the revelations made later by M. Paléologue.

Next day the officers of the garrison of St. Petersburg were received in the Winter Palace. After a Te Deum the Tsar formally took the oath not to conclude peace so long as an enemy remained on Russian soil.

After this there were ovations for M. Paléologue, the Ambassador of our chivalrous ally.

My son had succeeded in reaching the frontier by the last train from Berlin. Noticing that the Russian officers were being arrested, he jumped out of the train and crossed the frontier on foot, under fire from the German sentinels.

A few weeks later he was at the front; there, in 1915, he met the death of a brave man, falling during an attack near Marienburg.

THE LAST AUDIENCES

In August 1916, at Mohilev, the Emperor sent for me to come to his study and told me that he intended to appoint me Minister Plenipotentiary at Bucarest. This appointment would coincide with the entry of our troops into Roumania.

Seeing my astonishment the Tsar explained why he was making the appointment.

He had received information, he said, to the effect that the Queen of Roumania, his cousin, was very, disturbed about the possible relations between the Russian army command, the King of Roumania, and the population of the kingdom. The Emperor's own view was that the army leaders do not give sufficient attention to the suggestions made to them by diplomats who are not themselves soldiers. It was necessary, therefore, to appoint to Bucarest somebody of sufficient weight for effective collaboration with the commander of the Russian troops. After the many years I had spent in the Sovereign's suite, I should be well qualified for imposing my will on whoever was to direct military operations in Roumania.

All I could do after these explanations was to say how sorry I should be to be no longer in the immediate entourage of my Sovereign.

The Tsar added that he did not want to upset Count Freedericksz, with whom I had worked on such friendly terms. He was not to be told, therefore, of my appointment, and the Tsar would himself undertake to explain to him that my departure would only be on 'a temporary mission'. The ukase appointing me Minister Plenipotentiary would mention that I still held my post of Head of the Court Chancellery.

Shortly after my arrival in Roumania, the Queen asked me whether I thought the Tsar would consent to a marriage between the heir to the throne, Prince Carol, and one of the Russian Grand Duchesses, the daughters of Nicholas II. I left for Petrograd to present a very confidential report on this subject.

After my statement, the Tsar said to me:

'I agree with your view of the proposal, but I do not know what the Empress will think of it.'

'When might I present myself again, to learn the answer that I am to make to the Queen?'

'I shall not say anything to the Empress. Ask for an audience with her; give her the Queen's compliments, and make your report to her.'

'I will do so, Sire.'

'Why, you seem frightened! Have I not made you a diplomat? This is your business both as Minister Plenipotentiary and as an officer of the Court. So, make your report to the Empress.'

The audience took place at four o'clock on the following afternoon, at Tsarskoe Selo. On leaving Her Majesty I was told by a servant that the Emperor was in the garden and wanted to see me.

I gave a full account of the audience. The Empress intended to invite Queen Marie and Prince Carol to stay over Easter at Tsarskoe Selo. Then we should see whether the marriage could be considered.

'Of course,' I added, 'that is if Your Majesty approves the plan.'

'I did not think you would be so successful in your mission. You have the art of persuasion.'

In spite of this praise, I had the feeling that the Emperor would have been better pleased to learn that the Empress had replied with a refusal. That would not have faced him with the prospect of separation from his daughter.

A few days later I left for Roumania. That was the last time that I saw Their Majesties.

THE ATTEMPT TO SAVE THE IMPERIAL FAMILY

In 1918 I was at Kiev, in the Ukraine. The country was under German occupation, with a Hetman (Skoropadsky) at the head of a shadow government.

At Kiev I met Prince Kotchubey, my colleague in the Ministry of the Court, and Duke George of Leuchtenberg, a former brother officer in the Horse Guards.

Our one and only thought was for the rescue of the Emperor and his family from their prison in Ekaterinburg.

The Duke of Leuchtenberg undertook to speak on our behalf to the German authorities; he was a cousin of the heir to the Bavarian throne, and that fact secured him access to General Eichhorn, the Commander-in-Chief of the army of occupation, and to General Groener, his Chief of Staff.

The Germans came to our aid with the utmost readiness. They opened credits for us and promised to supply us with machine-guns, rifles, and motor-cars. Our plan was to freight two vessels, which would be sent with officers in our confidence to steam up the Volga and the Kama, its tributary. They were to stop about forty miles from Ekaterinburg, where further instructions would be given.

We sent two officers into the town as scouts; one belonged to the detective staff formerly in attendance on the Tsar, and the other to the Horse Guards.

They were to get into touch with German agents then secretly in the town, whose help would be of the utmost value to us.

I knew that the Tsar would not consent to exchange his captivity under the Bolsheviks for captivity in Germany. To make the position clear, I wrote a letter to William II, and entrusted it to Count von Alvensleben, who was attached to the person of the Hetman. The Count was to leave that day for the German G.H.Q.

In this letter I asked the German Emperor to place in my charge a letter addressed personally to the Tsar, guaranteeing that he would be enabled to reside in the Crimea, without having to submit to captivity in Germany.

It may be imagined with what feverish impatience we awaited the return of Count von Alvensleben.

On his return to Kiev he gave no sign of life. Next day I went to see him. He seemed very embarrassed. According to him, the Kaiser was unable to reply without consulting his Government. Alvensleben advised me to see Count von Mumm, the diplomatic representative of Germany with the Hetman.

Count von Mumm categorically refused to help me. He told me he was astonished to learn that the German military authorities had promised to give us their assistance. From now on I must no longer count on the Germans.

I made desperate efforts for more than two hours to get Mumm to listen to reason. I explained to him that in Germany's own interest he must save the Tsar of Russia.

I had no success.

Shortly afterwards we learned the news of the tragedy at Ekaterinburg.

ALEXANDER II† 1818–81   m.(1) 1841 Marie of Hesse 1824–80   m.(2) Catherine Dolgorouky, 1880 cr. Princess Yourievsky 1847–1922

Children of Alexander II:

- Alexandra 1842–9; Nicholas 1843–65 *no issue*
- ALEXANDER III 1845–94 m.1866 Dagmar (Marie) of Denmark 1847–1928
- Vladimir 1847–1909 m.1874 Marie of Mecklenburg-Schwerin 1854–1920
- Alexis 1850–1908 m.1870(?)** Alexandra Zhukovsky 1842–99
- Marie 1853–1920 m.1874 Alfred, Duke of Edinburgh 1844–1900
- Serge† 1857–1905 m.1884 Elizabeth of Hesse‡ 1864–1918 *no issue*
- Paul† 1860–1919 m.(1) 1889 Alexandra of Greece 1870–91; m.(2) 1902 Olga von Pistolkors cr. Princess Paley 1866–1929

Issue:

- NICHOLAS II‡ 1868–1919 m.1894 Alix (Alexandra) of Hesse‡ 1872–1918
  - Alexander 1869–70; George 1871–99; Xenia 1875–1960; Michael‡ 1878–1918; Olga 1882–1960
- Vladimir issue: Alexander 1875–7; Cyril* 1876–1938; Boris 1877–1943; Andrew 1879–1956; Helen 1882–1957
- Alexis issue: Alexis, Count Belevsky-Zhukovsky† 1871–1932
- Marie issue: Alfred 1874–99; Marie 1875–1938; Victoria Melita* 1876–1936; Alexandra 1878–1942; Beatrice 1884–1966
- Serge issue: Marie 1890–1958; Dmitri 1891–1942
- Paul issue: Vladimir‡ 1897–1918; Irina 1903–90; Natalia 1905–81

George 1872–1913 m.1900 Alexandra von Zarnekau 1888–1957 m.diss.1908

Boris b.&d.1876

Olga 1873–1925 m.1895 Nicholas von Merenberg 1871–1948

Catherine 1878–1959 m.(1) 1901 Alexander Bariatinsky 1870–1910 m.(2) 1916 Serge Obolensky 1890–1978 m.diss.1924

*Cyril married Victoria Melita in 1905
** marriage disputed; if took place, never officially recognized
† assassinated before revolution of 1917
‡ put to death during or after revolution

Other reprints available in this series

Life of Alexander II, F.E. Grahame
Alexander III, Tsar of Russia, Charles Lowe
The Emperor Nicholas II as I knew him, Sir John Hanbury-
  Williams
The Intimate Life of the Last Tsarina, Princess Catherine Radziwill
My mission to Russia and other Diplomatic Memories, Sir George
  Buchanan
The reign of Rasputin: An Empire's Collapse, M.V. Rodzianko
*Collected Works: Once a Grand Duke, Always a Grand Duke,
  Twilight of Royalty*, Alexander, Grand Duke of Russia
Memories of Russia 1916-1919, Princess Paley

Frederick, Crown Prince and Emperor, Rennell Rodd
Letters of the Empress Frederick, edited by Sir Frederick Ponsonby
*Between two Emperors: The Willy-Nicky Telegrams and Letters,
  1894-1914*
My Memoirs, Princess Victoria of Prussia
Potsdam Princes, Ethel Howard

Emperor Francis Joseph of Austria, Joseph Redlich
The Story of my Life (Vols. I-III in one volume), Marie, Queen of
  Roumania
*A Royal Tragedy: Being the Story of the Assassination of King
  Alexander and Queen Draga of Servia*, Chedomille Mijatovich
My Past, Marie Larisch

The Witchery of Jane Shore, C.J.S. Thompson
Richard III, Sir Clements Markham
His Royal Highness The Duke of Connaught and Strathearn, Sir
  George Aston

*The Complete Works: The Journal of a Disappointed Man,
  A Last Diary, Enjoying Life and other Literary Remains*, W.N.P.
  Barbellion

For further details please see *amazon.co.uk/amazon.com*

More titles are in preparation

Printed in Great Britain
by Amazon